Girls for Sale

Girls for Sale

Kanyasulkam

A Play from Colonial India

Gurajada Apparao

Translated from Telugu by
Velcheru Narayana Rao

INDIANA UNIVERSITY PRESS
Bloomington & Indianapolis

This book is a publication of

Indiana University Press
601 North Morton Street
Bloomington, IN 47404-3797 USA

http://iupress.indiana.edu

Telephone orders 800-842-6796
Fax orders 812-855-7931
Orders by e-mail iuporder@indiana.edu

The paper used in this publication meets the minimum requirements of American National Standard for Information Sciences—Permanence of Paper for Printed Library Materials, ANSI Z39.48-1984.

Manufactured in the United States of America

Library of Congress Cataloging-in-Publication Data

Apparao, Gurajada Venkata, 1861–1915.
[Kanyasulkam. English]
Girls for sale : a play from colonial India = Kanyasulkam / Gurajada Apparao ; translated from Telugu by Velcheru Narayana Rao.
p. cm.
Includes bibliographical references.
ISBN 978-0-253-34899-9 (cloth : alk. paper)—ISBN 978-0-253-21913-8 (pbk. : alk. paper)
I. Narayanaravu, Velceru, date II. Title. III. Title: Kanyasulkam.
PL4780.9.A5957K313 2007
894. 8'2725—dc22

2006103353

1 2 3 4 5 12 11 10 09 08 07

For Ramesh and Srilata Vemuri
Friends beyond words

deśamaṇṭe maṭṭi kād 'oy.
deśamaṇṭe manushul 'oy.

A country is not its soil.
A country is its people.
—Gurajada Apparao

CONTENTS

Acknowledgments

This translation has been long in the making. I have been talking about my reading of the play for more than a decade now, to anyone willing to listen, until they are tired. Pressed by friends that I should write my ideas down, I realized that before I presented my reading of the play, I had to translate it. Over the long period of time I have worked on the translation, I have incurred a number of debts, many that I cannot repay with words of thanks.

Wissenchaftskolleg zu Berlin is the first on my list. A fellowship at the Kolleg during 2000–2001 gave me an opportunity to produce the first draft of the translation. It was fortuitous that David Shulman, Sanjay Subrahmanyam, Muzaffar Alam, and Partha Chatterjee were at the Kolleg at the same time. Their company was energizing and also provided the necessary corrective to many errors I would have committed in my enthusiasm to quickly produce a complete translation. Muzaffar helped me with the Urdu words and songs in the text. Sanjay and Partha read the first draft and by their silence told me it needed a lot of work. I set to work on improvements and the more I reread the draft, the more changes I began to make. In June 2003, David read the complete draft with me and suggested improvements on practically every page.

I knew the translation was not anywhere close to publication. Many words were unclear and contexts unknown. My work on improving it continued. Apparao's language faithfully reflects the regional dialects of Vizianagaram. I come from the same area of northern Andhra that Apparao does and comfortably understand the language he uses in the play, but the distance of time has made some of his expressions opaque. Dictionaries did not help, and people I was able to contact long distance from Berlin were not particularly helpful either. These words and references do not interfere with the enjoyment of the play as such, so even admirers of Apparao read on without thinking about them, but for one who is translating the play, they pose serious hurdles. I continued to pester my friends for books and information.

Attaluri Narasimharao and Chandu Subbrao of Visakhapatnam,

India; Paruchuri Sreenivas of Düsseldorf, Germany; and Paranandi Lakshmi Narasimham of Columbus, Ohio, responded to my requests patiently and sent me valuable material that helped in writing my notes and afterword ("The Play in Context").

A senior fellowship from the Institute for Research in Humanities, University of Wisconsin–Madison, gave me the time free from teaching to rework with undivided attention on my translation, afterword, and notes. I am deeply thankful to my colleagues at the Institute and director David Sorkin for their support.

Sylvia Dakessian worked with me all along, fixing my wording to make it more colloquial and carefully editing my text draft after draft.

Sanjay came to my aid again to read my afterword and suggested a number of improvements to make my argument work better.

I used a version of my afterword in Oxford, England, when I gave Radhakrishnan Lectures at All Souls College, in Hyderabad when the Anveshi group invited me to talk about *Kanyasulkam,* and at the Institute for Research in Humanities. I am grateful to the audiences at each place for their feedback.

Veluri Venkateswara Rao explained the card game in the fifth act and sent me a note about it, which I include here as an appendix.

Just when I thought I had a text ready to be sent to publishers, my friend and colleague Charles Hallisey offered to read it on his plane journey to Boston. He brought the manuscript back with a number of suggested improvements written in longhand. His sensitivity to spoken English was very helpful, and no words of thanks are enough to express my debt for the time and attention he gave to the text. My only solace is that I was able to make his plane journey less boring with a text which he said he enjoyed reading. Gyan Pandey gave a very careful reading to my afterword and suggested a number of changes for which I am deeply thankful.

I sent the manuscript to a former student, Rebecca Glowacki, who read it, "painting houses during the day and reading the play at night, finding myself laughing out loud." After a few days she sent me a long e-mail with corrections only her careful eye could catch and suggestions for improving the dialogue, many of which I adopted.

The most valuable editorial comments came from Rebecca Tolen, the editor at Indiana University Press, whose gentle style made working on this book with her a truly delightful experience.

Last but not least, I am immensely benefited by the meticulously careful copyediting of Kate Babbitt.

Introduction

Until recently, English translations of late-nineteenth- and early-twentieth-century literary works from India have been almost exclusively from Bengali or Hindi. The writers from Bengal in particular taught us how India became modern. They wrote of social reform, moral rejuvenation, and the cultural revitalization of a great civilization, which had its glory in the ancient past but gradually deteriorated during the medieval period until colonial education opened it to the West. Bengali social reformers Rajah Rammohun Roy and Kesab Chandra Sen and Bengali writers Bankim Chandra Chattopadhyaya and Rabindranath Tagore are hailed as the harbingers of the Indian Renaissance, which then spread to other Indian languages.

This story of Indian modernity would have been told differently if Western scholarship had been acquainted with the works of a great writer from Andhra, Gurajada Apparao, especially his play *Kanyasulkam.* Witty, humorous, serious, and devastatingly honest, this is the first realistic play, perhaps in any Indian language, which depicts a society undergoing radical changes under the influence of colonialism. From the day the play was first staged in 1892 (published in 1897, followed by a second and revised edition in 1909), it captured the imagination of generations of audiences and readers in Andhra, scholars and ordinary people alike. The 1909 edition is immensely superior to the first edition and has been celebrated as one of the greatest works of Telugu literature. It has been so popular among educated Telugus that memorized lines from the play are often quoted in conversations. Characters from the play have grown as familiar to people as their next-door neighbors and have acquired a life of their own in the popular imagination. Often compared to Sudraka's classical Sanskrit play *Mṛcchakaṭikam* (The Little Clay Cart), *Kanyasulkam* depicts a vibrant upwardly mobile society with people from all walks of life–from Veda-chanting Brahmins to whoring widows, from corrupt police officers to idealistic lawyers, from smart courtesans to pseudo-yogis, from cunning village politicians to dashing English-speaking dandies and intelligent people from a variety of castes and professions.

The Plot

The plot of the play revolves around the desire of an elderly Brahmin, Lubdha Avadhanlu ("Miserly Brahmin"), to buy as his new bride the very young daughter, Subbi, of another Brahmin, Agni-hotra Avadhanlu ("Fiery Brahmin"). Agni is determined to go through with the deal, but the girl's mother is staunchly opposed since her elder daughter, Bucc'amma, is already widowed. She begs her brother, Karataka-sastri, to stop the match or else she will kill herself. Karataka-sastri thinks of a ruse. He disguises a young boy, his disciple, as a girl and offers to sell her to Lubdha for a cheaper price. This disciple is already well trained in the art of playing women's roles in the theater. The drama of masquerade is managed by the deft manipulations of the courtesan Madhura-vani, who is a central character in the play. To make the plan work, she manipulates her lovers and others who are drawn to her charms. After the wedding is completed, the new bride (the boy) disappears. A corrupt police establishment charges Lubdha with murder. A staunch social reformist and idealist lawyer, Saujanya Rao, defends Lubdha but finds his case in deep trouble because there is no evidence to prove the innocence of his client.

Interwoven with this plot is another plot, the love life of Girisam, another central character, who is a young and handsome con artist with a glib tongue and a flair for English. He preaches social and moral reform in public but has a secret affair with a young widow who runs a restaurant and also keeps Madhura-vani as his pleasure-woman. Owing money to everyone in town, he escapes to Agni's village under the pretext of tutoring Agni's son in English during the summer vacation. He cons the family into believing that he is a highly educated man. This is right at the time when Agni has made all the arrangements to marry his little daughter to a seventy-year-old man against the wishes of the women of the family. Girisam pretends to help the women escape this disaster, seduces Bucc'amma, and elopes with her the night before the wedding.

The last act has Madhura-vani, in a man's guise, going to Saujanya Rao's house at night, where Girisam has been staying. He has just eloped with Bucc'amma and, pretending to be a sincere young activist in the movement for social reform, is seeking Saujanya Rao's support to marry her. The unexpected stranger (Madhura-vani) who shows up as they are talking in Saujanya Rao's bedroom tells the lawyer that he (she) has come on an important and sensitive business matter and enters into a conversation with them. The play ends with a double surprise and the memorable line by Girisam: "Damn it, the story has taken a wrong turn."

The Author

Gurajada Venkata Apparao was born in 1861, the same year Rabindranath Tagore was born, but that is where the similarity stops.[1] He was a sickly child, very small and delicate. He entered the Maharaja's College in Vizianagaram, and after passing his matriculation in 1882 and his FA in 1884 found himself unable to continue his education. Apparao then held a series of minor positions, including that of a school teacher for a brief time, married in 1885, and managed to complete, with the generous help of Principal Chandrasekhara Sastry, his BA (in philosophy and Sanskrit) in 1886. The maharaja was the great patron in town, and anyone of any talent or aspiration gravitated to his palace to seek his *darśan.* The maharaja appointed Apparao as a Level IV lecturer in his college on a salary of 100 rupees per month, with an extra allowance of 25 rupees to read newspapers for the maharaja every day. From that day until his death in 1915, Apparao served the royal family in various capacities: as a newspaper reader for the maharaja, as the royal epigraphist (*samsthāna śāsana pariśōdhaka*), and, after the death of the maharaja, as the personal assistant and adviser to the Maharani of Rewa, the maharaja's widowed sister, and also for a time as the de facto Diwan of the kingdom.

During his school days, Apparao published poetry in English and wanted to establish himself as an English poet. Encouraged by friends, he started writing in Telugu. Apparao closely followed developments in the world theater and studied Sanskrit playwrights. A man of short stature and delicate health, he keenly observed everything around him with his sharp eyes. He met with Rabindranath Tagore and corresponded with him. An entry in his diaries suggests that he may have corresponded with George Bernard Shaw.

In addition to the two versions of *Kanyasulkam,* Apparao wrote two more plays, *Bilhaṇīyam* and *Koṇḍubhoṭṭīyam,* both left unfinished. He wrote a few short stories and a small number of poems and songs. He died on November 30, 1915.

Critics who have written about this play in Telugu have consistently maintained that it was written in strong support of social reform against a number of social evils, including the tradition of selling girls as brides, the custom which prohibited widow remarriage, and the prevalence of "nautch girls" (i.e., women who gave sexual services to men in return for money), and hailed Apparao as the harbinger of a cultural renaissance in Telugu following Bengali social reformers. I contest this position and discuss this in the afterword, where I present an in-depth analysis of the play and the cultural context in which it is written.

The Text

Available editions of *Kanyasulkam* carry a number of errors and other casual alterations. I based my translation on the 1909 edition, a copy of which I acquired from the British Library in London. This is the most reliable edition, since it was published under the author's personal supervision. Consulting *Moṭṭtamŏdaṭi Kanyasulkam* (Kanyasulkam, the First Version), superbly edited by Bangorey with elaborate notes, was very helpful. K. V. Ramana Reddy's biography of Apparao, *Mahodayam* (The Great Dawn), is a gold mine of information on Apparao's life, and his little booklet *Kanyasulkam: Ṭīkā-Ṭippaṇi,* (Kanyasulkam: A Glossary) identified sources of some unknown references. There is a substantial output of articles and books on Apparao, from which I have derived great benefit. However, the primary material that would have been extremely valuable, Apparao's personal diaries, letters, and other papers, all of which he wrote in English, have mysteriously disappeared, except for a few at the Andhra Pradesh State Archives, Tarnaka, Hyderabad. After repeated attempts to trace them, I gave up and depended upon the Telugu translations of Avasarala Suryarao, even though I had been warned that they were not always accurate. As for Apparao's other writings–his poetry, short stories, essays, and his two unfinished plays–the only editions available are by Visalaandhra, who should be thanked for their service in keeping Apparao's books in print as best they can. Apparao is a celebrity in Andhra today. Praise is showered upon him and statues commemorate him; let us hope that his work will be scientifically edited and properly annotated.

Note on Translation and Transliteration

Translating Apparao into English is a challenge. One of the main characters in the play, Girisam, uses a lot of English in his conversations. I retain his English words as well as the English words used by other characters, setting them in italics to distinguish them from the English of my translation. I also retain a number of Telugu, Sanskrit, Hindi, and Urdu words, songs, and poems from the original, and they are shown in italics as well, with their translation in the notes.

Every character in the original speaks in a dialect of Telugu specific to his or her caste, social status, gender, educational level, and individual style. Determined to use the language as it is spoken in real life, Apparao took care to spell every word as it is pronounced by the character. He even made a few orthographic innovations to indicate the precise sounds. I made no effort to reflect the dialect variations in my translation.

No diacritics are used in the text for the names of characters or for modern names of people. No diacritics are used for proper names of locations in the play, other locations mentioned in the play do use them. Names of deities in the play use diacritics, but all other personal names do not. All foreign words are given with diacritics throughout the text. Names of the characters and places are given with diacritics in an appendix along with a guide to pronunciation.

Girls for Sale

Dramatis Personae

In alphabetical order

AGNI-HOTRA AVADHANLU: A Vaidiki Brahmin, traditionally learned in the Vedas who lives in the Brahmin village Krishna-raya-puram. Short-tempered and gullible.

ASIRI: A low-caste man who is a servant at Lubdha Avadhanlu's house.

BAIRAGI: A non-Brahmin religious guru who pretends to have supernatural powers. Smokes marijuana and drinks. Has a following among low-caste people. "Bairagi" means "a person who renounced the world." He has no given name.

BHUKTA: A Brahmin landowner who appears during the card-playing session at Madhura-vani's house in Act Five.

BUCC'AMMA: A young virgin widow; daughter of Agni-hotra Avadhanlu and Venk'amma.

BUCC'ANNA: A low-caste follower of Bairagi.

DAY-MEAL-WOMAN: A young Brahmin widow who runs a Day-Meal-House (i.e., restaurant, where one pays for each meal) for Brahmin men only. Apparently she has no family to take care of her following the death of her husband, so she cooks for Brahmin men to make a living. Girisam has a secret affair with her.

DISCIPLE: A student who is learning Sanskrit from Karataka-sastri. Plays girls' roles in theater. Karataka-sastri dresses him as a girl to marry him to Lubdha Avadhanlu in place of Subbi. He also appears as a religious street singer. His personal name is Mahesam.

GIRISAM: A cousin of Lubdha Avadhanlu who is educated in English. Young, handsome, and successful with women. He has a glib tongue and can turn any situation to his advantage. Cons people and lives by pretending to be a very learned and influential man.

HAVALDAR ACC'ANNA: A retired army man. A high-caste non-Brahmin, nephew of the Village Head. Havaldar is a rank in the colonial Indian army, which has become his title.

HEAD CONSTABLE: Head of the police in Rama-chandra-puram. Neither his name nor his caste is identified. He has a high social status and in all likelihood comes from a high caste; he may be a Brahmin.

KAMAYYA: Junior constable.

KARATAKA-SASTRI: Venk'amma's older brother and Agni-hotra Avadhanlu's brother-in-law. He is a Sanskrit scholar and actor who is famous for his role as a clown in Sanskrit plays.

KAM-BHOTLU, KONDI-BHOTLU: Young adults from Brahmin families. The Bhotlu at the end of the names suggests that they are Vaidikis.

LAKSHMANNA: A low-caste follower of Bairagi.

LUBDHA AVADHANLU: A Vaidiki Brahmin who is learned in the Vedas. A rich man known to be a miser. Lives in the Brahmin village Rama-chandra-puram.

MADHURA-VANI: A pleasure-woman in Vizianagaram, probably in her twenties. For most of the duration of the play, she is kept by Ramap-Pantulu, and she moves to Rama-chandra-puram with him. In the end she moves to Visakhapatnam, the headquarters of the district.

MANAVALLAYYA: Belongs to the Satani caste of non-Brahmin Vaishnavites. Frequents the village bar in Rama-chandra-puram.

MINAKSHI: Young widowed daughter of Lubdha Avadhanlu.

POLI-SETTI: A rich merchant in Rama-chandra-puram. Komati by caste.

PRIEST GAVARAYYA: Vaidiki Brahmin. Ritualist who performs weddings in Rama-chandra-puram. He also controls spirits with his chants.

RAMANNA: A low-caste follower of Bairagi.

RAMAP-PANTULU: A Niyogi Brahmin who is the *karaṇam* (hereditary revenue officer) of Rama-chandra-puram. Thinks he cleverly manages village politics. He enjoys good things in life and keeps Madhura-vani as his pleasure-woman. As a Niyogi, he assumes a proud style and demands to be served and respected.

SAUJANYA RAO: Advocate. Known to be incorruptible, he has staunch *anti-nautch* principles and is an idealist social reformer. Comes from a Niyogi Brahmin family.

SHOPKEEPER: His given name is Ramam-dasu. He owns the village bar in Rama-chandra-puram and is a shrewd businessman. Comes from an unspecified low caste.

SIDDHANTI: Vaidiki Brahmin. Makes birth charts and fixes auspicious times for weddings and other occasions in Rama-chandra-puram. Siddhanti is a professional title indicating that he is an expert in astrology. His personal name is not known.

SUBBAMMA: (Doesn't appear on stage.) The second daughter of Agni-hotra Avadhanlu and Venk'amma; called Subbi by family members. Her marriage to Lubdha Avadhanlu is the center of action in the play.

VENK'AMMA: Agni-hotra Avadhanlu's wife and innocent village woman.

VENKATESAM: Agni-hotra Avadhanlu and Venk'amma's son. Goes to high school in the city because his parents want to give him an English education.

VILLAGE HEAD: Hereditary Village Head of Rama-chandra-puram. A high-caste non-Brahmin. His given name is Somi Nayudu, but no one calls him by his name.

VIRESA: Belongs to the Jangam caste of non-Brahmin Saivites. Frequents the village bar in Rama-chandra-puram.

YOGINI: A young low-caste temple woman who has been religiously initiated. Serves liquor at the village bar in Rama-chandra-puram.

An honorific suffix -garu is added to the name if the speaker wishes to be respectful toward a person.

Act One

SCENE ONE. Hill of Lies[1] in Vizianagaram

(Enter Girisam.)

GIRISAM: It's evening. I took twenty rupees from the Day-Meal-Woman, told her I'd get her some groceries from the market, and spent the money on the dancing girl.[2] That was a month ago, and this morning she made a big fuss about it. I was so mad that I wanted to smash her head. But you know, as Poor Richard[3] said, we can't win in this world unless we are patient. This is not the first time I used her money, but she never said anything before. I suppose she got wind of the dancing girl. Some jealous bastard must have squealed. Considering what happened this morning, it doesn't look like she'll feed me anymore. My game is up in this town. Anybody you can name, I owe them money. One of these days, I'm going to get beat up for the love letter I sent to Venku Pantulu's daughter-in-law. But then,

Can Love be controlled by advice?
Will cupid our mothers obey?[4]

The only smart thing to do is pack up and leave. But it's hard to leave my love, Madhura-vani.

It is women that seduce all mankind.[5]

That poor woman thinks I'll land a big job and live a princely life with her happily ever after.

Who's that coming? Oh, it's my favorite disciple, Venkatesam. Yes, today is the beginning of Christmas vacation.[6] I can see by his face that he's failed his exams. I'll console him and escape to his village with him. I'll tell him I'll tutor him through the vacation. That'll solve a lot of knotty problems. As in the story, gain time, ask to begin chopping from the other end.[7]

(Venkatesam enters.)

What's the matter *my dear Shakespeare*![8] You look sad.

VENKATESAM: I don't want to talk to you. My teacher said I wasted my time in your company and I failed my exam because of you.

GIRISAM: *Nonsense.* I knew he would say that from day one. Your teacher doesn't like me. I knew that from day one. That's why he failed you. You, failing an exam? No way! You know how it all began between me and your teacher? All that he teaches is a bunch of bullshit. I tore him to pieces in the press. Since then, he hates my guts.

VENKATESAM: All I learned from you is how to smoke cigars. Have you ever taught me a single lesson?

GIRISAM: *Damn it!* I get furious when you speak such nonsense. *This is base ingratitude.* Just talking to me is an *education.* Look, does your teacher know as much English as you know? How many *lectures* did I give you about *widow marriage,* about the *nautch question*? Not a single student of mine has failed in life. When I was a student in Deccan College at Poona,[9] I gave a *lecture* on *the Eleven Causes for the Degeneration of India* for three hours nonstop, and all the *professors* were astounded. Did a single person open his mouth the other day when that Bengali man gave a *lecture* in this town? Our people are total idiots. You should thank me for teaching you how to smoke cigars. I'm a little surprised you don't appreciate the charms of smoking. It's because of smoking that the English have become our bosses. Have you ever seen an Englishman who doesn't smoke? It's on the principle of the cigar that the white man invented the steam engine and such things. How else could he think of them? You know what our ancient texts say?

> When the Lord of Birds brought the elixir of eternal youth,
> it bubbled over and a drop fell down, that's the truth.
> It became tobacco for all to smoke. If you say no,
> in your next life you'll be born as a big buffalo.[10]

Bṛhannāradīya, chapter 4.[11] But leave that alone. I'm furious with your teacher for failing a brilliant student like you. When I catch him alone, I'll beat the daylights out of him. But what are your plans for the vacation? Are you here or are you going home?

VENKATESAM: I want to go, but my father will beat me to death if I tell him I failed.

GIRISAM: I'll tell you how to escape that danger. Will you promise to do as I say?

VENKATESAM: (Falling on Girisam's feet.) Have I ever disobeyed you? My father has a terrible temper. If he finds out I didn't pass, he'll break my bones. (He wipes away his tears.)

GIRISAM: *That's tyranny.* You know what a Bengali boy would do in your place? Father or grandfather, he'd pick up a big stick and hit him back. Tell me, are there any other kids from your village in your school?

VENKATESAM: Not one.

GIRISAM: Let me tell you a way out of your problem. I will come with you to your village and tell your folks you passed the exams. Tell them I came to tutor you during the vacation. At the end of the vacation I'll get you admitted in the town school in the next higher grade.

VENKATESAM: If you come, I'm saved. My mom even said to bring you last vacation.

GIRISAM: I would love to come, but then I'll lose a lot if I leave here. The munsiff[12] said he will pay me *fifty rupees* if I teach his kids during vacation. But that's all right. I'm willing to lose anything for your sake. There's only one little problem. Your people are *barbarous,* and they may not treat me well. You have to recommend me strongly to your mother. Now why don't you make a list of the books we need? We need some cash for cigars, you know. Get a pencil and your notebook.

Royal Reader
Manual Grammar
Ghose Geometry
Bose Algebra
Srinivasa Ayyar Arithmetic
Nala-caritra
Rajasekhara-caritra
Shepherd General English
Venkata Subbarao Made Easy

How many are there?

VENKATESAM: Nine.

GIRISAM: Add one more, to make it ten: *Kuppusamayyar Made Difficult.*[13] That's enough. If your folks should ask you to speak English, recite without fear whatever you remember from the books you've read. Do you have any change in your pocket? I only have large bills. Get a pound of Banaras sweets.[14] I won't eat dinner tonight. Go to the market, hire a cart, put my traveling suitcase on it, and wait for me here. I have a few important things to do and I will meet you here no matter how late in the night. *Go at once my good boy.* If you obey my word, I will train you to be as great as Surendranath Banerjea.[15] Don't let any other soul know that I am coming with you. Take care.

(Exit Venkatesam.)

GIRISAM: This matter is settled. But I can't leave without a *parting visit* to Madhura-vani.

(Sings:)

Your sight
is my delight
if I don't
embrace you tight
it's a sad plight,
like a moonless night

(A servant enters.)

SERVANT: I'm the servant of the photographs man. He needs his bill paid. He asked me to get the cost of the photographs you owe him. Now.

GIRISAM: (As if he hasn't heard:)

Full moon is light
jasmine is white
forget the moon
forget the flower
your face is bright
brighter than bright
bright, bright, bright[16]

SERVANT: He has sent a number of his people to collect, but you didn't pay up. I'm not going to leave without getting that money out of you.

GIRISAM: Oh, yes, go straight; this is the right way to the lake.

SERVANT: He is truly the king of the deaf. (Loudly:) Hey, can you hear me?

GIRISAM: You are asking for a grocer's shop? There's none here, you have to go to the Kaspa Bazaar.

SERVANT: (Speaking right into his ear:) Are you or aren't you going to pay up the cost of the photographs?

GIRISAM: Yes, you can comfortably stay at the travelers' inn.

SERVANT: (Even louder:) You had photographs taken with your whore one year ago. You haven't paid the bill yet. My master said pay now or else.

GIRISAM: Oh, is it you? I mistook you for someone else. Talk softly. Talk softly. Come to the Day-Meal-Woman's house tomorrow morning at 8:00 sharp. I will pay the money in full, to the last penny. Doesn't your master care for friendship and goodwill?

SERVANT: Promises are no good; collect the money right now, that's what my master said.

GIRISAM: You're a reasonable man. You shouldn't lose your cool. And your father was a reasonable man. Look at this cigar. See how beautifully it burns. The white masters call it Havana. Come tomorrow in the morning, I will give you a couple of packs.

SERVANT: As you please, sir. But sir, what about the money?

GIRISAM: I told you, didn't I? If I don't pay you tomorrow, call the outcaste man's son an untouchable.

SERVANT: He *is* an untouchable, anyway, isn't he?

GIRISAM: If you don't trust me, I will take an oath on my sacred shoulder string and the Gayatri chant.[17]

SERVANT: As you say, sir, but if you don't pay tomorrow morning, my credibility is lost.

GIRISAM: Your credibility is as good as mine. Trust me.

(Exit servant.)

GIRISAM: At last, I've found a use for the shoulder string. You never know. As the theosophists[18] say, every old custom of ours has been put in place for a purpose. You'll know the truth only by experience. This devil of a servant—it took all my strength to get rid of him. I should get out of here fast. I'm a dead duck if I don't. I should go visit Madhura-vani. As the Englishman says: *Make hay while the sun shines.*[19]

SCENE TWO. A room in Madhura-vani's house.

(Ramap-Pantulu seated on a chair. Madhura-vani stands facing him.)

RAMAP-PANTULU: (Takes a cigar, bites off its end.) Give me a light, honey.

MADHURA-VANI: (As she strikes a match and lights the cigar, Pantulu pinches her cheek. Madhura-vani drops the match even before the cigar is lit and steps back angrily.) Anyone, man or woman, should have principles. I told you not to touch me, but you wouldn't listen.

RAMAP-PANTULU: Everything has been finalized. I'm keeping you as my woman, and I'm just waiting for an auspicious day to take you to my village. Why do you still act as if you were under some nincompoop's hold? What's this pretense of chastity?

MADHURA-VANI: Just because I'm a pleasure-woman, you can't take me lightly. Even *we* have our morals. I'll call my master Girisam-garu and tell him, "Sir, I'll go my way and you go your way." I'll cut myself loose from him. But until that time, consider me *his* woman. You might make fun of him because he was born in a Vaidiki[20] family, he might be Christianized,[21] and maybe he kept that Day-Meal-Woman. Still, for all these days that great man has been my patron. You're a far better lover than he is and you have stolen my heart, but I must have some gratitude for him, right?

RAMAP-PANTULU: You use such big words. He kept no Day-Meal-Woman, that woman kept him. She feeds him gruel every day for his services.

MADHURA-VANI: That's unfair. He is truly a learned man and famous, too. He's going to land a big job one of these days.

RAMAP-PANTULU: (Laughing.) A-haha, how naive you are. You are too trusting to be a pleasure-woman. You call him Girisam-garu, with the honorific ending. I know him too well, he is Lubdha Avadhanlu's nephew. We used to call him Girradu.[22] You think he'll land a job with the couple of words of English every butler can speak?[23] There is only one job God made for him—to live in that Day-Meal-Woman's house for free food and to slave for her like a Tamilian.[24]

MADHURA-VANI: May I ask him if this is true?

RAMAP-PANTULU: By all means. You can also tell him that I told you to ask him.

MADHURA-VANI: Anyway, what do I care if he is great or small? He's my master. I'm blind to his faults.

RAMAP-PANTULU: If so, when are you going to divorce him?

MADHURA-VANI: As soon as you give me the two hundred you graciously offered. I'll pay off my debts and get rid of him this minute.

RAMAP-PANTULU: Take it, then. (He pulls two hundred rupees from his pocket and gives them to her. As Madhura-vani reaches for them, Ramap-Pantulu pulls her hand toward him. Madhura-vani releases her hand from his grip, throws the rupee bills at him, and stands at a distance.)

MADHURA-VANI: This isn't working. I can't trust a person who doesn't stand on principle.

RAMAP-PANTULU: Forgive me. I'm very sorry. (He picks up the bills and gives them to her.) Count them.

MADHURA-VANI: No need to count. I trust you. If I didn't, I wouldn't go with you. What a fine lover you are! You don't even know me. Keep your money. I'm not in it for the money. (She tries to give the money back.)

RAMAP-PANTULU: No, no, no. I was just trying to know your mind. This Girisam is a good-for-nothing fellow. You don't really think he's a great man, do you?

MADHURA-VANI: If you think you can insult him in front of me, please leave. (She opens the door with one hand and shows the way out with the other.) Hold on; here he comes, you can tell him yourself.

RAMAP-PANTULU: You must be joking.

GIRISAM: (From outside:) *My dear!*

RAMAP-PANTULU: (To himself:) God, he came at the wrong time, this bastard. What if he beats me up? How do I get out of here? I'll hide under this bed. (He hides under the bed.)

(Enter Girisam.)

GIRISAM: *Well, my dear empress!* (He tries to pat her on her shoulder.)

MADHURA-VANI: (Avoiding him.) Don't touch me.

GIRISAM: (Amazed.) Why, what's this new game?

MADHURA-VANI: The very last one.

GIRISAM: (To himself:) How did she know that I am running away? Maybe women have a secret spirit that keeps them informed. (Openly:) If you are menstruating,[25] go take a shower and come back quick.

MADHURA-VANI: What's the rush? I'll take an oil bath[26] later.

RAMAP-PANTULU: (To himself:) What an honest woman! What a ploy to avoid the bastard!

GIRISAM: We Englishmen don't care about menstrual pollution and such nonsense. Come closer. (He reaches close to her.)

MADHURA-VANI: (Warning him with her finger.) Stop there. You may have gone Christian, but I've not, at least not yet. Someone told me just now that you're a Christian.

RAMAP-PANTULU: (To himself:) My God, I hope she doesn't tell him that I said that.

GIRISAM: Someone told you! Who is that man? What man on earth has the courage to enter this house? Who has the boldness to tell you these slanderous tales? And how dare you listen to them and repeat them to me?

RAMAP-PANTULU: (To himself:) He'll beat me up. How did I get into this mess?

MADHURA-VANI: Why should it be a man? Don't women have mouths?

GIRISAM: (To himself:) That slut, the Day-Meal-Woman, is slandering me. (Openly:) A woman told you? God made woman live by her loud mouth. But then, why would a respectable woman come to your house?

MADHURA-VANI: When respectable men come, why can't respectable women come here? Sit down. You can be angry later. Have a cigar. Here are the matches.

GIRISAM: If you can't touch me, don't I even deserve to get a light from you? I came with a lot of joy, and you've ruined it all.

MADHURA-VANI: What's so joyful?

GIRISAM: Here in my pocket is the *firman*[27] from the Nizam of Hyderabad. My buddy, Nabob Sadar-adalat Bavur Alli Khan Ispahanjang Bahaddar, recommended me for the position of a *musayib*[28] on a salary of one thousand *sikka* rupees.[29] My job is to constantly offer my company to the Badshah.

RAMAP-PANTULU: (To himself:) Wow, what a lot of bull!

GIRISAM: I bring you such great news and you keep me at a distance. Not fair. Will you go to Hyderabad with me?

MADHURA-VANI: (Shaking her head.) Why me? Take the Day-Meal-Woman.

GIRISAM: (Amazed.) Is she making a stink?

MADHURA-VANI: You should know.

GIRISAM: I can't stop laughing at your stupidity. You seem to believe whatever anyone says against me. Whoever is telling these ugly lies about me, don't think he can get away with it. Even if he runs beyond the seven seas, I'll catch him by his hair and shoot him with a pistol—*ḍha ḍha ḍha*—and riddle his body with holes. If I don't, my name's not Girisam and the roaring conch of the great warrior Arjuna is not Devadattam.[30] *Kabaḍdār!*

MADHURA-VANI: You don't have to take the trouble of traveling overseas; the man who said those things against you will tell you to your face.

RAMAP-PANTULU: (To himself:) God, this slut's going to reveal my name!

GIRISAM: (To himself:) Thank God it wasn't the Day-Meal-Woman. (Openly:) If that good woman should hear such painful words, she would be badly hurt. And you will bear that sin. What a chaste woman she is, serving her husband faithfully.

MADHURA-VANI: At long last, now I hear that a widow is serving her husband!

GIRISAM: No. That's not what I meant. She has no husband, it's true, but you can't call her a widow.

MADHURA-VANI: How can she be a widow while you are there for her?

GIRISAM: Nonsense. (To himself:) Let's make up a story to delight her. (To Madhura-vani:) Listen. This is what happened. While the Day-Meal-Woman was a little girl, barely walking, her folks decided to marry her to a decrepit old man. Either just before he tied the marriage knot[31] or immediately after, the old fellow kicked the bucket right on the wedding seat. A question arose whether the wedding was completed or not. Some said he tied the knot and others said he didn't. The bride's father sued the heirs of the groom for a share in the groom's property. The priest took a bribe from the groom's heirs and testified in court that the groom didn't tie the knot. The case was lost. But then no one else married her.

MADHURA-VANI: But you had to.

GIRISAM: What are you talking about? I don't understand what you are saying. It isn't funny any more. If you're teasing me, anything you say is fine. But if you really mean it, you'd better watch out. Tell me this minute what son of a bitch is prattling this nonsense.

MADHURA-VANI: *Rāma . . .*

RAMAP-PANTULU: (To himself:) God, I am dead. She has revealed my name!

MADHURA-VANI: *Rāma Rāma,*[32] God's name as my witness, the whole world is talking about you and her. Why name a single person? (A woman's voice from the street:) Open the door!

GIRISAM: (Turning pale.) Don't, don't open the door. The woman is insane. She will hurt people.

MADHURA-VANI: The door isn't locked.

GIRISAM: Run and lock it.

MADHURA-VANI: Well, she is coming in, kicking the door open.

GIRISAM: Throw her out. Throw her out.

MADHURA-VANI: Wait a minute, by her style she looks like your chaste woman. (Goes into the front porch.)

GIRISAM: (To himself:) Let's get under the bed. (He hides under the bed.) (To himself:) Dirty slut, she hid a customer under the bed. I thought she was a good woman. The hell with her. I would pull her hair apart and kick her in the head, but this is not the time for it. Anyway, I'm leaving. Why should I bother? (Softly to Ramap-Pantulu:) Who are you, sir? You look like a gentleman.

RAMAP-PANTULU: Son, it's me, Ramap-Pantulu.

GIRISAM: Is that you, sir? Why hide under the bed for this? If you had asked me, I would have donated a score of sluts to you.

RAMAP-PANTULU: (To himself:) Thank God, he isn't angry with me. (To Girisam:) So you are the person who has kept her. If I had known, I wouldn't have come anywhere near her.

GIRISAM: I can't hear you. Come closer.

(Ramap-Pantulu moves closer and Girisam moves over and gets near the wall.)

GIRISAM: Sir, never trust this bitch. She can hide twenty more customers like us.

RAMAP-PANTULU: She milked me out of two hundred rupees.

GIRISAM: Throw in some sesame seeds too. At least you will get the merit of gifting.[33]

RAMAP-PANTULU: What a fool I was.

GIRISAM: You can say that again!

(Enter Madhura-vani and the Day-Meal-Woman with a broom under her sari.)

MADHURA-VANI: I told you that the man you are looking for is not here, but you won't listen.

DAY-MEAL-WOMAN: The people on the street told me he entered your house, and you want me to believe what you say? What do I care if the bastard is in your house or not, just give me back the twenty rupees he gave you.

MADHURA-VANI: Ask the person you gave the money to.

DAY-MEAL-WOMAN: If I see the bastard, I'll knock his block off. Where have you hidden him?

MADHURA-VANI: Why should I hide anybody? I'm neither a wife nor a widow. The man who visits me comes like a prince, openly. (Gestures with her eyes to show under the bed.)

DAY-MEAL-WOMAN: Maybe he's hiding under the bed. (Bending to look under the bed.) So this is where your glory shines; come out. (She hits Ramap-Pantulu with the handle of her broom.)

RAMAP-PANTULU: *Ayyo!* Why did you hit me, you bitch?

MADHURA-VANI: Hey, why did you hit my man? Who are you to make a fuss in my house?

DAY-MEAL-WOMAN: Then why is he hiding under the bed?

MADHURA-VANI: That's none of your business. That's our love game.

DAY-MEAL-WOMAN: Well, this is my broom game.

RAMAP-PANTULU: (Feeling his back.) I will cut your braid off, you whore. If you weren't a woman, I would have killed you. Why did you hit me instead of your lover? Is that why the bastard moved toward the wall and pushed me to the front?!

DAY-MEAL-WOMAN: So the bastard is under there too. Come out of there, you dog!

GIRISAM: Come here, my crazy sister, and let me cure you of your madness.

DAY-MEAL-WOMAN: You bastard, am I your sister? You think I'm scared of you? Let's see if your whore can save you. (She goes under the bed from one end, while Girisam gets out from the other end, hits Ramap-Pantulu on the head, runs toward the backyard, and escapes.)

RAMAP-PANTULU: *Ayyo.* I'm dead. (Holding his head in both hands.) How dare he! Madhura-vani, call the police.

MADHURA-VANI: Why make a public case of it and ruin your good name? You can hit him back one of these days and take revenge. (She hugs him and kisses his head and rubs it.) He's bad, and if he were a man, he would stand up to you in an open fight, not hit you from behind like a coward. You will teach him a lesson one of these days.

RAMAP-PANTULU: There's a constable paid by the government for this job. Why should I put my body on the line for it? I'll drag this bastard through all twelve courts.[34] If I don't, my name isn't Ramap-Pantulu. You'll see what I can do.

MADHURA-VANI: (Kissing Ramap-Pantulu.) Hush. (Pointing under the bed.) He should be ashamed of hitting you behind your back.

RAMAP-PANTULU: But it still hurts. Why is that whore still under the bed? Take that broom away from her.

DAY-MEAL-WOMAN: (To Ramap-Pantulu:) When I heard a slap, I was wondering what happened. What a manly fellow you are! (She comes out from under the bed.)

(Exeunt omni.)

Act Two

SCENE ONE. The house of Agni-hotra Avadhanlu in Krishna-raya-puram, a Brahmin village.[1]

(Agni-hotra Avadhanlu is spinning shoulder threads. Karataka-sastri is being deloused by his disciple. Venk'amma is cutting vegetables.)

VENK'AMMA: The boy wrote that *kismis*[2] vacation started yesterday. I haven't seen him in ages. My eyes are aching to see him. He should be here any minute.

AGNI-HOTRA AVADHANLU: What's the point of feeling sad now? I said no, but you put him in this English school anyway. All the rent from the upland is spent on him. Last year he failed his exams. God knows how he did this year. I told you English studies are bad luck to us. My elder brother Dibba sent his son to Parvati-puram to an English school and a fever killed him in three days. They barely began considering sending Bucc'abbi's son to English school when he fell so sick that he almost died.

VENK'AMMA: You always say horrible things like this. All you worry about is your money. Hasn't the little kid of the Nemani family become a munsiff? Just yesterday he was playing marbles in the street with his messy hair.

AGNI-HOTRA AVADHANLU: Our idiot doesn't seem to be learning anything, but we will end up having to sell off our farmland in a couple of years to pay for his books and school fees. Then we will have to go around with a begging bowl to make a living. If he had stayed home, I would have taught him at least four sections of the Veda by now. I was saying no but you got him into this bastard English.

VENK'AMMA: If our boy becomes a magistrate or gets a police job, he'll buy up all the farmland of this village. You're hesitating to spend a paltry hundred rupees a year. Do you want your son to eke out a living by making shoulder threads like you? If you think his education is such a burden, I will sell the farmland my parents gave me as a wedding gift to pay for his schooling.

KARATAKA-SASTRI: Sister, why should you sell your land? Your husband has grown fat on our money. He should pay.

AGNI-HOTRA AVADHANLU: (To Venk'amma:) So now you're attacking me? If you do it again, even your brother here will not be able to save you.

(Enter Girisam and Venkatesam.)

VENK'AMMA: My son, my son, at last you've come! (Embraces Venkatesam.)

AGNI-HOTRA AVADHANLU: Idiot, have you at least passed this time?

(Venkatesam turns pale.)

GIRISAM: Yes sir, he passed at the top of his class. I worked hard to teach him.

AGNI-HOTRA AVADHANLU: Who is this Turaka?[3]

GIRISAM: *Turk? Damn it.* (To Venkatesam:) *Tell* him *man!*

AGNI-HOTRA AVADHANLU: (Teluguizing the English word:) *Mān*? Am I like *mānu,* the tree trunk? I'll shatter your eardrum.

VENKATESAM: (Shaking, looks at his mother.) Mother, this is my teacher.

KARATAKA-SASTRI: What's the matter with you, brother-in-law? When a respectable gentleman comes to visit, you talk like a lout. He says something to the boy in English and you assume he is calling you names—like the man in the story who brushes off his shoulders when someone talks about stolen pumpkins.[4]

(The cart driver brings the baggage inside.)

GIRISAM: (To Karataka-sastri:) Agni-hotra Avadhanlu is your brother-in-law! You don't know me, but I have seen you at the deputy collector's house many times. I used to tutor his kids. The deputy collector thinks the world of you.

KARATAKA-SASTRI: Yes, your face looks familiar. The *deputy collector* is surely a great lord.

GIRISAM: The *deputy collector* speaks highly of you. He says there is no one else who knows as many languages as you, that your Sanskrit flows like water in a clear stream and you play the role of the jester superbly.[5] Where can you find a greater connoisseur of poetry? He'd die to hear my poems. He made it possible for me to see the maharaja too.

AGNI-HOTRA AVADHANLU: (With a sour face.) I don't care for this mutual admiration. I see that this man plans to set up camp here. No way. We will not feed you here.

VENK'AMMA: Don't pay attention to what he says, sir. That's his way of talking. We will be grateful if you teach our boy a thing or two.

GIRISAM: It would be my pleasure. I came here because he is a smart boy with a good future and because he begged me to tutor him during the vacation. Not that I don't relish the food in the munsiff's house in the city or the good money he pays me.

VENK'AMMA: The boy lives away from us with no one to look after him. Our thoughts are always with him. We never hesitate to spend money, but that's all we can do. We only gave birth to him, but you are both his father and his mother. You have to take care of him like your son and teach him. We put the burden on you.

GIRISAM: You don't have to say it in so many words. Ask your son if I am a good teacher or not. The *deputy collector* himself commended me, I don't have to speak for myself. If your son is under my training for three more years, he'll pass the criminal exams all the way up to the police test.

AGNI-HOTRA AVADHANLU: Three more years! How much will it cost for books this year, son?

VENKATESAM: Fifteen rupees.

AGNI-HOTRA AVADHANLU: I won't give one *dammiḍi*.[6] Looks like these two will split that money between them to spend on their pleasures. I learned all eighty-two sections of the Veda without spending a single *dammiḍi* on books. You are trying to pull wool over my eyes.

KARATAKA-SASTRI: (Laughing.) Brother-in-law, your words are worth a million.

GIRISAM: (To Karataka-sastri:) *This is barbarous.* See how he insults a *gentleman* like me. It's no good staying here anymore. Good-bye.

VENK'AMMA: Enough of this. I'm always afraid something like this will happen whenever someone comes to the house. Sir, don't pay attention to his words. Please stay.

KARATAKA-SASTRI: Agni-hotra Avadhanlu, you're hesitating about spending a little money on your son's education. What did you do with the fifteen hundred rupees you got from selling Bucc'amma?

GIRISAM: *Selling girls, damn it!*

AGNI-HOTRA AVADHANLU: Every jackass says "you sold her, you sold her." Is she a vegetable to sell? If I hadn't taken that money, what would have happened to her now that her husband is dead?

KARATAKA-SASTRI: Well, you can't blame him for dying. He was literally on his deathbed when you married your daughter to him.

GIRISAM: (To Agni-hotra Avadhanlu:) So you are the famous Agni-hotra Avadhanlu of the Nulaka family. My people in Rajahmundry say that no one compares to you in the braided recitation of the Veda.[7]

AGNI-HOTRA AVADHANLU: So you belong to Rajahmundry! Why didn't you say so! Is Rama Avadhanlu well?

GIRISAM: He is fine, sir, he is my uncle, my mother's brother.

AGNI-HOTRA AVADHANLU: You don't say!

GIRISAM: My uncle speaks highly of you whenever we talk of this part of the country.

AGNI-HOTRA AVADHANLU: He and I are good friends. See, this anger of mine is a weakness. I said all those words not knowing who you are. Please don't mind them.

GIRISAM: Sir, elders like you can yell at kids like us; that's only fair.

KARATAKA-SASTRI: (To himself:) At last my firebrand brother-in-law has met his match.

AGNI-HOTRA AVADHANLU: Look here! What did you say your name is?

GIRISAM: People call me Girisam, sir.[8]

AGNI-HOTRA AVADHANLU: Listen Girisam-garu, this Karataka-sastri is a confused man. He doesn't understand what's good and what's bad. Our son-in-law died, right? But see how much we benefited from it. We sued for his lands, didn't we? By the way, could you do me a favor and read the *order* on the *petition* I filed recently. (He goes to the room, brings a paper, and gives it to Girisam.)

GIRISAM: (Looking at the paper.) Looks like some mindless clerk wrote it. The handwriting is shabby; it doesn't even look like English.

AGNI-HOTRA AVADHANLU: Our vakil[9] read it fluently.

GIRISAM: Not that I can't read even more fluently. For a scholar like me, who gives *lectures,* this is a piece of cake. I am just admiring the skill of the person who wrote it. Is it your command sir, that I should translate this and submit it to you like a peeled banana?

AGNI-HOTRA AVADHANLU: That would be more than helpful. (To himself:) I will have all my court papers translated for free.

GIRISAM: If you have any more English papers, throw them at me, and I will translate them for you.

AGNI-HOTRA AVADHANLU: That would be really good.

VENK'AMMA: Could you and my son please speak to each other in English? I'd just like to hear.

GIRISAM: Sure. *My dear Venkatesam,*

> *Twinkle, twinkle, little star!*
> *How I wonder what you are!*

VENKATESAM: *There is a white man in the tent.*[10]

GIRISAM: *The boy stood on the burning deck,*
Whence all but he had fled.[11]

VENKATESAM: *Upon the same base and on the same side of it, the sides of a trapezium are equal to one another.*

GIRISAM: *Of man's disobedience and the fruit of that mango tree, sing, Venkatesa, my very good boy.*[12]

VENKATESAM: *Nouns ending in "f" or "fe" change their "f" or "fe" into "ves."*

AGNI-HOTRA AVADHANLU: What's the meaning of what you are saying?

GIRISAM: We are discussing what we should read during this vacation and all that.

KARATAKA-SASTRI: Son, read a Telugu verse.

VENKATESAM: *pŏgacuṭṭaku sati moviki . . .*[13]

KARATAKA-SASTRI: Excellent choice!

GIRISAM: *Damn it, don't read that.* (Softly.) Read *nala-damayantul'iddaru.*[14]

VENKATESAM: *nala-damayantul'iddaru manah-prabhavânala dahyamānulai salipiri dīrgha-vāsara-niśal . . .*

KARATAKA-SASTRI: Hold on a minute. What is the meaning of *manah-prabhavânala*?

VENKATESAM: (Looks up toward the ceiling.)

GIRISAM: How can a young boy know the meaning of such difficult poems?

AGNI-HOTRA AVADHANLU: Don't they teach the meanings of poems?

GIRISAM: For now they make them chant the verses like the Veda. In the white man's school they don't care much for Telugu poems. All the time they bombard the students with *jāgraphī, gīgraphī, arthameṭik, alligībra, māthamaṭiks,*[15] and all that heavy stuff.

KARATAKA-SASTRI: (To himself:) Great. If we don't show the door to this fellow pretty soon, it'll be a total disaster.

AGNI-HOTRA AVADHANLU: They teach all that?

GIRISAM: Yes sir, all that and more. A boy who works hard like your son will not have a break even for a minute.

AGNI-HOTRA AVADHANLU: That's how education should be. If only you can keep him away from marbles, he will study really well.

GIRISAM: No marbles, no nothing, sir. I'll not permit such things. If you hold a book, you can't set it aside even for a minute. It should stick to the fingers and become a part of the hand. That's how strict I am.

AGNI-HOTRA AVADHANLU: If you make him work, he will pass all his exams. We even found him a bride free of cost.

VENK'AMMA: You only talk rough, but you really love your son. When there was smallpox in the city, you asked him to come home right away, asking for a leave of absence, didn't you? In your heart you are a loving father. Of course you know you've got to get him educated and get him married as well.[16]

KARATAKA-SASTRI: How are you going to marry your son without spending money? It's not like selling girls. You should be ready to shell out at least fifteen hundred to get a bride for your son.

AGNI-HOTRA AVADHANLU: Well, you will see for yourself how I will marry Venkatesam without spending money. You don't happen to know Lubdha Avadhanlu of Rama-chandra-puram, do you?

KARATAKA-SASTRI: No, I don't.

AGNI-HOTRA AVADHANLU: He is a millionaire. He asked to marry Subbi for eighteen hundred. They'll pay all expenses, for both the bride's party and the groom's, and celebrate the wedding in style. We just bring the girl to his house and give her away. We don't have to bear any of the expenses. I'll use the eighteen hundred to get a wife for Venka.

VENK'AMMA: How old is the groom?

AGNI-HOTRA AVADHANLU: What does it matter how old he is? Forty-five.

GIRISAM: Lubdha Avadhanlu is my cousin, sir. We would become relatives through this marriage and I love it, but the fact of the matter is that he is past sixty. Whatever his age, *selling girls,* that is, giving girls in return for money—*damn it*—is totally wrong. Sir, I gave a four-hour lecture, nonstop, on that topic when I was in Poona. If you bear with me, I will convince you that taking money for your daughter is a wrong practice.

KARATAKA-SASTRI: Brother-in law, if you make this match, I'll set fire to your house.

AGNI-HOTRA AVADHANLU: A pox on your house! Every jackass comes here and eats me out of house and home and then blames me. I already agreed to the match and gave the betel.[17] The contract is sealed. Go kill yourself if you want to.

VENK'AMMA: What! Without even telling me!

AGNI-HOTRA AVADHANLU: Consult with women! Stay out of this, you slut! If I don't go through with this wedding, call me lower than the outcaste village servant. (He storms off the porch.)

KARATAKA-SASTRI: How soft spoken!

VENK'AMMA: Brother, if this match is made I will throw myself in a well or a pit. We are bearing the pain of the older girl like live coals on our chest. This man is no child, but he has no sense of pain or suffering or he would not have fixed this god-damned match. If you want to see me alive, find a way to get out of it.

KARATAKA-SASTRI: This is really a tough problem. Your husband is a stubborn bastard. The more you oppose, the tougher he gets. I can't see a way out of this.

GIRISAM: Mother, don't you worry. If Avadhanlu has an hour's free time, I will give him a *lecture* and convince him that it is uncivil to marry young girls to old men for money.

VENK'AMMA: Sir, if that man is your cousin,[18] I beg you, please go talk to him and change his mind. I will give my skin as leather for your shoes.

GIRISAM: Mother, what can I say? He is a nut. He won't give up this opportunity on his own. It's rare luck he found a girl at all. If he lets this match go, he will never find another girl.

KARATAKA-SASTRI: Sister, I will tell you a way out. Come here.

(Exit Karataka-sastri, his disciple, and Venk'amma.)

GIRISAM: My dear Shakespeare, your father is really a firebrand. There's no one in your house with eloquence enough to subdue him. See my power. See what I'll do today. Bring me the speech written by Viresalingam on bride money. I should sharpen my weapons to *lecture* to your father.

VENKATESAM: Never mind your *lectures,* I am happy that I escaped death. If you hadn't come, my father would have beaten the skin off my back with a whip.

GIRISAM: Escaping such calamities, that's where smartness is needed. If we tell a lie to get out of a tight corner, it should be impenetrable even to god. That's the key to being a *politician.* What do you know? Here I am, unnoticed, unsung. If only our country were *independent,* I would have outdone Gladstone[19] with my power as its prime minister. Hey listen, from what I've seen of your father, it doesn't look like he will give us any money for books. We only have half a pack of cigars left. What to do?

VENKATESAM: If Father doesn't give, I'll get money from Mother.

GIRISAM: That's smart. Your intelligence is blossoming. If you get trained like this, you'll be a *politician* too.

(Enter Bucc'amma.)

BUCC'AMMA: Brother, Mother says come and eat, go wash your feet.[20]

GIRISAM: (To himself:) *How beautiful; quite unexpected.*

BUCC'AMMA: (To Girisam:) Sir, will you eat leftover rice?[21]

GIRISAM: *Not the slightest objection,* that means I have no problem at all. Please serve, and I'll be right there. I finished my morning prayers[22] at the river on the way.

(Exit Bucc'amma.)

GIRISAM: Is this your sister? Looks like a case of ruined-hair.[23]

VENKATESAM: Yes, she doesn't comb her hair properly.

GIRISAM: That's not what I meant. A ruined-hair means a widow; not not combing your hair and stuff. But then why didn't you tell me all these days while I was *lecturing* to you about widow remarriage? You have an *unfortunate beautiful young widow* right in your own house! How sad! My heart melts. If I were her father, I would have earned eternal fame by performing a remarriage for her. (To himself:) What a beauty indeed. I've never seen such charm. I was afraid I'd be bored in a village, but to have a chance for a major *campaign* here is really my good fortune.

VENKATESAM: My father will perform my wedding too.

GIRISAM: Today you escaped a big "wedding" by the skin of your teeth. If you can manage the rest of the vacation without your father making a drum out of your body, then I'll call you really smart. Now about the real wedding, you aren't going to marry some innocent child your father is going to fix for you, are you? If you don't marry a young fair-skinned beauty of a widow, *I should be ashamed of you.*

SCENE TWO. Temple.

(The Disciple sits in a pavilion in the flower garden, speaking to himself.)

DISCIPLE: If you open the book once in six months, the old verses and the new verses, they all look alike. If you ask me to find the place we stopped last time, how can I? I'll have to go to a clairvoyant to find it. I will open the book at random and read whatever appears on the page. (Reads:) *mṛgāh priyālu-druma-mañjarīṇ ām*[24]

This sounds vaguely familiar. Doesn't this mean that deer run? What a great discovery of the poet. Who cares if the deer run or don't run? Don't dogs run, and foxes and cats? There isn't a single useful thing in this book. How to balance accounts, how to calculate interest on interest and such things—what does Kalidasa know about them? That's the knowledge the white man possesses. If you want to know exactly where a certain city is or where a mountain range is, ask Girisam, he will answer right away. (Reads some more:) *priyā-mukham kimpuruṣas cucumba.*[25]

So the darned fellow kissed her. Well that's better than biting her nose.

(Enter Karataka-sastri from behind, unseen by the Disciple.)

varṇa-prakarṣe sati karṇikāram
dhunoti nirgandhatayā sma cetah[26]

This verse sounds familiar too. The poet doesn't like whatever that flower is. What the hell if he doesn't like it. My guru doesn't like *dŏṇḍakāya.*[27] But his wife cooks *dŏṇḍakāya* every day because she has a *dŏṇḍa* vine in her backyard. The likes and dislikes of people who are alive are not respected. Who wants to know the preferences of dead people? I'll put an end to this study and learn a little English from Girisam. That Venkatesam is so uppity because he knows English.

KARATAKA-SASTRI: What's that you say, young man?

DISCIPLE: Nothing, it's just about my life.

KARATAKA-SASTRI: I am your guru; why don't you share that with me?

DISCIPLE: What's there to say? You have time to make me play roles in the theater and make me memorize long Sanskrit compounds and Hindustani words without knowing their meanings, but you don't have time to teach a verse even once in four days. When we leave town for a visit to the villages every six months, that's when you ask me to pick up the book. How can I learn Sanskrit this way?!

KARATAKA-SASTRI: From now on, I'll teach you four verses a day. Now read on.

DISCIPLE: (Reads:)

> *asty uttarasyām diśi devatātmā*
> *himālayo nāma nagādhirājah*[28]

KARATAKA-SASTRI: You are back at the beginning?

DISCIPLE: Well, the beginning and the end look the same to me.

KARATAKA-SASTRI: All right, let's begin from the beginning.

DISCIPLE: What's the use? This verse is all lies.

KARATAKA-SASTRI: Who says that?

DISCIPLE: Girisam-garu says that.

KARATAKA-SASTRI: What did he say?

DISCIPLE: He said the Himalayas are not straight like a measuring rod reaching the oceans from the east to the west, like Kalidasa says here. He showed them to me on the map.

KARATAKA-SASTRI: Never mind the Himalayas. Shut that book and listen to what I say.

DISCIPLE: Whatever you say. (He shuts the book.)

KARATAKA-SASTRI: Who needs your Sanskrit these days?

DISCIPLE: Unlucky people like me.

KARATAKA-SASTRI: Well said. Do you want to learn English?

DISCIPLE: Who'll support me?

KARATAKA-SASTRI: I will.

DISCIPLE: Really?

KARATAKA-SASTRI: Really, but on one condition.

DISCIPLE: What's that?

KARATAKA-SASTRI: There is a major problem. I need your help to resolve it.

DISCIPLE: Are there major problems that *I* can help you resolve?

KARATAKA-SASTRI: This one can be resolved only by you. No one else can do it. Let me tell you. You have to become a girl for a few days.

DISCIPLE: But I left my falsies in the city.

KARATAKA-SASTRI: We won't need falsies for this role. If you comb your hair and put a sari on, you will look like a charming twelve-year-old girl. I'll take you and marry you to Lubdha Avadhanlu. Manage skillfully in his house for a couple of days, then take your costume off and run away. The real wedding day is much later.

DISCIPLE: That's easy.

KARATAKA-SASTRI: Don't take it lightly. If you overdo it, they'll be suspicious. If you are caught, our heads will roll.

DISCIPLE: Don't worry a bit.

KARATAKA-SASTRI: If you do this successfully, I will marry my daughter to you and keep you in my house as resident son-in-law.

DISCIPLE: Take an oath that you will keep your word.

KARATAKA-SASTRI: Here, I take the oath holding this book.

DISCIPLE: No, I don't believe in Sanskrit books anymore. We need something weighty. Should I go get an English book from Girisam-garu?

KARATAKA-SASTRI: Then I take an oath with the earth as my witness.

DISCIPLE: What can the dumb earth do if you go back on your word? I trust you. Your word is enough.

SCENE THREE. Street in front of Agni-hotra Avadhanlu's house.

VENKATESAM: How did your *lecture* to my father on selling brides go last night?

GIRISAM: What *lecture*? The whole house exploded. Your father is a veritable demon. Your *uncle* Karataka-sastri is a *scoundrel.*

VENKATESAM: What happened?

GIRISAM: All day your uncle kept egging me on to begin my *lecture* at suppertime. He promised to support me after I broached the topic. Noticing your father's mood, I didn't have the courage to open the topic and kept suppressing every word that came to the tip of my tongue. By the time we came to the curd-rice,[29] I thought time was running out and made bold to begin my *lecture.* I had hardly begun the introduction when a couple of English words slipped past my tongue. Immediately your father fell into a rage and yelled: "These dirty English words! All Brahmin-hood is ruined with this bastard learning. Morning prayers and chants to gods and goddesses have been lost long ago. Now you bark those profane words even at mealtime as if they were gods' tongue." I became a little hesitant and wondered if my effort would be like throwing pearls before swine. I looked at Karataka-sastri for support. You know what the *rascal* was doing? He was laughing to himself, hiding his face. I was utterly unable to continue my *lecture* and in fact I was unable even to eat anymore. I felt like leaving your house right away after that humiliating experience.

VENKATESAM: Don't tell me you are leaving.

GIRISAM: No, of course not. Listen, I finally *pocketed* your father.

VENKATESAM: I knew you would do that. You promised you would convince my father to stop this wedding.

GIRISAM: No, not even the creator god can stop this wedding. Even if Demosthenes and Surendranath Banerjea[30] should talk to your father, he would not listen. *Lectures* work only in cities, they don't have any effect in villages. If you *lecture* in a city like Poona, ten thousand people come to listen to you. If you have to hold a meeting in this village, you beat the drum, put out posters, stand on the street corner, and drag in passersby—even then you'll barely have fifty people. Villages are unfit for *lectures.* I harangued the bullock-cart driver for two hours about the National Congress, and the bastard asks, "Will the Congress transfer the head constable? And if so, when?" *Lectures* are no use in *villages,* and you can't even mention the word "*lecture*" to your father.

VENKATESAM: But then how did you pocket my father?

GIRISAM: That's *politics.* Listen to what happened afterward. After yelling at me he was still burning with rage and began squeezing curds and rice furiously. Just at that time your sister came and said in her beautiful voice, sounding like a cuckoo, "Father, spend my money for brother's wedding but don't ruin my sister's life by giving her to Lubdha Avadhanlu." Your father exploded with fury, and without even reciting the closing chants[31] to end the meal, he picked up his curd rice and poured it on your sister's head. When Karataka-sastri tried to stop him, he emptied a pot of water on his head. Karataka-sastri left in a huff for his hometown with his disciple.[32]

VENKATESAM: So is this your style of pocketing my father?

GIRISAM: *Patience.* Listen to the very end. I was happy the *scoundrel* Karataka-sastri left, but I was saddened by your *sister's fate.* If I were her *husband,* I would have shot your father with a *revolver* right there. Your mother sat in a corner weeping. I put firewood in the stove, heated water for bathing, and asked your *sister* to bathe. As I sat on the porch to have a smoke, your father walked in in a mood of regret, sat right near me, and kept chatting, effectively preventing me from having even one *cigar.* At last we became friends.

VENKATESAM: How did you do that?

GIRISAM: I used a powerful *political* weapon.

VENKATESAM: And what's that weapon?

GIRISAM: Just agreeing with everything he said. That's the most powerful charm of all, you know!

VENKATESAM: So instead of giving a *lecture* and making my father agree with you, you agreed to everything he said. Is that what you did?

GIRISAM: See, if you can't measure rice with the vessel set straight, try measuring it with the vessel upside down. You'll at least catch a few grains of rice on the top. Come to think of it, *infant marriage* doesn't sound too bad.

VENKATESAM: But all these days you said it was bad.

GIRISAM: You are not a *politician* unless you *change* your *opinions* now and then. Listen to this new argument: There are no *young widows* unless there are *infant marriages.* There's no room for *marriage reform* unless there are *young widows,* right? If the test of *civilizational* progress is *widow remarriage,* progress of *civilization* is *halted* if there is no supply of *widows.* The civilization cannot go forward even one foot. Therefore we should encourage *infant marriages.* What do you say? This is a new *discovery* of mine. Second, I would argue that giving child brides to old men is also desirable.

VENKATESAM: You aren't saying that giving Subbi to Lubdha Avadhanlu is right? If that match is made, mother says she will throw herself in a well and commit suicide, you know.

GIRISAM: Women are *fools,* I say. Every woman threatens to kill herself, but actually no one does. The whole thing is nonsense. If your father gives her a nice gold ornament, your mother will forget all about those threats. But listen to my argument.

VENKATESAM: Go on.

GIRISAM: Is marriage an auspicious event or an inauspicious event? A good thing or a bad thing?

VENKATESAM: It is a good thing.

GIRISAM: Very good. If marriage is a good thing, the more marriages that take place the better, right? Therefore, marry a child bride to an old man and if he dies, to another old man—marriage after marriage and dowry after dowry—in this way a thousand from this man and a thousand from that man and yet another thousand from yet another man—bread on butter and butter on bread—make plenty of bride-money and finally if the woman marries a handsome young man like me—that would be heaven indeed. How does that sound?

VENKATESAM: Now you seem to be saying that bride-money[33] is good too.

GIRISAM: You are absolutely right. Never do anything half-heartedly. If you want to do anything, go all the way. Don't stop halfway, like the barber on Tirupati hill.[34] With this weapon, your father fell into my trap. The Englishman said, "*Think.*" You don't understand the truth unless you think. If you think well, you will see there's no marriage in the world that doesn't involve paying for the bride.

VENKATESAM: How so?

GIRISAM: I'll tell you. Is cash the only form of bride-money? What about contracts that say you should give the bride a gift of so much gold, so much silver? Aren't such things bride-money? That's exactly what all the big Brahmins in Niyogi[35] families do. Right?

VENKATESAM: That's right.

GIRISAM: The English are worse. My God, their wedding costs are exorbitant. The gifts to the bride—clothes, perfumes, jewelry—practically bankrupt the groom's house. Not to mention the marriage settlement which stipulates that certain property should be given to the bride. When I said this, your father felt very happy. Let me tell you the best argument in favor of giving your younger sister to that old man Lubdha Avadhanlu.

VENKATESAM: What's that?

GIRISAM: Lubdha Avadhanlu is old and loaded. In a couple of years, he *kicks the bucket,* that is, he dies. Your sister will become a *rich widow.* When you grow up, you can perform a *widow remarriage* and easily earn lasting fame. What do you say?

VENKATESAM: That sounds right.

GIRISAM: And one more thing. If this marriage takes place, you and I will be relatives.

VENKATESAM: That I like very much.

GIRISAM: Your father said last night that he will pay for your education up to *high court vakāltī.*[36] I brought up the matter of money for books, but he said he will give it after the wedding. If we don't find money to buy cigars soon, we will die. Do you have any small change on you?

VENKATESAM: No. All morning mother was in a bad mood. So I stole a bunch of tobacco father saved for making snuff.

GIRISAM: *That's politics.* Why didn't you tell me? We'll roll cigars and smoke here in the temple tower.

VENKATESAM: Can we smoke in a temple?

GIRISAM: That's the best place to smoke. Incense is nothing compared to cigar smoke. Here, give me the tobacco. (Sniffs.) Wow. What fine tobacco. *Country life* has its charms. The best tobacco, best curds, excellent ghee—that's why *poets* crave the *country life.*

VENKATESAM: You are also a *poet,* aren't you?!

GIRISAM: Of course. That's why I love *country life.* However, there are no *beautiful shepherd girls* and falling in love like in England. There are plenty of *grass girls* here, but they *smell*. Moreover, there are no *maidens* in our country. You have to *love widows*, no other way.[37]

VENKATESAM: You said you would show me the poem you wrote on the widow, but you haven't.

GIRISAM: If I give it to you as soon as you ask, it becomes cheap. Also, you are too young to understand the beauty of it. However, I will make an exception in your case and teach it to you. Take a notebook and write.

(Girisam dictates, word by word, with cigar in hand, smoking and taking breaks as he dictates.)

The Widow

She leaves the bed at A.M. four,
And sweeps the dust from off the floor,
And heaps it all behind the door,
The Widow.

Of wondrous size she makes the cake,
And takes much pain to boil and bake,
And eats it all without mistake,
The Widow.

Through feasts and fasts she keeps her health,
And pie on pie she stores by stealth,
Till the town talks of her wealth.
The Widow.

And now and then she takes a mate,
And lets her hair grow on her pate,
And cares a hang what people prate,
The Widow.

I love the widow—however she be,
Married again—or single free,
Bathing and praying,
Or frisking and praying,
A model of saintliness,
Or a model of comeliness,
What were the earth,
But for her birth.
The Widow.[38]

When I published this in *The Reformer*,[39] Tennyson turned green with jealousy. (Finishing the cigar.) Let's go home. We have spent a long time here. (They walk a few feet, when they bump into Agni-hotra Avadhanlu.)

AGNI-HOTRA AVADHANLU: Sir, what did you say your name is?

GIRISAM: Elders call me Girisam, sir.

AGNI-HOTRA AVADHANLU: Look here, Girisam-garu,[40] you really think that we will win the lawsuits we were talking about last night?

GIRISAM: I'll bet my earlobes that we'll win. You are no small strategist. Moreover, as the book says, *yato dharmas tato jayah,* wherever the truth is there goes victory. The truth is on your side. There is a Jabalpur high court judgment[41] very strongly favorable to us regarding Bucc'amma's case. My uncle won a similar case recently.

AGNI-HOTRA AVADHANLU: The problem is that we had to file the suit in Kakinada. I sent Karataka-sastri to handle the case for me and he gave the brief to a good-for-nothing lawyer. This lawyer writes only for more money but doesn't say anything about the progress of the case. It is not like a nearby town that I can go to every few days.

GIRISAM: If you allow me, I'll go on the *steamer* and settle that matter. My uncle is the most intelligent lawyer in Kakinada.[42] He has won every single case he took up.

AGNI-HOTRA AVADHANLU: If you go, it is as good as my going there. Never mind what it costs, we will give the case to your uncle. What do you say?

GIRISAM: You wouldn't need to pay him any *fee,* sir, just take care of the expenses, and I will see that he works for free.

AGNI-HOTRA AVADHANLU: I knew you would say that. We'll give you a nice gift when we win.

GIRISAM: That won't be necessary, sir.

(Enter Bucc'amma.)

BUCC'AMMA: Father, Mother says to take your bath, the meal is ready.

(Exit Bucc'amma.)

AGNI-HOTRA AVADHANLU: Whatever you say. (Girisam looks at Bucc'amma from the corner of his eye.) I'll give you the relevant papers after we eat. Take a look at them at your leisure. We brought a suit on our neighbor Ramavadhanlu about the wall that separates both our houses and the munsiff dismissed it. I know he was bribed. We appealed but our advocate took bribes from the other party and ruined our case. If I'd had the support of a person like you I would have pulled Ramavadhanlu's hair off his head. You tell me, if the east wall that separates his house from ours is his, the west wall should be ours, right? See how he built his roof over that wall? Bhukta advised me to file a criminal case.

(Enter Bucc'amma again.)

BUCC'AMMA: Father, Mother says to take your bath.

AGNI-HOTRA AVADHANLU: What a nuisance. I am talking business with important people, and you keep interrupting like the idiot in the street play.[43]

GIRISAM: We should certainly file a criminal case. Should we file it under *Criminal Procedure Code section 171* or *section 172*?

AGNI-HOTRA AVADHANLU: Can't we bring both *sekshans*?

GIRISAM: Criminal entry and occupation, both the sections will work. I have seen it with my own eyes and I can give strong evidence that the wall belongs to you. It clearly looks like your wall, after all.

AGNI-HOTRA AVADHANLU: There's no doubt about that. I overlooked the matter all these days. Come, I'll show you the other wall. I won the case against the blacksmith Akka-battudu by twisting his nose. But then I had to sell my farmland in Siripuram to pay for the litigation. But if only I had won the suit against Ramavadhanlu, I wouldn't have regretted the loss of property.

(Exeunt omni.)

Act Three

SCENE ONE. Front room in Ramap-Pantulu's house in the Brahmin village Rama-chandra-puram.

(Enter Madhura-vani.)

MADHURA-VANI: This Ramap-Pantulu may look shiny on the outside but he is hollow inside. People say his properties are mortgaged to his debtors. He has borrowed up to his neck and can't raise any more loans. He gets people to fight among themselves and makes a living from their quarrels. I should make as much money as I can in this village and find another branch to hold on to, the sooner the better. (Sings:)

Oooo, was I deceived!
Was I naive . . .
Oooo, was I deceived!

(Ramap-Pantulu enters as she is singing.)

RAMAP-PANTULU: I wonder how you were deceived? Sing the next line.

MADHURA-VANI: There is no next line. I was deceived because I trusted you.

RAMAP-PANTULU: Why do you say so? I didn't do anything to deceive you. In the city, I paid you two hundred rupees as agreed. I paid your monthly salary in advance. Is that deceiving you?

MADHURA-VANI: You take a strange view of things, Pantulu-garu! You seem to think that the only thing I care for is money. I treat money as trash, a piece of straw. I wouldn't have accepted your two hundred if I had known that your lands are mortgaged to your debtors. You should cut down on your expenditure, begin saving, pay off your debts, and put your house in order. I get a good name only if people say that Pantulu-garu so-and-so kept such-and-such a pleasure-woman and flourished from her love and care. This is my family tradition, Pantulu-garu! I am not like all the other pleasure-women in town.

RAMAP-PANTULU: Land under mortgage? I don't know who told you these things. It's all a big lie. I live like a prince.

MADHURA-VANI: I know that. Because you looked like a prince to me, I left everything, came away with you, and offered you my life and honor. Don't dump me now. A huge sin will engulf you if you do so.

RAMAP-PANTULU: Do I look like a cheat?

MADHURA-VANI: Then tell me why did you fix a match for the old man Lubdha Avadhanlu? This move is entirely for your own pleasure. And you think I don't see it?

RAMAP-PANTULU: Ha ha ha. Is this what you suspect? I hope you don't think I'm an old man too, just because I have a few white hairs in my beard.

MADHURA-VANI: Trees get stronger when their trunk gets darker and men get younger when their hair gets grayer. Beauty lies in the occasional gray hair—like stars in a dark sky.

RAMAP-PANTULU: What a lovely image! Give me a kiss. (He tries to kiss Madhura-vani.)

MADHURA-VANI: (Hiding her face in her hands and turning her face away.) Don't you have any sense of timing? I won't let you kiss me until you undo this match you have fixed for Lubdha Avadhanlu.

RAMAP-PANTULU: It's too late, it's not within my power to stop the wedding. (Kisses Madhura-vani by force.)

MADHURA-VANI: You're rough, just because you are strong!

RAMAP-PANTULU: What do you know about my strength? In my youth, I used to hit the base of the temple flagpole with my hand and the bells would ring for a whole hour. Ever since I fell sick, I have become a little weak.

MADHURA-VANI: A little weak? Look at my hand. It's all red. You're really rough.

RAMAP-PANTULU: A torn rug is still big enough to sit on. Your tender body can't bear even my present strength.

MADHURA-VANI: If you don't break up this match, I won't talk to you.

RAMAP-PANTULU: You are like the crazy person in the proverb who says: "I am perfectly sane now, bring the pestle and I'll wind it around my head like a turban." For two years[1] I have used all my tricks to fix this match for him. How can I undo it now?

MADHURA-VANI: What are these tricks?

RAMAP-PANTULU: I would love to tell you so you'll know that I am strong in my mind too. This Lubdha Avadhanlu is a miser. His name truly translates his qualities. He is literally Lubdha, "miserly." I had someone tell him that he will come into a lot of money if he marries.

MADHURA-VANI: How did you perform that miracle? If a person marries, he usually has to spend money. How can he make money from a marriage?

RAMAP-PANTULU: What do you know about my political skills? I make impossible things possible and possible things impossible. I bribed Siddhanti to read Lubdha's horoscope. He looked at it from top to bottom and said he saw a marriage very soon and a lot of money from it too. Since then the old man has been pulled both ways. The hope of getting money pulled him forward and the fear of spending money pulled him back. Meanwhile the master astrologer Panda came to town. I tutored him to say the right things. Lubdha showed his horoscope to him for a second opinion. What did Panda say? "Marriage and fortune are linked here. But then you are an old man. Who'll give their daughter to you? When such impossible events are indicated in a horoscope, it often means that a great calamity will happen instead. Either you will die or suffer a huge loss of money. Do a ritual to pacify the planets and feed a lot of Brahmins. The evil will subside with a minor sickness or some such small thing." When Panda finished, Lubdha's heart broke into two pieces and he began to seriously look for a bride.

MADHURA-VANI: What a sham!

RAMAP-PANTULU: Wait, there's more to the story. Now there's Agni-hotra Avadhanlu's daughter in Krishna-raya-puram. How is her horoscope? It's lucky beyond words. The house she enters will grow into ten houses. Whatever she touches will turn to gold.

MADHURA-VANI: Is this true or is this your doing too?

RAMAP-PANTULU: No, this time it's not my doing. Agni-hotra Avadhanlu fixed the horoscope himself. This is common among us Brahmins. Not one horoscope we show for matchmaking is true; every one of them is fixed.

MADHURA-VANI: What a fraud!

RAMAP-PANTULU: Call it politics.

MADHURA-VANI: What's the difference?

RAMAP-PANTULU: If a person trusts you and you deceive him, it is fraud. If a person doesn't trust you, it's politics.

MADHURA-VANI: Why don't you just say it's fraud if someone else does it and politics if you do it? It's all lies anyway.

RAMAP-PANTULU: What did you say? It's all lies? God created a profession called management. What's that profession? Telling lies that look like the truth and making money. How can someone like you understand these subtleties of dharma?

MADHURA-VANI: You're right. How would I know? But tell me, how do you make money from this marriage?

RAMAP-PANTULU: (To himself:) She is cross-examining me, the slut. (Openly:) I fixed a dance performance for you. Isn't that making money?

MADHURA-VANI: What a clever person you are, Pantulu-garu! (Hitting him with a betel leaf.) Two years ago you dreamed that I was going to enter your life, so you made a huge effort to arrange this marriage so I could make money by performing at the wedding? Let me tell you exactly how you are going to make money from this marriage. You're going to seduce the bride, make her your girl, and through her, swindle the old man of all his money. I may be naive, but I can imagine that much. Otherwise, why won't you cancel this wedding when I beg you to? With your savvy, I don't believe there's anything you can't do.

RAMAP-PANTULU: That's true. But do you think I do everything just for money? I worked on this marriage to help the old man.

MADHURA-VANI: There is a story called "Strange, Strange, Stranger Than Strange." That's how everything you do looks.

RAMAP-PANTULU: Tell me that story. I love stories.

MADHURA-VANI: No, stories shouldn't be told in the daytime. Come, first tell me this story of your wondrous plan to help the old man.

RAMAP-PANTULU: No, I shouldn't tell you. I won't.

MADHURA-VANI: I won't let you go without telling me.

RAMAP-PANTULU: What will you do if I don't?

MADHURA-VANI: I'll hit you with my braid. That's the weapon *Kāmasūtra* advises women to use.

RAMAP-PANTULU: Wait, I can't handle violence. Put your texts away and don't think of using force. I don't mind telling you, but you shouldn't hear such gossip. It's really not much. This Lubdha's widowed daughter Minakshi is a loose woman. Every once in a while she gets into a crisis. Police threaten Lubdha and make a few rupees. That miser of a father almost dies when he has to part with money. He says that Minakshi wastes money even in managing the house. If the old man gets a wife, there will be a check on her.

MADHURA-VANI: It's amazing to hear you say that Minakshi's morals are loose. What woman can keep her morals once you set your sights on her?

RAMAP-PANTULU: See, that's why I didn't want to tell you in the first place.

MADHURA-VANI: I don't care for all your tricks. Just stop the wedding.

RAMAP-PANTULU: I'll get you a little money for your dance at the wedding. Stay quiet.

MADHURA-VANI: (With her index finger straight on her nose, indicating "no, no":) Me, dancing in front of Lubdha Avadhanlu! What are you talking about?

RAMAP-PANTULU: He sits there only in name. The real dignitary is me, right?

(Enter the Head Constable smoking a cigar. He comes and sits down.)

HEAD CONSTABLE: Hey, Ramap-Pantulu, you even pulled the wool over the inspector's eyes, didn't you?

RAMAP-PANTULU: (In the Head Constable's ear:) Say "-garu," show some respect.

HEAD CONSTABLE: What "garu"? That's garish. No "garu," no nothing.

RAMAP-PANTULU: Brother, you shouldn't barge in where there are women.

HEAD CONSTABLE: You say "women." Including yourself? (Laughs.)

RAMAP-PANTULU: There is a time for humor.

HEAD CONSTABLE: I didn't come here for laughs. You grabbed twenty-five rupees from Rami-nayudu using the name of the inspector. How many others have you swindled like this? The inspector asked me to drag you to the police station by your pigtail. He left for Palem and will be back soon.

RAMAP-PANTULU: The inspector and I were classmates. He can drag me by my pigtail and I can drag him by his. That's all fine. The word about Rami-nayudu is a lie. You go ahead, sir. I'll come on horseback and meet you at the station.

HEAD CONSTABLE: I have things to do. I can't come to the station, Pantulu. I'll send a constable to take you.

RAMAP-PANTULU: (In his ear:) I beg you, don't address me without the "-garu" in my house.

HEAD CONSTABLE: Is that the problem? Whatever you say, Pantulu. (Exits.)

RAMAP-PANTULU: (To himself:) See, he still says "Pantulu" and not "Pantulu-garu." (Openly:) Anyone there?

SERVANT: (Enters.) Sir.

RAMAP-PANTULU: Get a horse ready.

SERVANT: Yes, sir. (Exits.)

RAMAP-PANTULU: See, Madhura-vani? It rains money wherever I go. I had some five or six thousand rupees given to the inspector after he was transferred to this part of the district. Close the door behind you and practice your music. There's nothing more valuable than a good skill. (He goes out a few feet and comes back.) Good, you are already at your vina. Look, Madhura-vani, there are all kinds of bad people in this village. People will come saying they are my friends or relatives, but don't let them in. (Closing the door from behind him.) Lock it from the inside.

(Exits.)

SCENE TWO. Bedroom in Ramap-Pantulu's house.[2]

MADHURA-VANI: (Sits on a rug and plays the vina, completing her song.) "There is nothing more valuable than a good skill." Of course. Except for one thing. Money. If a skill doesn't bring money, it's poverty itself. People won't give a penny in this village, even if Narada[3] himself sings. So let's put this vina away. The Head Constable winked before he left. He doesn't part with cash, but he'll stand up for me if anyone causes trouble.

(A knock at the front door.)

MADHURA-VANI: This is probably him. (Going to the door.) Who are you? Relatives?

(Karataka-sastri in disguise and his disciple dressed as a girl are on the other side of the door.)

KARATAKA-SASTRI: A good relative is one who helps you when you're in trouble. We're not your relatives, but you could be ours.

MADHURA-VANI: Are you friends?

KARATAKA-SASTRI: (To himself:) This voice sounds familiar. (Openly:) We came to make friends with you.

MADHURA-VANI: With what?

KARATAKA-SASTRI: (To himself:) Is this Madhura-vani? The voice sounds like hers. But then it could be someone else with a similar voice. (Openly:) There's only one thing to seal any friendship.

MADHURA-VANI: What would that be?

KARATAKA-SASTRI: Gold.

MADHURA-VANI: If you are neither relatives nor friends of my Pantulu-garu, I am allowed to open the door for you.

KARATAKA-SASTRI: (To himself:) What a surprise, this *is* Madhura-vani![4]

MADHURA-VANI: (With a finger on her nose:[5]) How strange!

KARATAKA-SASTRI: What is strange?

MADHURA-VANI: This guise of yours.

KARATAKA-SASTRI: This is the dress God gave me. Anything to feed the belly.

MADHURA-VANI: So you hide things from me too. Who's this girl?

KARATAKA-SASTRI: My daughter.

MADHURA-VANI: So the theater died and you are doing street guises[6] now. You are a rich man; why do you have to stoop to this?

KARATAKA-SASTRI: God has blessed me with enough to live on. I just came to see you.

MADHURA-VANI: I am grateful that you remembered this poor woman.

KARATAKA-SASTRI: There is no one else like you, Madhura-vani. I haven't seen you for days, but not because I lost interest in you. When I heard that the *deputy collector's* darling son had taken you for his woman, I was afraid that he would chop my head off if I came to your house. I have been praying for the day when the *deputy collector* would be transferred and I could see you again. When did you come to this village?

MADHURA-VANI: A couple of months after the *deputy collector* dispatched his son to Madras for higher studies, the young man sent me money through Girisam-garu. Later Girisam-garu himself kept me, but he was frequently short of cash. They were all afraid that the deputy collector might be watching my house to keep tabs on his son, so no respectable man came to see me. I wanted to leave town until the memory of the Sanjiva Rao affair faded, so I came here.

KARATAKA-SASTRI: (With his finger on his nose:) Did Girisam keep you? He is now in my sister's house under the pretext of tutoring my nephew. I should see that he is thrown out.

MADHURA-VANI: (With her finger on her nose:) What's wrong with Girisam keeping me? You yourself regret you've been unable to come to see me and blamed it on the *deputy collector.* It was all right for you to see me and wrong for Girisam? Frankly, your wife should have driven you out of the house.

KARATAKA-SASTRI: She didn't actually drive me out, but she might as well have, the way she treats me.

MADHURA-VANI: (Smiling.) If my Pantulu should see this young woman, that will be the end of her life with her husband.

KARATAKA-SASTRI: You are assuming she is married. I brought her to you to get her married.

MADHURA-VANI: To Pantulu?

KARATAKA-SASTRI: "One woman, beautiful or ugly"[7]—that's what the wise men say. When he has you, the most beautiful woman in all three worlds, why does your Pantulu[8] need a wife?

MADHURA-VANI: Then who do you want to marry her to? To me? If so, I'm ready. I'll dress myself as a man and sit on the wedding seat. How else can I marry a wife like this and become the son-in-law of the world-famous Karataka-sastri-garu? You think I am flattered when you call me the most beautiful woman in all three worlds? Compared to this girl, people like me fade like oil lamps before floodlights. It takes a woman to see beauty. Men are blind. All right, then. Give me my wife and go your way. Good-bye. (Pulls the Disciple by the hand.)

DISCIPLE: Look, Dad, she's pulling me!

MADHURA-VANI: (Laughing uncontrollably.) Great! Is that how a good wife behaves? If you don't go to your husband, what will the neighbor women say about you?

DISCIPLE: She'll probably beat me. Let's go home, Dad.

MADHURA-VANI: My, how you pretend innocence! Fine, I'll marry you later; first give me a kiss. (Kisses the Disciple.)

KARATAKA-SASTRI: You are spoiling an innocent girl.

MADHURA-VANI: He can teach a hundred people like me and spoil all of them. I know whose disciple he is. This girl's mouth smells a little like cigars.

KARATAKA-SASTRI: That's why my cigars keep disappearing from the box! Madhura-vani, God has put you in my path. I wanted to talk to you alone. Listen to my problem before Pantulu returns and get us out of the trouble we are in.

MADHURA-VANI: What's the trouble you are in, and what can I do to help you?

KARATAKA-SASTRI: It's not a small problem. In this village, there is an old man, a cousin of Girisam's, called Lubdha Avadhanlu. My brother-in-law decided to marry my little niece to him. If this marriage goes through, my sister says she will kill herself. Help me find some way out of this wedding and save my sister's life.

MADHURA-VANI: If you sell this girl for a cheaper price, Lubdha Avadhanlu will gladly marry her. Why him? I would gladly buy her myself.

KARATAKA-SASTRI: You grasp things with a hint. I don't need to tell you more.

MADHURA-VANI: But how to foil a match that is already fixed?

KARATAKA-SASTRI: There's nothing your brains can't achieve, and there is nothing money can't buy.

MADHURA-VANI: Brains can't do a thing, but money can do everything. Pantulu hopes to make a couple of rocks[9] from this wedding.

KARATAKA-SASTRI: If he fixes it for my girl, I will give him a couple more.

MADHURA-VANI: That's fine. Humor works well in a play. But if it enters the players' lives, have you thought of what it might lead to?

KARATAKA-SASTRI: You have nothing to lose and I have nothing to lose. Once we are through this, I'll wash off this beard and mustache and go my way, and my disciple will throw his sari in your house and go his way. You can wonder with all the other women of the neighborhood how this has come to pass. For now, think of a strategy to make this happen and talk Pantulu into doing this for us.

MADHURA-VANI: This can't be done with Pantulu alone.

KARATAKA-SASTRI: Then tell me who else I need to get.

MADHURA-VANI: After you talk to Pantulu, go see my friend Minakshi. She is Lubdha Avadhanlu's daughter. See her when her father is away and offer her two gold coins. Then see Siddhanti and offer him a similar bait. Siddhanti is critical in this matter. I will play the rest of the game from behind the curtain.

KARATAKA-SASTRI: And as for you, I don't even have to mention it. It's my duty to reward you suitably.

MADHURA-VANI: I am saddened when you say this. By profession I am a pleasure-woman. I take money for my services wherever I can. But did you think Madhura-vani has no kindness or compassion? Do I expect money to save your sister? Let's tell the Head Constable some of the facts; he will take care of matters if things go wrong. He should be here any minute. I'll talk to him. You sit here.

KARATAKA-SASTRI: I hope he is a friend, or the whole thing is done for.

MADHURA-VANI: A slave.

(She exits.)

KARATAKA-SASTRI: Let's sit here.

DISCIPLE: Sir, what's my name?

KARATAKA-SASTRI: God, you'll ruin everything. Your name is Subbi, Subbi. You must have lost your senses when you saw Madhura-vani.

DISCIPLE: I was just watching her to capture her laugh.

KARATAKA-SASTRI: If you remember *sabbu,* the word for soap, you will remember Subbi.

(Ramap-Pantulu gets off his horse and walks in.)

RAMAP-PANTULU: (Softly to Karataka-sastri:) Has anyone gone inside?

KARATAKA-SASTRI: Two or three people came, but your wife drove them away.

RAMAP-PANTULU: Who are you, and why did you come?

KARATAKA-SASTRI: I am from the Krishna coast. People call me Gunturu Sastullu.[10] I came to consult you on an important matter.

POLICEMAN: (From the street:) The inspector said that he will keep the horse under the banyan tree until I return. Give me the money, quick.

(Enter Madhura-vani.)

RAMAP-PANTULU: I heard someone come.

MADHURA-VANI: Who comes here? Your friends. Or so they say. I drove them out.

POLICEMAN: Hey, sir! The money!

RAMAP-PANTULU: (To Madhura-vani:) Give me the money I gave you the other day. I'll pay it back to you this evening. This devil is pestering me.

MADHURA-VANI: I already sent the money to town. If I keep it here, how can my mother live there?

RAMAP-PANTULU: You're lying.

MADHURA-VANI: (Takes the bunch of keys from her waist and throws it at Ramap-Pantulu.) Look for yourself.

RAMAP-PANTULU: (Rubbing his shoulder.) You have a bad temper. Can't you see that people get hurt if you throw things at them?

MADHURA-VANI: If you hurt me with your words, you get hurt too.

POLICEMAN: Hey Pantulu, should I go and tell the inspector that you aren't paying the money?

MADHURA-VANI: (Taking a gold chain from her neck.) Take this, pawn it, and get the money you want.

RAMAP-PANTULU: (To himself:) She's a good woman after all. I shouldn't suspect her too much.

KARATAKA-SASTRI: Sir, Pantulu-garu, how much do you need?

RAMAP-PANTULU: Twenty-five.

KARATAKA-SASTRI: Let me offer the amount. (Gives money to the constable.)

RAMAP-PANTULU: See, this is how money comes to a man who is born under a lucky star. What's the important business you came to see me about?

KARATAKA-SASTRI: This is my daughter. You must perform her wedding and accept the merit that comes from it.

RAMAP-PANTULU: I am not a Vaidiki to do weddings, I don't know those chants. (Takes a cigar and bites its end.) What do you say, Madhura-vani? Light.

MADHURA-VANI: (Lighting up the cigar, looks angrily at Pantulu and the Disciple by turns.)[11]

KARATAKA-SASTRI: Ritual chants of Vaidikis—what are they worth these days? Niyogis like you control the power of the word. Your words make things happen.

RAMAP-PANTULU: What do you say, Madhuram, shall I marry this girl? (Madhura-vani looks angrily at Ramap-Pantulu and the Disciple and exits into the house.) Beautiful women look even more beautiful when they are angry. Don't they, Sastullu-garu?

KARATAKA-SASTRI: We are Veda-chanting morons, what do we know about the beauty of women? If our wives get angry, broomsticks dance on our backs. We only read about love in books, we never find it in real life. Lord Sri Krishna says to Radha: "If you are angry with me, *ghaṭaya bhuja-bandhanam racaya rada-khaṇḍanam, yena vā bhavati sukha-jālam.*"[12] What's the great poet saying? Crush me in your arms and suffocate me in your embrace, bite my lips until they bleed. That's what he says.[13]

RAMAP-PANTULU: (Looking toward the doorway Madhura-vani went in.) Don't recite this crazy poetry to Madhura-vani. What she does is already more than enough, we don't need to make her any wilder. Delicate men like me don't like rough handling in love.

KARATAKA-SASTRI: Is she not your wife? The woman is better behaved than a wife. You are really a lucky man.[14]

RAMAP-PANTULU: Selection. It's all in choosing the right person. You didn't tell me what you came for.

KARATAKA-SASTRI: I hear that Lubdha Avadhanlu and you are good friends. People say that he doesn't go one step beyond your word.

RAMAP-PANTULU: That bastard is nobody's friend. His life is linked to money. He has no friend other than money. But then he doesn't know how to manage his affairs and is scared of the courts. So he can't live without my advice. Not just him; no one in this part of the country can win a case in court without my advice. No soup cooks here without my lentils.

KARATAKA-SASTRI: That's why I came here. Sir, I know you are the only one who can get me out of trouble. My cousin studied law. He is a deputy collector now, but he is no help to any of his relatives. If any of us sends a small gift to his wife or mother, he insists on returning it—refuses to eat until they return it. Only Niyogi lords like you are capable of giving or taking. You are worthy of your mustaches. The jobs we Vaidikis do are no better than dead wood. As the poet says,

> Only those who give or get others to give
> should sport a mustache, no one else.
> Doesn't the catfish have a mustache
> long as your arms outstretched?[15]

RAMAP-PANTULU: As English education spreads, not just Vaidikis but people of all kinds of castes are getting jobs. But no matter how many exams you pass, how can you Vaidikis get our skill and finesse? The skill of managing affairs comes naturally to us, while you have to acquire it with effort. Borrowed clothes do not fit well. Because you people don't have the courage to take bribes, you pretend to be Mr. Clean.

KARATAKA-SASTRI: As the saying goes, if that is a pendant, I would have sold it for money. My people are good for nothing, and that's why I am here. If my cousin had recommended me to a few of his clients, I would have made a little money and I would have been out of trouble.

RAMAP-PANTULU: What's the trouble you're in?

KARATAKA-SASTRI: Debts. I owe money to a lot of people. If I don't repay an IOU before the next full moon, they'll sue me. Everything was settled, I was going to sell this girl to Venkata Dikshitulu of Nallabilli, but in the end he said he had no money at the moment and would pay a month after the wedding. So I cancelled the match. I heard that Lubdha Avadhanlu is looking for a bride and I came to you for help. If you arrange this match, I will present you with ten gold coins.

RAMAP-PANTULU: No, I am not the kind of person to enter into forty-fifty-rupee matters.

KARATAKA-SASTRI: I would give any amount for your help. My debts add up to about sixteen hundred rupees. Anything you get above that is yours.

RAMAP-PANTULU: No ifs and buts with me. Lubdha Avadhanlu is paying eighteen hundred to get Agni-hotra Avadhanlu's daughter. He wouldn't go for your girl unless you agree to give her for half that price. And that's hardly enough to pay your debts, let alone pay me. In any case, it's too late now. If you had come ten days ago, I would have fixed that match for you. I was the one who arranged the match for Agni in the first place. But Poli-setti stole the commission from me. I had to bend over backward to get him to pay for Madhura-vani's dance at the wedding. Let's think of another plan. Do you have sons who are minors?[16]

KARATAKA-SASTRI: My youngest son turned eighteen three years ago.

RAMAP-PANTULU: Then it's easy. We'll say that the boy is a minor, and you don't even have to pay your debts.[17]

KARATAKA-SASTRI: How can we prove that, and with what evidence?

RAMAP-PANTULU: Ohoho! Do you know anything? I have handled matters like this before—as many as I have hairs on my head. Perhaps you don't know. It's official now. False witnesses are paid at the same rate the Zamindar of Urlām pays Sanskrit scholars.[18] If a person has pundit earrings,[19] he gets a rupee extra.

KARATAKA-SASTRI: But there's the birth chart. How can you change it?

RAMAP-PANTULU: If it's written on paper, light a match to it. If it's palm leaf, put it in the boiler. It's a matter of minutes to produce a new birth chart. Let's pray that the astrologer Siddhanti lives long. I have tons of old palm leaves, unwritten ones, in my attic. I have paper dating back thirty years and different kinds of ink. Give me a hundred rupees for my fee and pay for the expenses. I will run the show.

KARATAKA-SASTRI: I already gave you the money I brought for my travel expenses. I have nothing left even to pay the barber to shave my head clean. Courts cost money. How can I go round the courts with this girl here hanging like a weight around my neck? I don't believe there is anything you can't achieve. Please have the previous match cancelled and fix my daughter for the old man. Take ten percent of what he pays and give the rest to me. Once the girl goes to her husband's house, I'll be free. Then we can follow through with your plan.

RAMAP-PANTULU: Ten percent is not acceptable. I always get fifty percent.

KARATAKA-SASTRI: If I give you half, how can I pay my debts?

RAMAP-PANTULU: I was telling you, we will find a way so you don't have to repay your debts. And don't imagine that the money is in your hands already. It takes a lot of work on my part to change the scene in your favor.

KARATAKA-SASTRI: What can I say? I'm willing to sell flesh and blood. Why am I doing this if I am not getting enough money into my hands? My financial affairs are in bad shape and the girl is somewhat out of control—that's why I am in a bit of a rush to settle. I would have made a couple of thousand rupees on her if I had a little more time.

RAMAP-PANTULU: I told you I don't like these ifs and buts. One-fifth. What do you say?

KARATAKA-SASTRI: Should you really ask for a share of this blood money?

RAMAP-PANTULU: Blood money becomes good money when it passes through me. I don't need this money for myself, it's only for giving to others.

KARATAKA-SASTRI: Whatever you say.

RAMAP-PANTULU: Now see what miracles I will perform. Madhuram, honey, bring paper, pen, and the inkwell. Not the ordinary inkwell, the big one in the niche.

MADHURA-VANI: You found a sweeter honey than me. Why do you need me?

RAMAP-PANTULU: She's jealous. That's fun too. What do you say?

KARATAKA-SASTRI: You have a real jewel.

RAMAP-PANTULU: She's a jewel all right, but because of her city habits, she's bored if she doesn't talk to men.

KARATAKA-SASTRI: You should give her that freedom. Such women shouldn't be forced against their will.

RAMAP-PANTULU: What will she do if I force her?

KARATAKA-SASTRI: If her pride is hurt, she'll kill herself by jumping into a well or something.

RAMAP-PANTULU: Is that so?

KARATAKA-SASTRI: Yes, sir. You can be sure of that. You should handle a sensitive woman gently, like jasmine.

RAMAP-PANTULU: How do you know about such gentle touches?

KARATAKA-SASTRI: It's all from books, sir. If the hero rejects her, the heroine kills herself by hanging from the vines in the pleasure garden. Great poets described such things in their books.

RAMAP-PANTULU: She can talk to anyone she wants to, but tell her not to talk to that Head Constable. You are like her father, you can tell her.

KARATAKA-SASTRI: *Ptcha!* If only I was that lucky! If I had a daughter like her, I would have sold her for four thousand rupees, paid off all my debts, and lived happily ever after. Even this girl of mine, if I had shown her around, I would have made two or three thousand already. But her mother was keen on marrying her to her brother's son. That was what ruined all our chances. I had to bring this girl here into this part of the country without telling her mother.

RAMAP-PANTULU: You have all my support.

KARATAKA-SASTRI: Then I have nothing to fear.

RAMAP-PANTULU: Come here young lady, show me your palm.

(The Disciple withdraws, pretending to be shy.)

KARATAKA-SASTRI: Ammi, show him your palm, don't be afraid.

(Karataka-sastri pushes the Disciple closer to Ramap-Pantulu. Ramap-Pantulu grabs the Disciple's palm and examines the lines. The Disciple keeps pulling his hand back. Madhura-vani comes with paper, pen, and inkwell and stands behind Ramap-Pantulu.)

RAMAP-PANTULU: Wow, what a lucky hand! Look at her wealth line, and here's the line of children; she will have many.

MADHURA-VANI: Once you hold her hand, why would she lack children?

(She empties the ink from the inkwell onto Ramap-Pantulu's face and storms out of the room.)

SCENE THREE. Agni-hotra Avadhanlu's house in the Brahmin village of Krishna-raya-puram.

GIRISAM: (Stands at the front door and hums.)

Desire hits me with his arrow of flower[20]
How do I bear the pain, my love,
How do I bear it ever!

Who said that they are flowers, who'll believe such lies? The truth is that they are made of iron, with a sharp *diamond* at the tip, dipped in *poison,* and Desire hits you using a spell so no one can see the blow. It is like police torture, your body is in severe pain, but no wounds show. The *beauty* of this *widow* is killing me. But she is not the kind of woman who'll follow your ideas. The old tricks are not helping. With all my *experience* in dealing with women, my *love signals* are doing no good. I haven't seen such innocent *simplicity* ever. God, she doesn't have any idea of love. If I say charming things, she looks blank with those beautiful eyes. *I am dreadfully in love with her.* From the moment I saw her, I have had nothing but hatred for *dancing girls* and *city women.* I *positively abhor* them, their cunning words, their double dealings and deceitful ways. *Damn it.* They are all *insincere.* I wonder how I was such an ass and fell into Madhura-vani's trap. There's no *comparison* between Madhura-vani and this woman. Madhura-vani is a cheap piece of colored glass, and this woman is a *pure diamond.* If any idiot doesn't agree, I'll pull the hair off his scalp. I shouldn't defile this woman. It won't work even if I try. I should try a new and more honest way. I should manage to elope with her and marry her. That would give me happiness and fame as well. *Two birds at one shot.* Convincing an *utterly innocent widow* to elope and marry me would be a thrilling achievement. What's the fun in marrying a whore who has been pregnant once or twice and is ready to elope with any low-caste Turaka or Dudekula[21] fellow? That would be *hell.* Marrying a widow like the Day-Meal-Woman is no *widow-marriage.* That's more like a whore-marriage. This woman is Bucc'amma! She is a pure, chaste widow. *WIDOW* written in *golden letters*! But then, should His Exalted Royal Richness *Maha-Raja-Raja-Sri* N. Girisam esquire marry at all? *To marry a widow or not to marry—that is the question.* I am puzzled just as Shakespeare was, aren't I? As they say about the Haji Saheb who became a Turaka in haste,[22] a sensible man like me shouldn't do anything in haste. I should consider the pros and cons, do a cost-benefit analysis, and *decide. Let's see.*

First off. *Debit:* My family throws me out if I marry a widow. *Credit:* They don't take me in even now. Balance: nil. Absolute zero.

Account number two: *Debit:* Society will outcast me. *Credit:* I will outcast society myself after taking the best thing it can offer me—i.e., this widow. Balance: *Negative advantage, having nothing to do with this pauper world. Positive advantage: Possessing all its wealth.*

Account number three: *Debit:* Society will call my wife a widow. Question. Is this really a debit item? I should ask the audit department for clarification. Meanwhile, the considered opinion of the *Maha-Raja-Raja-Sri* His Exalted Royal Richness, Girisam Esq., is: What's a widow? It's an attribute. Is it written on the face of a woman? Who can tell a widow from a married woman if both of them are dressed up and stand before you? No one. So where's the widow? It's in the minds of mocking fools. The *credit* on this account is that no one casts an eye on your wife because they think a widow is unlucky and dangerous.

Account number four: It's all *credit* with no *debit*. Girisam's fame tops the world, so people would say:

> Like clusters of stars,
> like crystals of camphor,
> your fame floods the world
> with bright white light.[23]

Girisam marrying a widow makes headlines in newspapers.[24]

Account number five: *Credit:* The Association for the Support of Widow Marriages gives a little money. Bucc'amma has property too. *Debit:* You don't get a penny from her property until you sue your father-in-law Avadhanlu for it.

Considering all the pros and cons, marrying this widow is eminently desirable. But how? I should somehow build an asses' bridge[25] and reach the shore. (Lifting his face upward and thinking.) Ever since I jumped bravely into the well and saved Venk'amma when she tried to kill herself after a fight with her husband, the entire village treats me like some kind of folk hero. They believe I am an honest man, as honest as Harischandra of classical mythology. Why shouldn't they? I am surely as honest as Harischandra, except that occasionally my mind kind of wanders. This Girisam sticks his neck out for friendship. So people aren't going to be suspicious even if I am intimate with Bucc'amma, as long as I don't cross the line. She listens with great interest when I tell stories from the *Arabian Nights, Tales from Travel to Kashi,* and the *Stories of Madana Kāmarāju.*[26] I have told some tales of love too. Now that some groundwork is done, let me start talking to her about the merits of widows remarrying. If this game succeeds, hurry to Rama-varam[27] and make merry marrying her. Let me begin the campaign at once. (Peeps through the keyhole.) She is sewing leaf-plates in the hall. Let's start with a little tune. (He hums the tune. "Desire hits me with his arrow of flower . . ." and calls:) Sister-in-law Bucc'amma-garu,[28] open the door. (Bucc'amma opens the door.) Sister-in-law, *well,* where's Venkatesam?

BUCC'AMMA: He's in the backyard, playing marbles.

GIRISAM: His education suffers when he's in the village. In the town, I never let him leave his desk. Will you p . . . p . . . please call him. It's time for his lessons.

(Bucc'amma leaves to get her brother.)

GIRISAM: Oh God, the moment I stand before her alone, I start *trembling*. I want to say one thing but end up saying something else. There's no one around and she is alone with me—this is the best time to reveal my heart to her. And I tell her to bring that monkey. How stupid can I get! Well, let's start a little lecture before the lesson.

(Enter Bucc'amma with Venkatesam.)

Hello *my dear brother-in-law*, Venkatesam, you seem to have taken a vacation from your studies. If you stay here any longer, you will forget all that you have learned. Go get your textbook. (Venkatesam brings his textbook.) Open the lesson *God's Works. Read on, my good boy!*

VENKATESAM: (Reads haltingly:) *There—is—not—an—object—in—creation—which—does—not—serve—a—useful—purpose.*

GIRISAM: Stop, stop there. What does the word "*creation*" mean?

VENKATESAM: *Creation* . . . means . . . means . . . COWS.

GIRISAM: *Nonsense.* Looks like the more you read the stupider you get. You say cows because they are right in front of you. Think again.

VENKATESAM: What was the word? Say it again.

GIRISAM: *Creation.*

VENKATESAM: Oh, that one? *Creation* means the world. When I see these cows in front of me, I think of curds. It's only for another month that I get to eat these curds here at home.

GIRISAM: *One thing at a time.* Think of the lesson now. You can talk for an hour on this one word: *creation.* How is the world? *Kapitthākāra bhūgoḷā,* says Manu's Law Code. What's *kapittha*?

VENKATESAM: An orange.

GIRISAM: Very good. Do you know the verse for it from Amara's Dictionary?[29]

VENKATESAM: No, I don't. Tell me, I will write it down in my notebook.

GIRISAM:

> They are big as *badarī* fruit.
> They are big as *māreḍu* fruit.
> Bunches of lotus buds are their pair as well.
> But,
> only the temples of an elephant firm and full
> stand up to the towering breasts
> of that stirring girl.

Tell me what else we have in this world.

VENKATESAM: Cows.

GIRISAM: *Damn nonsense.* Always cows. Think.

VENKATESAM: Water buffalos.

GIRISAM: *That will not do.* Think.

VENKATESAM: Then I don't know.

GIRISAM: *Widows.* You don't even know the answer to such a simple question. The most important of all things in the world is a woman whose husband has died. You can talk for hours about her. There is a deplorable custom in our society. A man can marry again if a wife dies, but a woman can't marry again after the death of a husband, no matter how young and beautiful she might be. Is this unfair or what?

VENKATESAM: Absolutely unfair.

BUCC'AMMA: Sir, Girisam-garu, if a widow remarries, is she not living in sin?

GIRISAM: How naive you are! The texts say clearly that widows should remarry. Parasara's code says that, even the Veda says that. Pandits in Rajahmundry established it as the law. Widows in the old times did remarry. Hey, Venkatesam, read that verse from the *Story of Nala* about Damayanti's second marriage.[30]

VENKATESAM: I don't know that verse.

GIRISAM: You don't know such an important verse. Note it down in your book. *damayanti rĕndo-pĕḷḷki dharanuṇḍe rājul'ĕlla daḍa-daḍa vaccirī.*[31] Kings from all over the world came running to win Damayanti's hand the second time around. You see, kings themselves came to marry a widow. (Looking at Bucc'amma.) Do you see? Not only do all the law books approve, they even say that it is wrong for a widow not to remarry. The high priest Sankaracarya even made a proclamation about this.[32]

BUCC'AMMA: But then why do all the elders say that widows cannot remarry?

GIRISAM: All that is to get you to work for free in the kitchen. You are made to labor from four in the morning until late in the evening, like a donkey. They don't let you eat more than once a day. You may be beautiful, a goddess, but they don't let you wear nice clothes or jewels. They even shave off that lovely dark hair which flows like a row of bees. (Turning to Venkatesam.) *For example,* if only your sister had a dot of *kumkum* on that face of hers which is as brilliant as the moon, wouldn't God himself fall in love with her? What a pity, my heart melts at her plight. Anyway, what other things are there in this world?

VENKATESAM: Cookies.

GIRISAM: *Damn nonsense,* all the time food! *Bachelors.* There are also *brahmacārins,* unmarried young men, in the world. What's their duty?

VENKATESAM: Studying the Veda and bringing grass for the cows.

GIRISAM: *Nonsense.* Those are the duties of disciples who study with your father. The real duty of a bachelor is to marry a widow. What else is there in *creation*?

VENKATESAM: I don't know.

GIRISAM: There is a council in Rama-varam which pays a stipend of one hundred rupees a month to those who marry widows. So far, five thousand widows have remarried and turned into respectable housewives. *All right.* Let's move on. We are done with the word "creation." Read that sentence and translate.

VENKATESAM: I will read after you.

GIRISAM: *All right,* God made everything in the world to be useful in one way or the other. What did he make cookies for?

VENKATESAM: To eat.

GIRISAM: *That's right.* Why did God make cows?

VENKATESAM: To give us milk.

GIRISAM: *Perfect.* Why did he make women?

VENKATESAM: To cook.

GIRISAM: *Nonsense.* To marry and beget children. Therefore, widows who do not remarry are transgressing God's command and are committing sin.

(Enter Agni-hotra Avadhanlu.)

AGNI-HOTRA AVADHANLU: Sir, Girisam-garu, are you busy teaching?

GIRISAM: That's what I have been doing for the last hour.

AGNI-HOTRA AVADHANLU: Let me hear what you teach. Please go on.

GIRISAM: *My dear boy. God made creation.* Who created the world?

VENKATESAM: God.

VENKATESAM: *Father is next to God.* Who is next to God? *Say "father."*

VENKATESAM: Father.

AGNI-HOTRA AVADHANLU: On the whole, your English education looks good. The language is different but they say the same things as we do.

GIRISAM: Venkatesam, what things are there in the world created by God? *Say "courts."*

VENKATESAM: Widows.

GIRISAM: *Nonsense. Say "courts."*

AGNI-HOTRA AVADHANLU: What? Widows? Is this what the English education teaches?

GIRISAM: No, sir. *Vidvos* is Latin for courts. (To Venkatesam:) What are courts for?

VENKATESAM: To sue.

GIRISAM: *That's right.* (To Agni-hotra Avadhanlu:) See, I am teaching your son about courts too.

AGNI-HOTRA AVADHANLU: Have you had a chance to see the papers I gave you about our court case?

GIRISAM: We will surely win the case. I am translating all the papers so you can read them yourself. I will go to Amalapuram and see that the case is won, whatever it takes, or my name is not Girisam.

AGNI-HOTRA AVADHANLU: I trust you and depend on you. Never mind how much it costs, all I want is to win the case. Also, I need your help for the wedding. I can't do anything without your support. Karataka-sastri left in a huff; he is still angry with me. He will not come back.

GIRISAM: Relax. I will take care of everything. You don't even have to get up from your chair, sir.

(Exeunt omni.)

SCENE FOUR.

(Venkatesam sits in a guava tree eating a guava.[33] *Bucc'amma draws water from a nearby well shaded by the branches of the tree.)*

BUCC'AMMA: Brother, is Girisam-garu a great man, as they say?

VENKATESAM: You bet he is, as great as Surendranath Banerjea.[34]

BUCC'AMMA: Who is *he*?

VENKATESAM: The greatest of all.

BUCC'AMMA: But why doesn't Girisam-garu have a job?

VENKATESAM: *Nonsense.* You are a woman. What do you know? You think having a job is great. You know what a job means? It means to be a *servant*.

BUCC'AMMA: What does *servant* mean?

VENKATESAM: A *servant* is like the fellow who takes care of our cattle and the maid who sweeps the floor. These are our servants. The policeman and the munsiff are the servants of the white man. It's no big thing to have a big salary. They are still servants. People like Surendranath Banerjea and Girisam-garu don't serve anybody—not the white man, not even God. You know what the collector says to the policeman? He orders him to stand. When Girisam-garu goes to the collector, he shakes his hand and offers him a chair. The Nabob of Hyderabad offered him a job with a salary of a thousand rupees per month, but Girisam-garu turned it down.

BUCC'AMMA: Is he married?

VENKATESAM: No.

BUCC'AMMA: He says that widows should marry. Why didn't he marry a widow himself?

VENKATESAM: (Softly:) You don't understand. (Loudly:) He gave up jobs, gave up marriage, to fix the world. Get it?

BUCC'AMMA: How does he do that?

VENKATESAM: By teaching kids like me. (Softly:) Teaching them how to smoke cigars. (Loudly:) The nautch question—that is driving the courtesans out of the country—that is one. The National Congress[35]—that is, to exercise the powers of a royal adviser—that's another. Now do you understand?

BUCC'AMMA: If he doesn't want to serve a master, which king does he advise as a minister?

VENKATESAM: Which king? You are a woman. Why do you need to know all these details?

BUCC'AMMA: So do you also want to fix the world?

VENKATESAM: Sure!

BUCC'AMMA: If so, will you marry a widow too?

VENKATESAM: If father doesn't beat me up. But then I don't want a widow if she has no hair.

(Enter Girisam.)

GIRISAM: Young lady, standing under the tree, you're like the goddess of the forest. (He stares at Bucc'amma.)

BUCC'AMMA: Did you hear? Brother wants to marry a widow.

GIRISAM: My favorite student and your loving brother—if he marries a widow, we'll all give him a gala welcome.

BUCC'AMMA: You are the guru. Why don't you marry a widow?

GIRISAM: You asked the right question and I have to answer it, but I shouldn't brag about myself. Also, young lady, there's another rather tricky problem. Your father and mother are steeped in the wrong notion that widow remarriage is bad. No matter how many texts you quote or arguments you provide in favor of widow remarriage, they won't listen. If you ever mention such ideas to them, they will beat you up. Your father knows only the Vedas, but I am an expert in all the *śāstra* law books. What does the law say: *bālād api subhāshitam.*[36] "Listen to good words, even from a child." But our elders do not follow the *śāstra* law books, no, not in the least. Furthermore, if you talk back to them, they pick up a big stick and beat you. I have a strong body, stronger than iron. If they beat me with a stick, the stick will break; nothing happens to my body.

But your body is soft and delicate. If they hit you, your bones will break. So listen to me carefully; the words I am going to say should be strictly between you and me and you shouldn't tell this to anyone, no matter what. What do you say?

BUCC'AMMA: Yes.

GIRISAM: It's not enough to say yes. Unless you promise you will never ever tell anybody what I will tell you now, I can't speak my mind to you.

BUCC'AMMA: I will not tell anybody.

GIRISAM: You must take an oath.

BUCC'AMMA: What oath?

GIRISAM: That my head will explode if you should ever reveal this to anybody.

BUCC'AMMA: No. You should live long. I'll take an oath that *my* head will explode, not yours.

GIRISAM: I would never let that happen. I would give my life to save yours.

BUCC'AMMA: I know you are capable of that. You saved my mother's life, risking your own.

GIRISAM: Well, since you yourself said it, let me tell you what I wanted to say. If I had a wife and children, would I have been free to jump in the well to save your mother? I wanted to devote my life to the service of others, and therefore I remained a bachelor until now. True, when people like you who are my well-wishers say, "Marry me," I cannot easily turn them down.[37] It's good to live for the world, but when I find a jewel of a woman, more valuable than this whole world, I should marry her. I never found such a woman until I came here. I shouldn't embarrass you, but I did find such a woman here. I know it's a fruit beyond my reach, and I've been trying hard to control my feelings for her. But my heart is beyond my control. I tell myself: "Girisam, you cannot get the woman you are in love with. She is a real pearl all right, but give up that thought, stay unmarried, and serve the world." Look, young lady, let's say for argument's sake we get married. We need money to run the family, right? All these years I've been a bachelor and I have been able to get away with eating whatever I get and sleeping wherever I find shelter. But once we are married, that style won't work. If we run away, go to Rama-varam and marry there, we get a hundred rupees a month from the Widow Remarriage Council. After a couple of months, I can easily get a decent job which pays a thousand rupees a month, either in Baroda or in Hyderabad. The Nabob of Hyderabad offered me a job a few days ago, but I rejected the offer. If I had known that you would want to marry me, I wouldn't have let the offer go.

BUCC'AMMA: Brother said you would never work for anyone.

GIRISAM: Yes, I did make a vow that I would remain a bachelor all my life and serve the world. But now I have found a beauty more valuable than all the world put together. If the world is silver, you are gold. Tell me what is more valuable, silver or gold?

BUCC'AMMA: Gold.

GIRISAM: You are gold. I should marry you and let go of the world, right? Let's say we are married. Then we need a lot of money. We can't get a lot of money unless I have a job.

BUCC'AMMA: Yes.

GIRISAM: You might ask, why do we need a lot of money? Listen. We need a house, right?

BUCC'AMMA: Yes.

GIRISAM: I can't live in a small house. I need a big house, a two-story house. We should have a garden around the house—mango trees, guava trees, banana plants—all kinds of trees. Venkatesam will climb those trees all the time like a monkey.

VENKATESAM: I'll have all the fruit for myself.

GIRISAM: Sure, they're all yours. In the course of time we will have children. We have to raise them well. As I sit in my office and write at my desk, the children will come and pull my hand and ask for this and that. You'll move around in the house bedecked with ornaments, like the goddess of wealth herself. One child hugs you from one side and another hugs you from the other side. We'll have ornaments and gold-embroidered clothes made for our children. The Nabob may invite our kids to his palace. We can't send them in shabby clothes, like what Venkatesam wears now. We should buy a vehicle for them. I forgot to tell you, Venkatesam will stay with us. We will take care of his education.

BUCC'AMMA: Then father doesn't have to spend money on him and father and mother will not fight about it.

GIRISAM: I'm not saying no.

VENKATESAM: You should buy me a horse cart.

GIRISAM: You don't need a cart. You can use the same cart our children use. You can also take care of them.

VENKATESAM: So are you really going to marry my sister?

GIRISAM: I'm just kidding. Don't think this is for real.

BUCC'AMMA: I knew it.

GIRISAM: What do you mean *I knew it*? How could I be so lucky? If either you or I say anything to your parents, they'll kick me out of the house. If Venkatesam tells, the whip is ready.

VENKATESAM: (Touching his back.) My lips are sealed.

BUCC'AMMA: My friend Acc'amma of the Rambhatlas said she will marry you if you consent.

GIRISAM: If I have to marry, I am not going to marry an Acc'amma or any such Amma. If a beauty like you takes pity on me and says, "Girisam-garu, marry me," I will marry her. I am not going to lose the great and noble life of celibacy for any old woman.

VENKATESAM: A perfectly ripe guava just fell; pick it up.

GIRISAM: (Picking up the fruit.) What a lovely fruit, young lady, the same shade as your skin. Take it.

BUCC'AMMA: Drop it in the water pot. (To Venkatesam:) Brother, come down and help me lift this pot.

GIRISAM: I'll help you. (Helps her lift the pot.) (To himself:) What a beauty! (To Venkatesam:) Hey, my dear disciple, throw me down a couple of guavas.

VENKATESAM: Father is coming through the back door. What should I do now?

GIRISAM: Hide behind the leaves. I'll start drawing water to divert his attention.

(Enter Agni-hotra Avadhanlu.)

AGNI-HOTRA AVADHANLU: Girisam-garu, why are you drawing water? We have a servant to do that. You are an English-educated man; you don't have to go to that trouble.

GIRISAM: Nothing in the world compares to hard work. One shouldn't sit idle, doing nothing. Drawing water is good for the plants and gives me exercise. The governor does gardening, and the English queen makes clothes for poor people. The Englishman doesn't tolerate idleness. You know what the greatest of their poets, Shakespeare, said: He said *dignity of labor.* It means the man who does physical labor is great—not the *collector,* not the *judge.* That is why all these white men work in the garden. They consider climbing trees a great skill. You know, the white man does nothing without profit. When the white man goes from town to town, he gets thirsty on the way. If he doesn't know how to climb a tree and get some fruit, he has to die of thirst. He is traveling in the hills, and suddenly there's a tiger. He quickly climbs a tree and saves himself. That's why they teach their kids how to climb trees as part of their education.

AGNI-HOTRA AVADHANLU: The training of these white men, it's a different world. What's Venkatesam doing, is he reading or writing?

GIRISAM: I have been teaching him all day and just sent him off to climb trees.

AGNI-HOTRA AVADHANLU: Are you out of your mind? What if he breaks his legs?

GIRISAM: So you want him to die from fear when he meets with a tiger as he travels along the hills in his capacity as the tahsildar of this area?[38]

AGNI-HOTRA AVADHANLU: You think this boy will become a tahsildar?

GIRISAM: Why not? If our boy doesn't know how to ride horses and climb trees, they will say: "Young man, you are no good for official travel. You better sit behind a desk and do your clerical job. Sorry, you can't be an officer." That's what they will say.

AGNI-HOTRA AVADHANLU: Ask him to climb small trees; don't make him climb big ones yet.

GIRISAM: That's why I asked him to climb the guava tree.

AGNI-HOTRA AVADHANLU: (Looking up.) You monkey!

GIRISAM: See, you are cursing him. If you want your boy to be educated like a white man, he should be trained like a white man. If you curse him, he'll get scared and fall down. If you don't approve of him doing things like this, stop his English education and get him to read your Vedic texts.

AGNI-HOTRA AVADHANLU: I'm sorry. I forgot about what you said. This training of the Englishmen, it's a crazy thing.

GIRISAM: I am surprised to hear a learned person like you say this. God gave them such a glorious empire because their character is good. We forgot what our old texts say and they stole our texts, practiced them truly, and gained control over us. You read the books, you tell me. What did the disciples do for their teachers in the olden days? They went to the forest, climbed trees, and collected firewood for the teacher's fire worship. They learned to accept a tough, hard life. And what do you say now? "My son will wilt if he is exposed to sunlight. My son will break his leg if he climbs a guava tree." Your own disciples climb those huge banyan trees and bring you leaves, don't they? The white man learns the secrets of our texts and moves up, and we let our texts gather dust and decline.

AGNI-HOTRA AVADHANLU: You know a lot of things. You are right, the skills of these white men are all stolen from our old texts. These trains and stuff are all in our Vedas. You have a good mind. I like the arguments you wrote to help win my court case.

GIRISAM: I would have written even better arguments. The record is not complete. I couldn't tell if you lost some papers or if your advocate kept them for himself.

AGNI-HOTRA AVADHANLU: I didn't lose any papers. The trouble is I don't know English.

GIRISAM: If only you knew English, you would outdo all the lawyers in the country. When I am done with watering this garden I will make a list of all your papers. Go have some rest.

AGNI-HOTRA AVADHANLU: You are a hardworking man. You take care of every detail in the household. I hope my son will grow up to be like you. Help him get down from the tree carefully. Better safe than sorry.

(Exit Agni-hotra Avadhanlu.)

VENKATESAM: (Softly:) Father has gone.

GIRISAM: Get down from the tree carefully.

VENKATESAM: (Jumps from the tree.) You saved me. (He is about to leave.)

GIRISAM: Hey, don't go yet. Bring the guavas over here.

VENKATESAM: Don't take my guavas. That's unfair.

GIRISAM: Big fruits for older folks and little ones for little kids. You ate enough already sitting up there anyway. (Girisam takes four big guavas and pats Venkatesam on the shoulder.) Just these four. That's enough for me. Now, young man, you can go climb trees as you please. The Englishman says: Study nature. When you climb a guava tree, *study* which of the fruit is ripe and which is not and pick only the ripe ones. Give me a few of them as teacher's fee. As the poet said, "Pick only ripe fruit."[39] Now *run away.* (Thinking.) Looks like my strategy is working. Oh, what a beauty!

Her breast-line curves
like the bend in the river.
Her skin
glows like gold.
Her legs are soft as lotus buds,
and dark as a rain-cloud is her braid.
Her waist
vanishes into space,
and the ultimate secret
is the hair below.[40]

(Exit.)

Act Four

SCENE ONE. Ramap-Pantulu's porch.

(Ramap-Pantulu sits on a chair and Madhura-vani gives him betel leaves rolled with areca nut.)

RAMAP-PANTULU: If only I had learned English during my school days, I would have a field day before the judges. I have Jupiter in the house of speech in my horoscope. That's why I am successful even if I don't know English.

MADHURA-VANI: Take a talking dog hunting—you say sic'em, he says sic'em back to you.

RAMAP-PANTULU: Am I a dog?

MADHURA-VANI: I'm just joking; don't take it seriously.

RAMAP-PANTULU: Are you really joking?

MADHURA-VANI: If I don't joke with you, do you want me to joke with everyone in town?

RAMAP-PANTULU: You know what will happen if you do that.

MADHURA-VANI: That's why I have only you to call a dog or a pig. I can't call anyone else that. I have a right to call you whatever I want. And as for your skill in words, what can I say? I was taken by your words and I fell for you, right?

RAMAP-PANTULU: If only I knew English, English women would run after me.

MADHURA-VANI: Aren't we Telugu women good enough for your charming face? When you speak of English, I am reminded of Girisam-garu. People say he speaks like an Englishman.

RAMAP-PANTULU: Never mind what people say—what do people know? He speaks pidgin English like the cooks in the Englishman's kitchen. If he utters such words in the court, the judges will shoo him away.

MADHURA-VANI: You should know such things better. I hear that Girisam-garu is Lubdha Avadhanlu's cousin. You never told me.

RAMAP-PANTULU: Why is he in your thoughts? What is it to you if he is Lubdha's cousin or not?

MADHURA-VANI: Thoughtless mind and mindless thought.

RAMAP-PANTULU: You think I am mindless?

MADHURA-VANI: No. It's me that's mindless.

RAMAP-PANTULU: Why do you say that?

MADHURA-VANI: Because I am worried.

RAMAP-PANTULU: What are you worried about?

MADHURA-VANI: If Girisam-garu is Lubdha Avadhanlu's cousin, he will go to the wedding. If he goes, he'll find some pretext to pick a quarrel with you and beat you up.

RAMAP-PANTULU: Yes, that's true. Good you reminded me. But Lubdha is a miser, you know. He won't invite any of his relatives to his wedding.

MADHURA-VANI: Girisam-garu doesn't need an invitation.

RAMAP-PANTULU: So you must have asked him to come.

MADHURA-VANI: Why would I have anything to do with him? You may have no principles, but I have mine.

RAMAP-PANTULU: Then how do you know he will go to the wedding?

MADHURA-VANI: At this very moment Girisam-garu is at the bride's house under the pretext of tutoring her brother. He is in charge of all the wedding arrangements. That's why I assume he will attend the wedding.

RAMAP-PANTULU: If he comes, what to do?

MADHURA-VANI: You're asking me?

RAMAP-PANTULU: What if the wedding doesn't take place?

MADHURA-VANI: How is that possible?

RAMAP-PANTULU: Well, I planned a strategy.

MADHURA-VANI: Then you fulfilled my wish.

RAMAP-PANTULU: How can Ramappa live without obeying your orders?

MADHURA-VANI: Give me a kiss. (Kisses him in appreciation.)

RAMAP-PANTULU: But Madhuram, what if my strategy fails and he shows up at the wedding after all?

MADHURA-VANI: I am a woman and you ask me for advice?

RAMAP-PANTULU: A woman's mind is subtle. If it's a court battle, I can outwit anyone. If it's a fistfight, I am paralyzed.

MADHURA-VANI: Close the doors behind you and stay in the house until the wedding is done.

RAMAP-PANTULU: Great idea. I told you, women think well.

MADHURA-VANI: But I'm afraid of one thing. What if he locks the door from outside and sets fire to the house?

RAMAP-PANTULU: That's instant death all right. Surely, Girisam is capable of arson.

MADHURA-VANI: What will you give me if I tell you a way out?

RAMAP-PANTULU: I will worship you as the very goddess who saved my life.

MADHURA-VANI: (With a finger straight on her nose.)[1] No, no, you shouldn't say such things.

RAMAP-PANTULU: If you save me from this, I will give you four gold coins.

MADHURA-VANI: I didn't ask for money, I asked for your appreciation. Saving you is like saving myself—my life. Why should I be paid for it?

RAMAP-PANTULU: I was going to give you money in appreciation. What's wrong with that?

MADHURA-VANI: Of course it's wrong. I may be a pleasure-woman, but does that mean I don't have a heart?

RAMAP-PANTULU: I am sorry, I'll punish myself. (Slaps himself on his cheeks.)

MADHURA-VANI: Hire the Day-Meal-Woman as a cook for the wedding feast.

RAMAP-PANTULU: What a great idea. Give me a kiss. (Stops halfway.) But what if Girisam beats up both me and the Day-Meal-Woman?

MADHURA-VANI: No need to fear on that account. If Girisam-garu as much as sees the Day-Meal-Woman, he'll run for his life. She has a very sharp tongue.

RAMAP-PANTULU: Not just her tongue, her hand is sharp too. You don't know how hard she hits. Your advice is excellent. Give me a kiss.

(While Ramap-Pantulu is kissing Madhura-vani, Lubdha Avadhanlu enters with a letter in his hand.)

LUBDHA AVADHANLU: Don't you have any sense of decency?

(Ramap-Pantulu looks back, startled.)

RAMAP-PANTULU: Father-in-law, we're young and, besides, this is my girl. I can kiss her in the middle of the street. Who can question it?

MADHURA-VANI: Left to you, you would kiss on top of the roof. There should be a limit to being naughty. I bow to my brother-in-law, sir. Please come and sit down. (She brings a chair.)

RAMAP-PANTULU: Lubdha is my father-in-law. How can he be your brother-in-law?

MADHURA-VANI: For a pleasure-woman, every man is a brother-in-law.[2] In what way is he your father-in-law, anyway?[3] (To Lubdha Avadhanlu:) Please sit down. I don't know why, but my brother-in-law is angry today. Maybe after your wedding, you will kiss your wife, first making sure all the doors are closed. It's true, your son-in-law still behaves like a teenager.

RAMAP-PANTULU: How can I pretend to be an old man when I am in the prime of my youth? Lubdha, are you upset?

LUBDHA AVADHANLU: I don't want this marriage.

RAMAP-PANTULU: (In Madhura-vani's ear:) See Madhuram, my strategy is working already. (Openly to Lubdha Avadhanlu:) It's final now. No whining. You can't wiggle out of the marriage now.

LUBDHA AVADHANLU: I'm not whining. I do not want to marry.

MADHURA-VANI: (In Ramap-Pantulu's ear:) What's that letter?

RAMAP-PANTULU: I forged it in Agni-hotra Avadhanlu's name.

MADHURA-VANI: (In Ramap-Pantulu's ear:) What did you write in it?

RAMAP-PANTULU: "You are an old man, we don't want to give our girl to you."

MADHURA-VANI: Really? I will tell him.

RAMAP-PANTULU: (In Madhura-vani's ear:) You must be crazy. You were the one who pestered me to foil this wedding and I did this to please you. Don't be stupid.

MADHURA-VANI: (To Lubdha Avadhanlu, privately, in his ear:) Pantulu is trying to trick you into this marriage. Don't listen to him.

RAMAP-PANTULU: (To Madhura-vani:) How dare you! (To Lubdha Avadhanlu:) Don't for a moment believe anything she says. She makes up things. Plus, a woman's advice ruins you, you know.

LUBDHA AVADHANLU: (Shaking the letter in his hands.) This is all *your*[4] doing.

RAMAP-PANTULU: (Looks at Madhura-vani angrily and turns to Lubdha Avadhanlu, but doesn't show any interest in reading the letter.) I don't know anything about that letter.

LUBDHA AVADHANLU: You are the one who did it. If you don't know, who does?

RAMAP-PANTULU: Look, if you use that insulting tone and keep accusing me of fabricating the letter, I am not going to take it. You'll soon see what Ramap-Pantulu can do.

LUBDHA AVADHANLU: What does it matter if you did it or someone else did it? It's my fault to begin with. Why should I deal with bastard middlemen?[5] I will go straight to Agni-hotra Avadhanlu and talk to him myself.

(Lubdha Avadhanlu storms out.)

RAMAP-PANTULU: Watch your words. (To Madhura-vani:) Who's he calling a bastard middleman, me?

MADHURA-VANI: It can't be me, I'm not a man.

RAMAP-PANTULU: You made me a triple bastard. My name is in the pits.

MADHURA-VANI: What did I do?

RAMAP-PANTULU: You told that bastard that I forged the letter, didn't you?

MADHURA-VANI: No, I did not. I swear.

RAMAP-PANTULU: Then how did he know that I forged the letter?

MADHURA-VANI: I don't understand what you are talking about.

RAMAP-PANTULU: This bastard will take the letter and show it to Agnihotra Avadhanlu. And he will sue me for forgery. I'll lose my neck.

MADHURA-VANI: Wait; if things are out of hand, I'll fix them. (Goes out into the street.)

RAMAP-PANTULU: Where is she going? She really did tell him I forged that letter. I should never have shared the secret with her. I was a fool. Should I run and snatch the paper from his hands? What if he bites? Better still, I should go beg Minakshi to get the letter back for me.

(Reenter Madhura-vani holding the letter in one hand and Lubdha Avadhanlu's hand in the other.)

MADHURA-VANI: Enough of your wit and wisdom. Brother-in-law has no one to go to, no brothers, no cousins, no one. He comes to ask you for advice, and what do you do? Pick a fight with him. (To Lubdha:) Sir, sit down. (Makes Lubdha sit on the chair and gives Ramap-Pantulu the letter.) Read the letter carefully and see what it says.

RAMAP-PANTULU: (Looks at the letter and says to himself:) Thank God, this is not the letter I wrote. Like a fool who fears his own shadow, I got worked up over nothing. (Openly:) Lubdha Avadhanlu, why did you have to start making angry accusations? If you ask me gently, I will do anything for you.

LUBDHA AVADHANLU: Write to him, then, that we don't want all that show. If he wants that, he has to pay for it.

MADHURA-VANI: (Unties Lubdha Avadhanlu's hair and cleans it of dust.) So much dust. It's all because you have no one to take care of you. (She brings scented oil and a comb from the niche and combs his hair.)

RAMAP-PANTULU: (Turning the page to see the end of the letter.) "*Your servant and brother, Girisam.*" Oh, it's this fellow?

MADHURA-VANI: Read it out.

RAMAP-PANTULU: So if it's your Girisam, I should read it out loud?

MADHURA-VANI: If you don't want to, read it to yourself and enjoy it.

LUBDHA AVADHANLU: Why did you say "your Girisam?"

RAMAP-PANTULU: That's a different story.

LUBDHA AVADHANLU: Please read it aloud.

RAMAP-PANTULU: (Reading aloud:) "*Your servant, your dearest brother Girisam, salutes and obediently submits the following. I heard that you have decided to marry and settle in life in this venerable old age, and my heart jumped with joy at the gentle breeze of this joyous news."*

Oho, the young man is showing off his literary skills.[6]

LUBDHA AVADHANLU: Bastard, he calls me old. I just turned fifty.

MADHURA-VANI: You have no one to take care of you, or you would be in much better shape. Who calls you old?

RAMAP-PANTULU: (Continues to read:) "*Your future wife is the sister of my favorite student Venkatesam, and that makes me happy beyond words. I am here at Agni-hotra Avadhanlu's house and I am in charge of all wedding arrangements. He treats me like his own son. He is a great man but like the moon, which, with all its brilliance, is slightly blemished, he has two defects: a touch of greed and a bit of a short temper."*

Enough of this poetry. (Continues to read:) "*N.B. If you can avoid his presence when he is angry, your bones will be safe and your life will be out of danger. But his greed helps neither him nor you. Some scoundrel in town told him that you are a very rich man and will pay for a grand wedding. Therefore, Agni-hotra Avadhanlu has invited the entire village to the wedding. The bride's party will arrive in fifty vehicles. Also, he is borrowing from the Divan Saheb an elephant, three camels, and five horses. He is bringing a gold-trimmed palanquin too.*

N.B. It would be a feast for my eyes to see you ride in a wedding parade on the golden palanquin followed by elephants, camels, horses, and all the regalia, but your well-wishers like me worry that it is a waste of your money. What has Ramap-Pantulu to lose? Like the saying goes, the crow enjoys pecking at the bull's wound."

RAMAP-PANTULU: Bastard, why does he have to talk about me? (Still reading:) "*Just between us: This Ramap-Pantulu is like a* jackal *in playing tricks on you, but in intelligence, he is a* big ass."

So, he is showing off his knowledge of English.

(Still reading:) "*To translate . . ."*

Wait, he is providing us with a gloss.

(Continues to read:) "*A* jackal *is a kind of fox,"*

Lousy bastard.

(Continues to read:) "*and* big ass *means———."*

I'll cut his topknot off. Who the hell does he thinks he is? I will sue him for damages.

(Madhura-vani laughs beyond control.)

RAMAP-PANTULU: Why are you laughing? Are you happy your husband is abusing me?

MADHURA-VANI: (Not able to overcome her laughter, but after some effort:) No, no. I swear. Cam . . . cam.

RAMAP-PANTULU: Why swear? You will live happily if I die.

MADHURA-VANI: (With her finger on her nose, goes to Ramap-Pantulu, embraces his head and kisses him.) *That* was a bad thought.

RAMAP-PANTULU: Then why are you laughing?

MADHURA-VANI: Cam . . . cam . . . cam.

RAMAP-PANTULU: What's that cam?

MADHURA-VANI: Cam . . . el.

RAMAP-PANTULU: Yes, camel. So what?

MADHURA-VANI: (Controlling her laugh.) Why camels?

RAMAP-PANTULU: How should I know?

MADHURA-VANI: Looks like you asked for them.

RAMAP-PANTULU: Me? What do I need a camel for?

MADHURA-VANI: (Still laughing out of control.) To ride on.

RAMAP-PANTULU: Me, riding on a camel?

MADHURA-VANI: Why not? You on a cam . . . el, brother-in-law on another camel, and Poli-setti, because he does wedding supplies, on the third camel. The three of you ride through the fields, and we will all watch you from the rooftops and enjoy. (Laughs even more. Controlling herself after a little while.) Sir, forgive me. But I couldn't help laughing at that stupid letter.

RAMAP-PANTULU: Stupid, stupid, he's a real jackass.

LUBDHA AVADHANLU: He also wrote that you requested a donkey.

RAMAP-PANTULU: No, there's no mention of a donkey anywhere in the letter.

LUBDHA AVADHANLU: Yes there is. I read it. Why did you ask for a donkey?

RAMAP-PANTULU: Are you out of your mind? I told you there's no donkey. (Madhura-vani laughs again.) You, you are out of your mind too? Who are you laughing at, at me? Or at Avadhanlu?

MADHURA-VANI: Why do you think I am laughing at you? There's a saying about a donkey and a camel.

RAMAP-PANTULU: Saying, shmaying.

MADHURA-VANI: The donkey says, "I am famous for singing and my sister, camel, for her looks."

RAMAP-PANTULU: So?

MADHURA-VANI: It just reminded me of that. It's been a while since anyone mentioned donkeys and camels together.

RAMAP-PANTULU: So?

MADHURA-VANI: It was just funny. Why don't you laugh too—without arguing?

RAMAP-PANTULU: I'm going to sue this fellow for damages.

MADHURA-VANI: (To Lubdha Avadhanlu:) Sir, why suspect my master Ramap-Pantulu-garu? He really wants to help you. There's a reason why Girisam-garu wrote those nasty things against him. I shouldn't tell you, but I have to, when your friendship is at stake. Your Girisam-garu used to teach me English. He kept me too, for some time. He bears a grudge against Pantulu-garu because Pantulu-garu took me away from him. That's why he wrote all those lies calling him a jackal and a jackass. Don't take his letter seriously.

RAMAP-PANTULU: It's not funny to call me a jackal and a jackass. He'll know the consequences when he pays for libel.

MADHURA-VANI: Sir, think of this too. What does Pantulu gain by bringing camels and donkeys? (Laughs again.)

RAMAP-PANTULU: I told you, there's no donkey.

MADHURA-VANI: Never mind, if there's no donkey, there are other animals, right? What does Pantulu-garu gain if all these animals are fed at your expense? Maybe Poli-setti has something to gain, because he sells the fodder.

LUBDHA AVADHANLU: You got that right. All this is Poli-setti's doing.

RAMAP-PANTULU: You thought he would be cheap and gave the supplies contract to Poli-setti. Now you know.

MADHURA-VANI: It's still not too late. Write a letter to Agni-hotra Avadhanlu telling him to invite no one to the wedding, just send the bride and we'll do it all for a few rupees.

LUBDHA AVADHANLU: What a good idea. Pantulu-garu, Madhuram is very intelligent.

RAMAP-PANTULU: Look, you shouldn't be so intimate, calling her Madhuram. Call her Madhura-vani.

LUBDHA AVADHANLU: I am sorry. But what if they send the bride alone?

MADHURA-VANI: What's the problem? Marry her.

LUBDHA AVADHANLU: I will never, ever marry her. Read the letter to the end, and you'll know why.

MADHURA-VANI: (To Ramap-Pantulu:) You stopped reading. Is there something that bothers you?

RAMAP-PANTULU: I am definitely filing for defamation. This letter is trash; what's there to read?

LUBDHA AVADHANLU: The bastard didn't insult me any less. Read to the end anyway.

RAMAP-PANTULU: (Reads:) "*Appendix: The girl has all the lucky features but she has a cowlick. People say it indicates she will become a widow. This is sheer* supa . . . super . . . sti . . . tion, *that is, an irrational belief. Wise people like us shouldn't believe in such things. However, there's an easy treatment for this: Take a pair of tweezers and pluck all the hair from that spot and apply a certain powder. She won't get a cowlick again. However, if she should really become a widow in the meantime, the hair is periodi-*

cally shaved off anyway, so there won't be any problem at all. Furthermore, if she should grow her hair, even as a widow, there's nothing anyone can do about it."

MADHURA-VANI: Stop it. Enough of this. Girisam-garu is really wicked.

RAMAP-PANTULU: Now do you understand his nature? (Reads on.) *"Note no. 3. These days there's a lot of talk of widows remarrying. I suppose you know about that. When you die and go to enjoy the gods' women in heaven,*[7] *she might want to remarry. Let me tell you that this is something I cannot prevent. If I tell her not to remarry, she might say, 'Your brother is sleeping with Rambha in heaven, and why shouldn't I have similar pleasures here on the earth?' "*

MADHURA-VANI: Enough already. Will you please stop?

RAMAP-PANTULU: You think I am going to read when you want me to read and stop when you want me to stop? (He continues to read.) *"Note no. 4. The rest of the details are quite good. You should really marry this girl. Your would-be mother-in-law is as respectable as Arundhati.*[8] *However, just between us, she's adamantly opposed to marrying her daughter to you. She is telling all her neighbors that she will jump into the well and kill herself to prevent this wedding from happening. But never mind her threats, we will hold her and tie her up during the wedding. If she wants to kill herself after the wedding, that's her problem. We don't lose a thing. However, we may have to bribe the police to prevent a criminal case. I write this in some detail in the interest of your welfare, and I hope you will keep this information to yourself. The bride's horoscope, they say, is really superior. That was of course fabricated by Rama—."*

MADHURA-VANI: Rama? Go on. What's the rest of the word?

RAMAP-PANTULU: It's not a word fit for women to hear.

LUBDHA AVADHANLU: Does he say that the horoscope was your forgery too?

RAMAP-PANTULU: You think his head has any clean thoughts in it? He won't learn a lesson until a defamation suit is filed.

LUBDHA AVADHANLU: I don't know, there might be some truth to what he says. Even Poli-setti says that the bride's mother is opposed to this wedding. Please let me bow out of this. I don't want this wedding.

MADHURA-VANI: That's fine. Write a letter to the bride's father, right away, that you do not want to go on with this wedding. Shall I bring a pen and paper?

LUBDHA AVADHANLU: No more discussions. Please draft a letter that we do not want this match. (He stands up and whispers privately into Madhura-vani's ear and Madhura-vani whispers back into his ear.)

RAMAP-PANTULU: What's this whispering and touching each other's faces?

POSTMAN: (From the street:) Is Lubdha Avadhanlu here? He has mail. (Madhura-vani goes out, brings an envelope, and gives it to Lubdha Avadhanlu, who gives it to Ramap-Pantulu.)

LUBDHA AVADHANLU: I didn't bring my reading glasses. Read it for me please.

RAMAP-PANTULU: (Reading silently.) The problem is solved. From the bride's father.

LUBDHA AVADHANLU: What does he say? No elephants and camels, right?

RAMAP-PANTULU: No. He doesn't want to give his daughter to you.

LUBDHA AVADHANLU: What? Why doesn't he? And exactly who doesn't want this match, he or I? Does he think I'm not good enough for him?

MADHURA-VANI: A minute ago you said you don't even want to marry. Are you now upset that he has declined to give his daughter to you?

LUBDHA AVADHANLU: Read on. What other drivel is there?

RAMAP-PANTULU: He says he heard that you are a miser.

LUBDHA AVADHANLU: Me? A miser? What miser shells out eighteen hundred rupees just like that? Has Agni-hotra Avadhanlu ever seen that kind of money in his life? If I am careful with my money, does that mean I am a miser? Anyway, why should he care what kind of man I am once he gets his money?

MADHURA-VANI: You are a fine kind of man, worth your weight in gold.

RAMAP-PANTULU: He has also heard that you are old, and you suffer from tuberculosis.

LUBDHA AVADHANLU: Me, old? I'll chop his hair off. Old, at fifty? I cough a little, of course. When I have paid a heap of money and bought the girl, why should he be concerned with my problems or her problems? Once he has accepted the money, he has to marry his daughter even to a corpse. That's it.

RAMAP-PANTULU: Yes. You said it right. What does it matter if you are old?

LUBDHA AVADHANLU: What do you mean, "What does it matter?" You think I am old too? *You* probably started all this crap.

RAMAP-PANTULU: Why do you need me? Your cousin Girisam is there to rake up every piece of crap in the world.

LUBDHA AVADHANLU: How did this fellow end up there, like the devil himself?

MADHURA-VANI: Strange are the ways of men. Until now you were sorry the wedding was on, and now you are sorry the wedding is off. Tell me, do you really want to marry?

LUBDHA AVADHANLU: I might or might not. That's a different matter. I will not suffer this humiliation.

MADHURA-VANI: What will you do?

RAMAP-PANTULU: What will he do? He will file for damages.

LUBDHA AVADHANLU: No, for god's sake, no court cases.

RAMAP-PANTULU: Or if you marry another girl from an even better family, and even cheaper, that's tit for tat for Agni-hotra Avadhanlu.

LUBDHA AVADHANLU: How do you get a cheaper bride?

MADHURA-VANI: Listen to me. Don't marry. Just live happily.

LUBDHA AVADHANLU: Why, do you also think I am old?

MADHURA-VANI: You? Old? Who says that?

LUBDHA AVADHANLU: I wish Agni-hotra Avadhanlu had your sense.

MADHURA-VANI: Not one tooth loose, and your vision is fine. Look at your muscles, they are so strong.

RAMAP-PANTULU: (Looks at his own muscles.) Lubdha works in the garden, so he has thick arms. My arms may be thin, but they are bars of steel.

MADHURA-VANI: (Measures Lubdha Avadhanlu's chest with the end of her sari.) What a wide chest!

RAMAP-PANTULU: (Yelling at Madhura-vani:) Hey, what are you doing?

MADHURA-VANI: Why are you reading the letter to yourself? Read it out loud.

RAMAP-PANTULU: Who made you my boss? We'll read the letter as we please. These are not words women should hear. Go to your room.

MADHURA-VANI: I won't move from here.

RAMAP-PANTULU: I will pick you up and put you in your room.

MADHURA-VANI: (Stands behind the chair and embraces Lubdha Avadhanlu's arms from behind.) I will hold my brother-in-law like Markandeya held Śiva.[9] We'll see if you can take me away.

LUBDHA AVADHANLU: (To himself:) How soft her hands are! She smells sweet when she is close. (Openly:) The texts say, *bālād'api subhāshitam,* "listen to good words even from a child." Let Madhura-vani stay. She is intelligent. She has an eye for truth.

RAMAP-PANTULU: Listen, then. (Reads:) *"It is strongly rumored that people outcasted you because of your daughter's loose morals."*

LUBDHA AVADHANLU: (Stays silent for a while.) You are the one that ruined my house.

MADHURA-VANI: It's Pantulu, right?

LUBDHA AVADHANLU: Why blame outsiders?

MADHURA-VANI: (Stays silent for a while.) Listen. I will come and live with you. Give up this marriage stuff. I'll take care of you better than any wife.

LUBDHA AVADHANLU: (Showing his happiness.) But I am a poor man. Can't pay you. A valuable thing like you only Pantulu-garu can afford.

MADHURA-VANI: I don't care about money. Will you feed me?

LUBDHA AVADHANLU: Happily.

MADHURA-VANI: Then let's go. Don't be fooled by this Pantulu's empty words. No marriage, no nothing—and we'll live a happy life.

RAMAP-PANTULU: (Looks angrily at Madhura-vani.) Isn't it time for your meal? Go eat.

MADHURA-VANI: The way you treat me feels like a hearty meal in itself. (Leaves angrily.)

LUBDHA AVADHANLU: Madhura-vani—she may be a pleasure-woman, but she is much better behaved than any housewife. I wish our wives were as sensible as she is.

RAMAP-PANTULU: Yes, she is surely sensible, but very short tempered. And she is easily jealous, and at such times, she loses all sense of decency. But listen, respectable people like you should not touch a pleasure-woman's body. If she brings her face close to yours—because she is too young to know what is proper—you should tell her to keep her distance. This is the only bad quality she has—she cannot live without talking to other men. City life has made her too social.

LUBDHA AVADHANLU: She's too young. Madhura-vani is like my daughter. Don't take it wrong if she touches me.

RAMAP-PANTULU: What do you have to lose? Do you see my point? If your kept woman touched another man right in front of you and started admiring that man—"Your muscles are strong, your chest is wide"—and so on, that would make you want to kill her, wouldn't it?

LUBDHA AVADHANLU: I am sorry, I made a mistake. I will punish myself. (He slaps himself on his cheeks.) Forgive me.

RAMAP-PANTULU: No point in slapping your cheeks. Slap her cheeks instead. She seems to have taken a little liking for you. Tell her off.

LUBDHA AVADHANLU: Liking for me! What are you talking about?

RAMAP-PANTULU: She wants to live with you. Take her home, then.

(Madhura-vani enters wearing a silk sari as the last words are spoken.)

MADHURA-VANI: Sure; he'll take me home, if you can't bear me. If I serve this great man, at least my afterlife is secure.

LUBDHA AVADHANLU: Pantulu is just kidding. He's not going to leave you, and I don't deserve you. No.

RAMAP-PANTULU: Make her eat grass, she's behaving like an animal.

MADHURA-VANI: (To Lubdha Avadhanlu:) Pantulu might be kidding, but I am not. Donkeys eat grass, human beings don't.

RAMAP-PANTULU: See, you're saying donkeys again. (Madhura-vani turns her head away to hide her laughter, enters the doorway, goes to the inner room, and laughs out loud.)

LUBDHA AVADHANLU: Madhura-vani respects you and adores you too.

RAMAP-PANTULU: True. But when she gets angry she treats people like trash. She doesn't even mind if there are visitors around.

LUBDHA AVADHANLU: Sir, I think it's desirable to drop this marriage idea. What's your advice?

RAMAP-PANTULU: Why do you need my poor advice? Madhura-vani already counseled you against marriage, and you want to obey her. I told you what the elders say: *strī-buddhih praḷayantakah.* A woman's advice leads to ruin.

LUBDHA AVADHANLU: I am seeking your advice because you wish me well. Do you think I want to drop the marriage idea because Madhura-vani said so? Anyway, this match failed, and I am pleased I saved some money.

RAMAP-PANTULU: We're back to square one. I told you umpteen times why you should get married, but all my advice gets thrown out and the final note falls on money. If you marry and have a child, your family flourishes. If you die single, who's going to get all your wealth?

LUBDHA AVADHANLU: You exaggerate my wealth. What do I have?

RAMAP-PANTULU: All right, you have whatever you have. But you should have a son to offer some water at your funeral, right?

LUBDHA AVADHANLU: Well, if that's an argument for marriage, why are *you* not married?

RAMAP-PANTULU: I am different. I've brought my inheritance to zero. And my afterlife? I am a devotee of the Primal Female Energy. I do yoga. I am free from all ritual bonds. I do my ancestral rites only for the benefit of the world. You might ask why I keep a pleasure-woman. You know the saying: *kāmi gāka mokṣagāmi kāḍu.* Only a man of desire can desire liberation. But what about you? One of these days your widowed daughter is going to dig up that buried wealth while you sleep and run away with her lover-boy. Lady Poverty is going to be your companion from then on.

LUBDHA AVADHANLU: So what do you want me to do?

RAMAP-PANTULU: Look for another girl to marry. Your daughter's games will be held in check by your wife's presence in the house and your wife will be kept under surveillance because of your daughter's presence in the house. Don't you agree?

LUBDHA AVADHANLU: What you say is true.

RAMAP-PANTULU: But it's also true that you have a habit of forgetting it and I have to keep reminding you. Don't you remember what your horoscope says? If you don't marry this year, you will face the risk of death.

LUBDHA AVADHANLU: No, I didn't forget. But the fact is that after a long search we only found this girl for eighteen hundred, and even this failed in the end. Is it going to be possible now to find another girl so cheap? Impossible! Impossible!

RAMAP-PANTULU: He came just yesterday from Gunturu, this Brahmin. I wonder if he is still here.

LUBDHA AVADHANLU: Looking for a match?

RAMAP-PANTULU: Yes. What a stupid thing I did! He asked me if there are any bridegrooms that I know of, and I said no. How would I know this match would fail? That Brahmin chants the Veda in braids[10] and comes from a very respectable family. Marrying his daughter would be a slap in the face for Agni-hotra Avadhanlu.

LUBDHA AVADHANLU: What's the asking price?

RAMAP-PANTULU: It's very cheap. That's why I'm sorry to have lost the chance. He comes from Gunturu. People there are new to our style of haggling. He settled for twelve hundred in Nandipalli, but the groom's family said that they couldn't pay until later. The Brahmin has debts to repay. If he doesn't pay before the due date, the case goes to court. So he is in a hurry to give away his girl. He found matches in a couple of places for a thousand rupees. But he is not willing to give her for less than twelve hundred.

LUBDHA AVADHANLU: We will raise it by a hundred and offer eleven hundred.

RAMAP-PANTULU: First, he should be here to raise it by a hundred or fifty.

LUBDHA AVADHANLU: Please find out where he is staying. It'll be a great help to me. Where are they staying?

RAMAP-PANTULU: Forget the money—money is nothing—but what a beauty, that girl! What lines of luck she has! She has a line of fortune extending from one end of her palm to the other. Her lines of progeny are very sharp. The girl is a star.

(Enter Madhura-vani.)

MADHURA-VANI: Star? What star?

RAMAP-PANTULU: We are looking at the stars in Avadhanlu's horoscope. They say that he will surely get married this year.

MADHURA-VANI: I don't trust your word. (Goes close to Lubdha Avadhanlu, puts her face very close to his, and asks:) Is it true?

LUBDHA AVADHANLU: Everyone says so.

MADHURA-VANI: What does the astrologer Siddhanti say?

LUBDHA AVADHANLU: Every astrologer says the same thing. I will marry this year. So far, my horoscope has been right. Not one prediction has been wrong.

MADHURA-VANI: Then suffer your fate. But don't listen to this Pantulu and marry that girl with the cowlick.

RAMAP-PANTULU: You came in the middle of your meal; what's so important?

MADHURA-VANI: I need the silver bowl.

RAMAP-PANTULU: Take it.

(Exit Madhura-vani.)

LUBDHA AVADHANLU: Why does this woman go on saying "Don't marry"?

RAMAP-PANTULU: Talk softly. Does a pleasure-woman ever advise marriage? She has her eye on you.

LUBDHA AVADHANLU: Her eye on me? Don't be ridiculous.

RAMAP-PANTULU: If you do not marry, she will come and sit in your house. She was saying it loud and clear; didn't you hear? Let me warn you. If you mess with her, you and I will have a fight.

LUBDHA AVADHANLU: What are you talking about? She is like my daughter. Please go and find out if that Brahmin from Gunturu is still around.

RAMAP-PANTULU: He was staying in the house across the street from here. I'll find out if he is still there. But let me check on Madhura-vani's meal first.

(He goes into the house, returns, and goes out into the street.)

LUBDHA AVADHANLU: This Pantulu thinks that I will take his woman away from him. *Aha ha.* (Inhales a pinch of snuff.) Only a pleasure-woman can sense the difference between man and man. If I grow a mustache and dye it, I'll be young again. If I can get this inexpensive match, there won't be anyone luckier than me.

(Enter Ramap-Pantulu dragging by the hand the Disciple dressed as a girl. He shows her palm to Lubdha Avadhanlu.)

RAMAP-PANTULU: You lucked out, Lubdha. Look at this line of fortune running up from the bottom of the palm all the way to the top. Here are the lines of progeny. See here on her neck—lines of ornaments.

LUBDHA AVADHANLU: Enough, no need to look too close.

(While the conversation goes on, Madhura-vani sneaks in from behind and empties a pot of water on Ramap-Pantulu's head.)

RAMAP-PANTULU: Hey, how dare you?

MADHURA-VANI: A ritual bath for the new groom. (Pinching the Disciple's cheek.) Don't you have any shame, you slut?

(Exit Madhura-vani.)

RAMAP-PANTULU: When she is upset, she loses all her sense. Next she'll attack us with a broomstick or a firebrand. Let's take this girl and get out of here.

(Walks toward the street holding the Disciple's hand.)

LUBDHA AVADHANLU: She can walk. You don't need to hold her hand.

RAMAP-PANTULU: Oh, I see, she is your wife-to-be.

(All three go out and enter the street.)

LUBDHA AVADHANLU: So you think I should marry this girl?

RAMAP-PANTULU: Never mind what I think. See for yourself. How does it feel to you? Does she touch your heart? Her looks, shape, and style, are they appealing? These are the things you look for.

LUBDHA AVADHANLU: We are family people, what do we need beauty for?

(Siddhanti enters rushing somewhere.)

SIDDHANTI: (To Lubdha Avadhanlu:) Father-in-law, who is this girl?

(Lubdha Avadhanlu doesn't answer. Instead, he points with his head to Ramap-Pantulu.)

RAMAP-PANTULU: She is ours.

SIDDHANTI: (Staring at her.) What a fortunate girl! She has all the features of luck.

RAMAP-PANTULU: What do you mean?

SIDDHANTI: Look at those wide eyes, well-shaped earlobes, curly hair. Young lady, may I see your hand? (Examining the Disciple's palm.) Whoever married her, he is a very lucky man.

RAMAP-PANTULU: She is not married yet.

SIDDHANTI: Then you are lucky. You can't find a more fortunate girl. She will bring wealth, fortune, and gold and she will have a long married life. See, here is her marriage line. This is her line of wealth. Pantulu, get the treasure chests ready. Young lady, turn your hand over. Children: (Counts:) one, two, three . . . (Leaves her hand and turns to Lubdha Avadhanlu.) Father-in-law, a little snuff. (Inhales.) Poli-setti's daughter is giving birth. I have to write the birth chart. I will seek your audience again. Bye.

RAMAP-PANTULU: Just a word. (Talks privately to Siddhanti. Siddhanti consults the almanac, says a few words, and rushes away.)

LUBDHA AVADHANLU: What did he say?

RAMAP-PANTULU: He thinks I am going to marry this girl. He says the next thirteenth day of the moon[11] is auspicious for the wedding.

LUBDHA AVADHANLU: I don't think there's an auspicious moment on that day for weddings.

RAMAP-PANTULU: The elders say: *śubhasya śīghram.* Good things should not be delayed. No need to be picky about an auspicious moment for a second marriage. It's enough if the day and the star are good. Here comes your would-be father-in-law.

LUBDHA AVADHANLU: See if we can get a good bargain.

KARATAKA-SASTRI: (To Ramap-Pantulu:) Looks like you poured holy water on your head. Where are you taking my daughter, sir?

RAMAP-PANTULU: Just a word. (Takes Karataka-sastri aside and they talk privately.)

RAMAP-PANTULU: (Now taking Lubdha Avadhanlu aside:) He is asking fourteen hundred. He has an offer for thirteen.

LUBDHA AVADHANLU: That's no help. (Angrily:) At least fix the bargain at the twelve he had asked for.

RAMAP-PANTULU: I am only trying to help. Don't be cross with me. If you want it badly, they hike up the price. What can I do? (He goes to talk to Karataka-sastri and returns to Lubdha Avadhanlu.) Lubdha, somehow I got him to accept. He insists, however, that you should give a gift of gold to the bride.

LUBDHA AVADHANLU: That I cannot do.

RAMAP-PANTULU: Shh. Say yes. I'll borrow the gold *kaṇṭĕ*[12] from Madhura-vani, put it around the bride's neck at the time of the wedding, and take it back later.

LUBDHA AVADHANLU: I don't want to know anything about that. That's your business.

RAMAP-PANTULU: All right, all right, it's my business. We'll manage the wedding supplies ourselves and finish it all without spending a whole lot. Don't ask Poli-setti to take charge. Now who will go to invite the elders from Peddipalem?[13]

LUBDHA AVADHANLU: Who else do I have? You have to help me with that too.

RAMAP-PANTULU: I need to dress up when I go to visit the townsmen. I'll get my best clothes washed.

(Exeunt omni.)

SCENE TWO. Lubdha Avadhanlu's house.

LUBDHA AVADHANLU: Yes, what you say is right. A single-night wedding[14] in a holy place is an accepted tradition.

KARATAKA-SASTRI: Even people in high offices are performing single-night weddings these days. God Kodaṇḍa-rāma-svāmi manifested himself here, and the monkey god Hanumān himself consecrated the temple. Who can say this is not a holy place?[15]

LUBDHA AVADHANLU: That is true, but so far no one has accepted this as a holy site or performed a single-night wedding here. What would people say if we went ahead and did it anyway?

KARATAKA-SASTRI: Once this is a holy place, who cares what anybody says?

LUBDHA AVADHANLU: All right, let's tell Pantulu.

KARATAKA-SASTRI: You must be visiting here from the age of truth. You think Pantulu and Poli-setti, who are waiting for a chance to make a little cash out of this wedding, will accept an abridged single-night affair? Don't even tell them until after the marriage knot is tied.

LUBDHA AVADHANLU: If I don't tell Pantulu, he will cause trouble.

KARATAKA-SASTRI: What are you afraid of? Is he your boss or what? If he makes trouble, I'll chop his head off.

LUBDHA AVADHANLU: Don't mess with him. Give Siddhanti a couple of rupees and he will take care of it. Pantulu is speechless before him.

KARATAKA-SASTRI: Every poison has an antidote. Even Pantulu must have one.

SCENE THREE. The backyard of Lubdha Avadhanlu's house.

MINAKSHI: Grandpa, I will take care of your daughter like a child in my womb.

KARATAKA-SASTRI: She is my little girl. I leave her in your hands. You are both her father and her mother. (Weeps.)

MINAKSHI: Don't feel sad. She will lack nothing in my care. I will take good care of her.[16]

KARATAKA-SASTRI: I gave her a gold coin to give to you. Make sure you take it from her.

MINAKSHI: No rush. She will give it to me in due time. If she has it, it is just as good as my having it.

(Enter Siddhanti.[17])

SIDDHANTI: I see only vegetables and groceries—no sign of anything needed for the ceremony. My assistant is sleeping like a log.

MINAKSHI: The auspicious moment is four *gaḍiyas*[18] after sunrise. What's the rush, Uncle?

SIDDHANTI: You remind me of the kid who was sent to school and came back stupider than before. The auspicious moment is at four *gaḍiyas* before sunrise.

MINAKSHI: Dad is always like this. He never tells me anything clearly. Dad, Dad!

(Enter Lubdha Avadhanlu.)

LUBDHA AVADHANLU: What are you yelling about?

MINAKSHI: Uncle Siddhanti says the auspicious moment is four *gaḍiyas* before sunrise.

LUBDHA AVADHANLU: What! I thought it is at four *gaḍiyas* after sunrise.

SIDDHANTI: You might as well think it is forty-four *gaḍiyas* after sunrise. Stop being stupid and get ready quickly. Go and take the ritual bath. I invited all the Brahmins in the village.

LUBDHA AVADHANLU: You're going to kill me. It's too cold now to take a bath. Ramap-Pantulu also assumed that the time of the wedding is four *gaḍiyas* after sunrise. He will probably invite the elders of Peddipalem to come at that time.

SIDDHANTI: *śatāndhāh kūpam praviśanti:*[19] "A hundred blind men walk into the well." Minakshi, please take the bride and give her a bath.

MINAKSHI: Yes, I'll give her a bath in no time.

(Exit Minakshi.)[20]

SIDDHANTI: Women are far better than these lazy men. I'll take care of things in the wedding hall.

LUBDHA AVADHANLU: Can we go on with the wedding without Pantulu?

SIDDHANTI: Whose wedding is it? Yours or Pantulu's? Don't be a wimp. Go bathe.

(Exeunt omni.)

SCENE FOUR.

(Lubdha Avadhanlu in bridegroom's clothes, the Disciple in a bridal sari. A few Brahmins sit on the porch. Ramap-Pantulu enters with musicians, load-carriers, and helpers.)

RAMAP-PANTULU: *Abbabba.* I'm dog tired. (To the servant:) Ask the trumpet player to stop. These palanquin carriers and drummers—they make a huge racket when they reach the village. My feet are aching. That stupid Peddipalem—it's a lot farther than I thought. (Looks at Lubdha Avadhanlu.) Wow, you are already all dressed up as a groom in yellow clothes and everything with the bride at your side. So you have asked to be formally made up as a groom! The older you are, the more fun you want, right?

LUBDHA AVADHANLU: I'm really sorry you weren't able to make it in time for the wedding.

RAMAP-PANTULU: (Startled.) What! What do you mean in time for the wedding?

PRIEST GAVARAYYA: We were all disappointed you were not present at the auspicious moment. We thought you were tied up with something very important. The assembly looked empty without you. (Reads a verse:)

An assembly without a Niyogi,
is utterly vulgar—alas—to compare
it is like a woman. . . .[21]

RAMAP-PANTULU: Shut up. How did you tie the knot before the prescribed time?

PRIEST GAVARAYYA: Siddhanti carefully calculated the movement of the stars, calculated the time, and had the knot tied at the precise moment, sir.

RAMAP-PANTULU: It's not four watches in the day yet.

PRIEST GAVARAYYA: The auspicious moment was four watches *before* sunrise sir.

RAMAP-PANTULU: But Siddhanti told me four watches *after* sunrise.

PRIEST GAVARAYYA: Who on earth can change the movement of the planets, sir? He may have said four watches before and you might have heard it wrong.

RAMAP-PANTULU: Hold your planets. In this god-forsaken village, Siddhanti makes all the rules. What treachery!

PRIEST GAVARAYYA: Siddhanti was very disappointed you didn't come. Avadhanlu was worrying the whole time, wondering what calamity prevented you from coming. Only when he heard the sound of the trumpets did he calm down.

LUBDHA AVADHANLU: It's true, sir.

PRIEST GAVARAYYA: And that Madhura-vani, she stood like a doll in the wedding hall, but no—she did not sing one song, even when all the Brahmins pleaded and begged.

KONDI-BHOTLU: All the time she stood chatting with the Head Constable. Why? Couldn't she sing a measly tune when so many of us begged her to?

ANOTHER BRAHMIN: You nincompoop, how could she sing when Pantulu-garu was not present?

PRIEST GAVARAYYA: What do you think she was talking about to the Head Constable? Pantulu-garu was traveling with valuables. Some accident might have happened or he would have been here. So she was begging the Head Constable to send his men to go look for him.

KONDI-BHOTLU: This Brahmin is making things up! All the time she and the Head Constable were laughing, falling all over each other. Gavarayya weaves poetry that she was worried about Pantulu.

RAMAP-PANTULU: Enough, enough of your Vaidiki nonsense. Just mind your business; don't poke your noses into others' affairs.[22]

PRIEST GAVARAYYA: Stay quiet, Kondi-Bhotlu. Show some respect to your elders.

RAMAP-PANTULU: (To the Wedding-Brahmin:) You have no respect yourself. You started the whole thing.

PRIEST GAVARAYYA: You know why they say VMIAC, sir? Vaidiki's Mind Is Always Crooked.

RAMAP-PANTULU: Where is he, that fellow, what's his name?

PRIEST GAVARAYYA: Who, sir?

RAMAP-PANTULU: That man, that Gunturu Sastullu. Where is he?

LUBDHA AVADHANLU: Oh, him! He . . . he left.

RAMAP-PANTULU: What nonsense! How could he leave while his daughter's wedding is still going on?

LUBDHA AVADHANLU: The wedding is over, sir.

RAMAP-PANTULU: Don't be an idiot. The tying of the knot is done—you managed that without me. But the damn wedding goes on for five days, doesn't it?

PRIEST GAVARAYYA: No, it's a one-night wedding, sir. So we did it all in two steps: the main fire offering and the concluding fire offering.

RAMAP-PANTULU: (Stunned, to Lubdha Avadhanlu:) You ungrateful bastard!

PRIEST GAVARAYYA: (Shutting Ramap-Pantulu's mouth with his hand.) Peace, peace! Sir. (To Lubdha Avadhanlu:) Fall on Pantulu-garu's feet and beg his forgiveness. (To Ramap-Pantulu:) Sir, you made this auspicious event possible. Don't utter inauspicious words now. Siddhanti and the bride's father discussed texts and decided on a one-night wedding ten minutes before the wedding began.

RAMAP-PANTULU: What a conspiracy! Don't tell me you paid him money.

LUBDHA AVADHANLU: He was in a rush to repay his debt, which comes due the day after tomorrow, or the lender will go to court. So he took the money and ran. He said he'll be back before the end of the week.

RAMAP-PANTULU: I mediated the whole bargain. How could you do this without me? Do you know how much of an advance I gave him? You colluded with your father-in-law and pulled the wool over my eyes.

LUBDHA AVADHANLU: You agreed to pay the money before the knot was tied. He refused to allow me to tie the knot unless we put cash in his hands. What could I do?

RAMAP-PANTULU: Your house was on fire and you had to tie the knot in a rush, right? Why couldn't you wait until I came? This guy is a con man. He wanted to grab the money before I came because he knew I'd catch him. What's his name?

PRIEST GAVARAYYA: His name . . . Lubdha Avadhanlu knows, sir.

LUBDHA AVADHANLU: I don't know his name.

RAMAP-PANTULU: You good-for-nothing! No doubt he's a con man.

LUBDHA AVADHANLU: You certified that he is a very respectable man. I trusted your word.

RAMAP-PANTULU: Who cares if you trusted my words or not? Cough up the hundred rupees I gave him for the wedding expenses.

LUBDHA AVADHANLU: If you gave him money, get it from him. Don't ask me.

RAMAP-PANTULU: All right, I won't ask you. I won't even talk to you. I won't even stay in your house a minute longer. (He stands up.) Listen everybody. This Gunturu Sastullu is a cheat, otherwise he wouldn't have grabbed the money this fool gave him and run away without even giving us his name. He got away with some of my money too. It looks like he sold a widow or a low-caste girl to this idiot and ran away with the money. Hey, watchman, go to the Head Constable and ask for a couple of policemen to be sent. I will have them chase after this fellow.

(Siddhanti enters as Ramap-Pantulu finishes and is about to leave and stops him by forcefully grabbing his arm.)

SIDDHANTI: Where are you going? Hold on a minute.
RAMAP-PANTULU: Why are you stopping me?
SIDDHANTI: You want the name of that Gunturu Sastullu?
RAMAP-PANTULU: I do.
SIDDHANTI: Peri Ramasastullu-garu. Why do you need his name?
RAMAP-PANTULU: He owes me money.
SIDDHANTI: He doesn't owe you a penny. I know it.
RAMAP-PANTULU: You are hurting my arm.
SIDDHANTI: Did you think that a Vaidiki's hands are soft? Tell me how much you skimmed off the money you took from Lubdha Avadhanlu for the wedding expenses.
RAMAP-PANTULU: Who are you to ask me? Why are you being so rude? Are you going to attack me or what?
SIDDHANTI: You said all those nasty things about the new bride—that she is a widow and things like that. We won't let you get away with that.
RAMAP-PANTULU: All right, she is not a widow; she is a virgin. Now let go of my arm.

(A frightened Lubdha Avadhanlu edges away from the Disciple in bride's clothes.[23])

SIDDHANTI: You can be angry but don't lose your business sense. You are our patron and I am your supplicant. I have something to tell you that should interest you. Please come over here.
RAMAP-PANTULU: If you show proper respect, I'll be nice to you too.
SIDDHANTI: Lubdha Avadhanlu-garu, come over here too.

(Siddhanti, Lubdha Avadhanlu, and Ramap-Pantulu confer secretly.)

RAMAP-PANTULU: (Joyfully:) Siddhanti, a pinch of snuff. (Takes a pinch of snuff from Siddhanti's snuffbox.) A Niyogi is always reasonable. Hey, you Brahmin cooks[24] over there, did you send snacks to my house? You, Kondi-Bhotlu, come with me.

(Kondi-Bhotlu goes to Ramap-Pantulu.)

KONDI-BHOTLU: At your command, sir.
RAMAP-PANTULU: Follow me to my house.
KONDI-BHOTLU: Yes, sir.
RAMAP-PANTULU: There are some fine jackfruits in my garden. Go get a couple of them. Your father loves jackfruit.
KONDI-BHOTLU: Yes, sir.

RAMAP-PANTULU: What's the news of the wedding?

KONDI-BHOTLU: Nothing, sir.

RAMAP-PANTULU: So Madhura-vani didn't sing?

KONDI-BHOTLU: She did, sir.

RAMAP-PANTULU: Is it true?

KONDI-BHOTLU: No, sir.

RAMAP-PANTULU: I see. I suppose she was busy talking to the Head Constable.

KONDI-BHOTLU: No, sir. She didn't say a word to him.

RAMAP-PANTULU: But you said she talked to the Head Constable, didn't you? You said she was laughing with him.

KONDI-BHOTLU: Yes, yes, but then . . . then . . . Kam-Bhotlu made me say so.

RAMAP-PANTULU: I'll teach him a lesson. No one plays games with me. You be good. I've known you since you were a kid. You're an honest fellow.

KONDI-BHOTLU: Yes, sir, I always speak the truth.

RAMAP-PANTULU: Yes, you do. But you didn't tell the truth in the case of the Head Constable. Swear by the deity in the temple and tell me truthfully—who are the people Madhura-vani spoke to?

KONDI-BHOTLU: Shall I tell you the truth, sir?

RAMAP-PANTULU: I am asking you because you speak the truth.

KONDI-BHOTLU: Well, she spoke with everybody.

RAMAP-PANTULU: Everybody—who is that everybody?

KONDI-BHOTLU: You are asking who? We left the wedding area and all of us gathered around Madhura-vani. She talked to Bhukta and then . . .

RAMAP-PANTULU: Who else?

KONDI-BHOTLU: Siddhanti stopped chanting the ritual chants and spoke secretly to Madhura-vani.

RAMAP-PANTULU: Who else did she talk to?

KONDI-BHOTLU: And then . . . and then . . . she talked to the Head Constable.

RAMAP-PANTULU: You idiot, didn't you just tell me she didn't?

KONDI-BHOTLU: Yes, she didn't.

RAMAP-PANTULU: Tell me truly, did she or didn't she?

KONDI-BHOTLU: God, I'm a goner.

RAMAP-PANTULU: I hate it when you tell lies. You know I have a bad temper. Take an oath and speak up. If you tell a lie, your head will crack open. Did she talk or not?

KONDI-BHOTLU: No. She didn't.

RAMAP-PANTULU: With God as your witness?

KONDI-BHOTLU: With God as my witness.

RAMAP-PANTULU: At last you've told the truth. Listen. You are still young. You should not say bad things against women, even if someone asks you to. Remember this.

KONDI-BHOTLU: Madhura-vani is a great woman, sir.

RAMAP-PANTULU: Do the people of the village think so?

KONDI-BHOTLU: Yes, sir. Everyone thinks so.

(In front of Ramap-Pantulu's house.)

RAMAP-PANTULU: I will knock on the door. Play this little trick for me.

KONDI-BHOTLU: Yes, sir.

RAMAP-PANTULU: Take this two-anna coin and tuck it in your waist. Go stand behind my back wall for about half an hour. If you see the Head Constable or anyone else coming out the back door, grab them and yell for me. I will meet you there. If you see no one, go your way.

(Exit Kondi-Bhotlu.)

(Knocks on door.) What's taking so long? She doesn't open right away. That's why I suspect her. Did the fellow speak the truth? How come she ran to the wedding on her own without waiting for me? (Knocks again.) She still hasn't come. (Madhura-vani opens the door.) What are you doing that's taking so long?

MADHURA-VANI: From now on, I will keep a log of everything I do from morning to evening. Come in.

(Both of them go into the house.)

(Enter Kondi-Bhotlu.)

KONDI-BHOTLU: Sir, Pantulu-garu!

(Enter Ramap-Pantulu and Madhura-vani.)

RAMAP-PANTULU: (To Madhura-vani:) You go into the house. (To Kondi-Bhotlu:) What happened?

KONDI-BHOTLU: Sir, I . . . I . . . couldn't do it.

RAMAP-PANTULU: Why not?

KONDI-BHOTLU: How can I catch an untouchable woman?

MADHURA-VANI: Why should you catch an untouchable woman?

KONDI-BHOTLU: Pantulu told me to catch anyone who comes out of the back door and yell for him.

MADHURA-VANI: How humiliating! The Brahmin is going insane.

RAMAP-PANTULU: (From behind Madhura-vani, he makes a sign asking Kondi-Bhotlu to leave.) You believe that chatterbox Vaidiki kid?

(He goes inside. As soon as Ramap-Pantulu goes in, Madhura-vani bolts the drawing-room door from outside, signs to Kondi-Bhotlu to come in, and kisses him.)

MADHURA-VANI: (Speaking softly:) You saved me.

KONDI-BHOTLU: Madhura-vani, here's the two-anna coin Pantulu gave me and the four-anna coin the Head Constable gave me, and here's the silver-trimmed snuffbox.

MADHURA-VANI: (Taking them.) You're a good boy. From now on we're friends—you know that? (She kisses him again.) Now you may go.

(Kondi-Bhotlu jumps out into the street and dances. Kam-Bhotlu enters.)

KAM-BHOTLU: Why are you so happy?

KONDI-BHOTLU: She kissed me!

KAM-BHOTLU: Don't tell lies. She kissed your monkey face?

KONDI-BHOTLU: You crazy ass, we're friends.

(Exeunt omni.)

SCENE FIVE. In the Brahmin village Krishna-raya-puram.

(Girisam is supervising the building of a pandiri in Agni-hotra Avadhanlu's backyard. Enter Venkatesam.)

GIRISAM: Why, my young man, your cheek looks bruised!

VENKATESAM: Father hit me.

GIRISAM: What did you do?

VENKATESAM: I didn't say my morning prayers.

GIRISAM: Couldn't you pretend you were praying?

VENKATESAM: I thought he wasn't watching.

GIRISAM: You should never do that. When you pretend, pretend all the time. Not just when someone is watching you. You know I meditate every day, like a heron in the lake.

VENKATESAM: What do you meditate on?

GIRISAM: On food. I say to myself, "God, please let this old man end his worship soon so I can get food on my plate."

VENKATESAM: You should pray to god with the right chants. Is it not a sin to ask for your meal?

GIRISAM: *Ignorance.* You don't know anything about religion. I should train you in religion after this wedding is over. I have studied all religions, taken the essence of all of them, and created a new religion. I am going to spread it in America. But let me answer your question now. What was your question? Is it right to meditate on food? See what your Upanishad says: *annam brahmeti vyajānāt.* It says, you fool, know that food is God. What does the white man pray for every day? *Father, give us our daily bread.* So what should we pray for? We should pray for rice and lentils. What does the Vedic *Camakam* say? *śyāmakās ca me.*[25] The *śyāmaka* rice is very delicious; that's what the prayer asks for. We can add anything we like in the *Camaka* text. Like "French fries *ca me,* chocolate *ca me.*" That's what I call religious reform.

VENKATESAM: "Thick curds *ca me,* cookies *ca me.*"

GIRISAM: Excellent. That's *originality.* Even your own mother will not give unless you ask. God doesn't either. Make a list of all the things you want and insert it into your chant.

VENKATESAM: Right, I am going to do *Camakam* regularly, starting tomorrow.

GIRISAM: Do it in your mind. If you say it aloud, your father—who is ignorant *of reason* and has no education—will break your eardrums to the chant of the violent Veda.

VENKATESAM: You stole a pack of tobacco from the Bhuktas. Won't God be angry with you for your sin?

GIRISAM: See, when I was young, my uncle—who was a firebrand like your father—twisted my earlobes and made me read the Upanishads. In one of those Upanishads—damn it, I forget the name—a student asks questions and a teacher answers them. You are the student and I am the teacher—just like in that Upanishad. If someone records your questions and my answers on a palm leaf, it will be a sacred text—after a couple of hundred years it will be known as *Tobaccopanishad.* What's so sinful about stealing tobacco? You just smoke it away, right? Moreover, it's good for the world to steal tobacco from those idiots who inhale snuff.

VENKATESAM: How's that good for the world?

GIRISAM: I'll tell you how. If you smoke cigars, the smoke goes to the sky like steam from a locomotive and turns into clouds that rain. If you inhale snuff, the sky gets dry from that pungent smell. Only your nose drips a few drops, making your clothes dirty. So we should, by all means, steal all the tobacco from those who inhale snuff and smoke it all as cigars. If God, however, says "Sir, Girisamgaru, you did commit a sin and you have to honor hell with your presence," I will give him a *lecture* and confuse him.

VENKATESAM: What's your lecture going to be on? I'm just curious.

GIRISAM: What will that be? O almighty God, did you create me to be independent of you or dependent on you? If I am created to be independent of you, I did what I did, and who are you to ask? If you trouble me with your questions, I will organize a National Congress in heaven. Or if I am created to be dependent on you, you are the one to take responsibility for my sins and you will be the one to be punished. Therefore, you go to hell yourself. If you give me power over heaven in your absence—for just six hours—I will fix a few mistakes in your creation.

VENKATESAM: What are those mistakes, sir?

GIRISAM: Serious mistakes. You yourself will agree. Is it not a mistake to create a stupid person like your teacher in the high school?

VENKATESAM: Yes, it is a mistake.

GIRISAM: Making a *beautiful young girl* like your sister a *widow.* Is it a mistake or not?

VENKATESAM: Surely a mistake.

GIRISAM: There are a million more like this. And how much of God's creation is wasteful? For instance, how many seas are there?

VENKATESAM: Seven.[26]

GIRISAM: Seven senseless seas. After creating a sea of milk, why do you need a sea of curds and a sea of clarified butter? This is *pleonasm*—redundancy. Now another stupid mistake: God dumped this totally useless salt-water sea in our neighborhood and placed seas of milk, curds, clarified butter, and sugar-cane juice in places impossible for anybody to reach. If God hands over his power to me for one year, I will bring the ocean of milk to Bhimunipatnam and the sea of sugar-cane juice to Kalingaptnam. I will make the entire Eastern Ghats[27] a tobacco forest.

When I give this lecture, you know what God will say? He will say, "This man is impossible to beat. He is far more intelligent than the man who asked the god of death if he was the original deity or his replacement." Then God will ask his angels to take me on a horse cart, show me around heaven, and let me choose the best house in the place. I will tell them that I want my favorite student Venkatesam to live with me. Then they will bring you on a sky chariot. We will live in heaven happily ever after. Enough religious instruction for today. Go play monkey-sticks on the temple trees.[28] In the evening, when your father comes, open the book and meditate on spicy pounded rice. That's a really delicious dish. *Run, my dear boy.*

(Exit Venkatesam. Enter Bucc'amma.)

BUCC'AMMA: Pieces of palm leaves from the *pandiri*[29] are falling all over this mortar. Could you please move it for me?

GIRISAM: That's easy. (Pulls the mortar away from under the *pandiri.*)

GIRISAM: (Sings:)

Praise the Lord
Praise the Lord
You Fool![30]

Why are you crying, young lady?

BUCC'AMMA: Me? Nothing.

GIRISAM: My heart melts when you cry.

BUCC'AMMA: What do you care? You are a lucky man. Our troubles shouldn't bother you.

GIRISAM: What cruel words you say. What use is life to me if I can't help you when you're in trouble? I'll do anything for you, give you anything I have, even my life. See for yourself. I am even willing to die for you. (Picks up a vegetable knife from the floor to kill himself.)

BUCC'AMMA: (Pulling the vegetable knife away from him.) You said you would stop this wedding, but you didn't.

GIRISAM: That's the one thing I wasn't able to do.

BUCC'AMMA: Then what good are you to me? You are so happy making all the arrangements for the wedding. My father doesn't care if my sister's life is ruined and you don't care either. Perhaps you are happy because the bridegroom is your cousin.

GIRISAM: Me? Happy? How cruel of you to say that! God knows how I grieve for your sister. I wrote a four-page letter to my cousin, berating him for wanting to marry your sister. He didn't care a bit. What else could I do? I don't even want to think of that sinful man. I'm working on the wedding arrangements so your father doesn't think I'm a burden, and I am hoping that one day you will be kind to me. But if you are not pleased with this servant of yours, I will quietly leave tonight without telling anybody.

BUCC'AMMA: Don't leave.

GIRISAM: But really, how can I leave? Many times I have said to myself: I am a failure. I haven't been able to stop this wedding, and I couldn't bring my Bucc'amma, the woman I love more than my life, back into married life. I lose hope, I decide to leave. My feet go forward but my heart pulls me back. How can I live without seeing my Bucc'amma? Even if you are not kind to me, I'll stay, just to be able to see you.

BUCC'AMMA: Brother says that if you talk to him, Lubdha Avadhanlu will give up this match.

GIRISAM: No one in the world would reject my advice. With two exceptions: your father and my cousin. They wouldn't even listen to God. Your father has a bad temper and my cousin is a miser. There is a practice called *slavery* in Africa. Human beings are sold like cattle in a public market. That's exactly what my cousin is doing in the name of marriage. He is buying your sister to serve him as an unpaid cook. I have another worry as well. I hope you will not get angry if I tell you.

BUCC'AMMA: I won't be angry, whatever you say.

GIRISAM: If you have that kind of trust, what else do I need? Those Brahmin men of Rama-chandra-puram are devilish. They won't let your sister live honorably after my cousin's death. She will become another Minakshi.

BUCC'AMMA: Why, what's wrong with Minakshi?

GIRISAM: What can I say? As the saying goes, if you spill your guts, your feet get filthy. But I shouldn't keep secrets from you. Every year she gets pregnant, and every year an abortion. Sometimes it is quite dangerous. There is a womanizer called Ramap-Pantulu in that village. He is a Niyogi. He keeps a pleasure-woman and has seduced a number of married women as well. He takes care of all my cousin's property. The moment my cousin dies, your sister will inherit her husband's property. She'll be independent and wealthy—enough to ruin herself, right? You might say, "Not all widows have affairs; look at me." But let's face it, your husband's property is not in your hands yet. And you haven't even left your parents' house.

BUCC'AMMA: That's true.

GIRISAM: You are still protected by your parents; no man can approach you. But your parents won't live forever. Once they are gone, you too will be independent. Who knows how your mind will work then? Once you stray from the straight path, you will regret not marrying Girisam the proper way. You will think: "If only I had married him, I would have children and wealth and all happiness." Where will I be then? In heaven, waiting for you. After this wedding, Venkatesam and I will return to the city. I will long for you and give up food and sleep. How long can anyone live without food and sleep? I will keep thinking of you and spend many sleepless nights. Then one day in the middle of the night, I'll be sitting in an easy chair. In front of me there will be an electric lamp and a life-size mirror and I will look at myself in the mirror and I will say to myself: "This handsome face, these wide eyes, this charming mustache—all these are of no use. What good are they when my Bucc'amma doesn't want them?" In despair I will open the drawer and pick up the double-barreled pistol, aim it at my heart, and shoot myself.

BUCC'AMMA: Don't, don't do that. If you say such things, I'll cry.

GIRISAM: Immediately the gods will send their sky chariot and take me to heaven. Will I be happy even in heaven? No. The gods' beauty queen Rambha will come bedecked with jewelry and will fall all over me cooing, "My sweet Girisam, I have never seen a more handsome man than you. Come, give me a kiss." And I will say to her: "Go away, I am *anti-nautch.* I won't touch a courtesan. This arm of mine is polluted by your touch. I have to clean it with Pear's soap.[31] You are Rambha, and they call you the most beautiful woman in heaven? You are nothing compared to my Bucc'amma. Get out of my way, *you damn dirty goose."* I will get rid of all the other women such as Menaka, Ūrvaśi, and Tilottama.[32] I will wear ochre robes and renounce the world, sit under the giving tree,[33] and meditate in the lotus position. After a while, my meditation will succeed and you will come—like moonlight into the garden of the gods. I will jump up and embrace you, my love. Your first husband—that dirty old man—will come with his snuffy nose and loincloth and will want to claim you for his wife. I will tell that bastard: "You are not fit for Bucc'amma; take your money and get out," and I'll kick the fellow out. We will live together in heaven happily ever after.

BUCC'AMMA: You make crying people laugh.

GIRISAM: If you marry me, we will live a life full of happiness, laughter, and pleasure. Would I let you mash lentils like this? We will have a lot of servants, attendants. We'll have gardens, yards, horses, carriages. Will I let you walk? I will carry you lovingly, like a delicate flower. Think of all the pleasures you will have.

BUCC'AMMA: Pleasures for me! Not in this life!

GIRISAM: Here I am, bowing to your feet and begging you to marry me, to be happy and make me happy. And what do you do? You spurn the easy path to pleasures of life and kick my life into the dust. What can I do?

BUCC'AMMA: What do you lack? You are a prince.

GIRISAM: Yes, I am a prince—if you marry me. Your words cannot be false. Come away with me. We'll elope.

BUCC'AMMA: No. No way. I can't do that.

GIRISAM: If you don't come, I'll die. You'll be free of me.

BUCC'AMMA: Please don't say that.

GIRISAM: What's wrong in saying what I know for certain? Never mind me, don't you have feelings for your sister?

BUCC'AMMA: What do you mean?

GIRISAM: Do you really love her?

BUCC'AMMA: Of course I do.

GIRISAM: If you do, you have the key to stop this match in your hands.

BUCC'AMMA: In my hands?

GIRISAM: Literally.

BUCC'AMMA: You are joking.

GIRISAM: See, I look like a joker to you because I love you, and only you, among all the women in the whole wide world. I totally give myself to you, and you make fun of me.

BUCC'AMMA: Please don't say that. I swear, I never meant it that way.

GIRISAM: I am glad. That gives me some confidence. Tell me honestly: If there is something you could do to prevent your sister's wedding, would you do it?

BUCC'AMMA: Definitely.

GIRISAM: I'm not so sure. Swear an oath.

BUCC'AMMA: What kind of oath?

GIRISAM: Take an oath on my life.

BUCC'AMMA: Swear on your life? Go on.

GIRISAM: Now listen. I wanted to tell you in private, but I didn't have the chance until now. Your father is out of town and your mother is out of the house.[34] I won't find a better time. Listen carefully. There is only one way to free your sister from this wedding: Elope with me and marry me. Don't have any second thoughts about it. If not, your sister's wedding is inevitable.

BUCC'AMMA: (Laughing shyly.) If I elope with you, my sister is saved? What strange things you say!

GIRISAM: I will tell you how. When all of us set out for the wedding, I'll give a little money to the cart driver and tell him to divert your cart to the Anakapalli road. My friends will arrange connecting carts from there to Rama-varam. We will run joyously to Rama-varam and get married there. And what will happen with your people? The morning after we elope, they'll look for your cart, won't find it, will search for it, worry, and raise an alarm. That will stop your sister's wedding. A couple of days later, they'll learn that we are married. That'll teach your father a lesson about the evils of giving his daughter to an old man. He will cancel your sister's wedding. Even if he doesn't, my cousin will refuse to marry your sister after hearing about what you did. That's it. Right?

BUCC'AMMA: Sounds plausible.

GIRISAM: So do you agree?

BUCC'AMMA: To what?

GIRISAM: To elope with me.

BUCC'AMMA: I can't do that, as long as there's life in my body.

GIRISAM: Well, if you can't do that, your sister's life is ruined and my life is ended too.

BUCC'AMMA: Don't say that.

GIRISAM: My death can't be avoided, even if I don't say it in words. I can't live without you, therefore I will die. You took an oath on my life and if you break your word, God will kill me. Either way, I die.

BUCC'AMMA: If you die because of me, I'll die too. Please don't die.

GIRISAM: Is it in my hands? Look, your brother is coming. There won't be time for us to talk about these things. Tell me one thing: Do you want me to live or die?

BUCC'AMMA: To live a thousand years.

GIRISAM: So it is certain you are coming away with me.

BUCC'AMMA: I will do whatever you want me to do.

(Enter Venkatesam holding a grasshopper in his hands.)

VENKATESAM: Look here, I caught a cow-girl.[35]

GIRISAM: Honey, your brother is not a kid anymore, he is chasing after girls.

BUCC'AMMA: (Laughing shyly.) It's a grasshopper. Cow-girl is what we call them.

GIRISAM: (To Bucc'amma:) At last the girl is in hand. (To Venkatesam:) Bring it here. Catching them is educational. This is natural history, the science of nature.

VENKATESAM: Sister, give me a taste of what you are making.

BUCC'AMMA: If Mother sees, she will hit you.

VENKATESAM: Don't worry, she won't see.

(Bucc'amma gives Venkatesam a little of the chutney she is making. Venkatesam licks it and jumps with joy.)

(Curtain.)

Act Five

SCENE ONE. Lubdha Avadhanlu's bedroom.

(Lubdha Avadhanlu is asleep in bed. He screams in his sleep and his hands and feet shake. He sits up in bed and shivers.)

LUBDHA AVADHANLU: Asiri, Ammi, I am dead; this fellow has killed me. God help me, help me, god. (Chants:)

rāma-nāma-tārakam
rāma-nāma-tārakam
rāma-nāma-tārakam

This slut was certainly married before. Her husband has turned into a spirit. He'll wring my neck and kill me. What do I do now?!

rāma-nāma-tārakam
rāma-nāma-tārakam

ASIRI: (From the other side of the door:) Sir, what's wrong? (Knocks at the door.)

(Enter Minakshi and the Disciple in woman's clothes.)

MINAKSHI: What happened, Father? Open the door.

LUBDHA AVADHANLU: (To himself:) I can't get up, and my hands are shaking. (Opens the door.) (To Asiri:) You bastard, don't enter the room.[1]

ASIRI: You called me; that's why I came.

LUBDHA AVADHANLU: (To Minakshi:) Don't let that slut enter my room.

MINAKSHI: (To Disciple:) You go to our room, dear. (Disciple steps out of the room.) What's the matter, Father?

LUBDHA AVADHANLU: My life is in danger. I'm dying.

MINAKSHI: What's the problem? You have a headache or a foot-ache or what?

LUBDHA AVADHANLU: My head is all right and so is my foot. But my life is in danger. I am the idiot who married a widow.

MINAKSHI: What ugly words. Who put this suspicion in your head?

LUBDHA AVADHANLU: It's not my suspicion. The entire village is talking.

MINAKSHI: It must be Ramap-Pantulu's doing. He starts these rumors. He gossips with everyone he meets, they tell others, and soon the entire village is buzzing. Don't scare the girl. She's a darling. She is sad that her father left; she cries for him day and night.

LUBDHA AVADHANLU: That bastard of a father. That son of a bitch hung this once-married slut around my neck and ruined me. I'm dead, I'll die.

MINAKSHI: You keep calling her a once-married slut as if you are blessing her. If you sing that song, the village will surely sing along. Just keep quiet.

LUBDHA AVADHANLU: How can I keep quiet? She doesn't belong to our village or our area. If she weren't a once-married slut, why would that bastard of a father have run away without giving his name?

MINAKSHI: He told Siddhanti.

LUBDHA AVADHANLU: Who knows what he said? That Siddhanti gives a new name every time you ask.

MINAKSHI: It's a new name, all right. We can't expect Siddhanti to remember names easily. Anyway, we have the girl in our house; what do we need her father's name for?

LUBDHA AVADHANLU: If this slut of a wife lives with me, that's death to me. I'll die.

MINAKSHI: Don't be crazy. Shut up and stay quiet. The neighbors will laugh. Your father-in-law is a great scholar and a respectable man. Don't hold stupid suspicions. That young girl will be confused.

LUBDHA AVADHANLU: You rotten woman, did he bribe you? Why are you defending him? You want me to die too?

MINAKSHI: You must have lost your senses, Father. He'll be back today or tomorrow. You'll have to eat your words.

LUBDHA AVADHANLU: Who is he anyway, Jack in the Jungle? Why would he come back? My death is ready and waiting.

MINAKSHI: What the hell is wrong with you? Suppose she has been married. Hush it up. Don't make a scene of it. Aren't many people happy these days marrying a woman who was married before? She is an intelligent and well-behaved girl. You are lucky to have her for a wife. Keep quiet.

LUBDHA AVADHANLU: Lucky, my foot. What devil has possessed you? Are you part of this conspiracy to get your father to marry a widow? (Addressing himself:) You Lubdha! You nincompoop who married a widow! What were you thinking? Where was your learning and where was your Veda? You're finished. (Minakshi laughs.) Why are you laughing, you ugly slut? You and your stepmother will kill me and escape to Rajahmundry and remarry.[2] What Girisam said was right. I am a moron, I didn't listen to him. All my money will go to pay for the atoning rituals. Go away, I'm going to sleep. (Lying on the bed.) God, he'll come again!

MINAKSHI: Who is he?

LUBDHA AVADHANLU: Go away. What do you care? That bastard will smother me to death. Your wish will be fulfilled.

MINAKSHI: When you talk like that, I cry. I won't move from here. Who, who on earth can smother you?

LUBDHA AVADHANLU: Then bring your bed and sleep here.

MINAKSHI: I will. Who is trying to kill you?

LUBDHA AVADHANLU: That slut's first husband. Before you came in, the bastard sat on my chest and grabbed my throat. I thought I was going to die.

MINAKSHI: You had a bad dream, Father.

LUBDHA AVADHANLU: You call it a dream? My throat was really twisted.

MINAKSHI: How did you know he was her first husband?

LUBDHA AVADHANLU: He told me himself. He threatened me. "Bastard, you married my wife. I will kill you," he said.

MINAKSHI: What does he look like?

LUBDHA AVADHANLU: He is the spitting image of Girisam.

MINAKSHI: That was a dream, Father. You were thinking of Uncle Girisam, and he came in your dream.

LUBDHA AVADHANLU: Who cares if I die?

MINAKSHI: Shall I ask the girl the truth?

LUBDHA AVADHANLU: No, don't.

MINAKSHI: You're yelling at me, you're scared that her first husband will kill you, why not clear away the doubt? We'll ask her if she was married once before. The truth will come out.

LUBDHA AVADHANLU: Why do you think she will tell you the truth?

MINAKSHI: She won't hide anything from me. She's an innocent girl. She's very good to me.

LUBDHA AVADHANLU: So you are spoiling her?

MINAKSHI: I hate you when you say such things. You must have been startled and frightened by something during the day. That's why you had this bad dream. Just don't go crazy yelling she was married once before, twice before, and so on. I'll call Priest Gavarayya. He will chant a mantra and give you some protective ashes. You can smear them on your body and go to sleep.

LUBDHA AVADHANLU: That'll be the end of my reputation. If he comes, what shall I say was the problem? Go, ask the girl to tell the truth.

MINAKSHI: Why should I ask when you call me all kinds of bad names? I won't even talk to her.

LUBDHA AVADHANLU: Please ask; you are my darling daughter.

(Minakshi leaves the room.)

LUBDHA AVADHANLU: What shall I do? Chant a section of the Veda? Chant the Gayatri? Vedas and Mantras are peanuts for these spirits. I wanted to learn the śāpara chants,[3] but I was afraid they would boomerang if I didn't practice them properly. God, what's the way? I'll chant Rāma's name.

Rāma-nāma-tārakam
bhakti-muki-dāyakam
jānaki-mano-haram
sarva-loka-nāyakam
rāma-nāma-tārakam
rāma-nāma-tārakam

I won't live if this slut stays in the house. Where are my beads? (He sits at the edge of the bed and feels under the bed, and as he is picking up the rosary, Minakshi enters.)

MINAKSHI: She says it's true, Father.

LUBDHA AVADHANLU: True? (He falls off the bed.)

MINAKSHI: (Helping him get up.) Father, Father, are you all right?

LUBDHA AVADHANLU: I'm all right. So it's true!

MINAKSHI: It's true. Just now, the husband appeared before her and warned her: "You whore, you married again? I will twist the throat of your new husband." That's what she said.

LUBDHA AVADHANLU: *Ayyo, Ayyo,* that Ramap-Pantulu—may his house turn into a funeral ground—why did he recommend this hell of a marriage? May his funeral offering go to the cats! What did she say her bastard of a husband looked like?

MINAKSHI: She says he appears to her every day. He has long hair and a mustache. He has brown skin.

LUBDHA AVADHANLU: It's him, it's him. I'm dead, I'm dead.

MINAKSHI: I'll call Priest Gavarayya.

LUBDHA AVADHANLU: No, don't! If he comes, he will eat me out of house and home.

MINAKSHI: Let him, if he wants to. Your life is more important now.

LUBDHA AVADHANLU: Why don't you listen when I say I don't want him to come? Bring your bedroll and sleep right next to my bed. Give me the *Bhāgavatam* text you read every day; I will put it under my pillow. (Minakshi leaves.)

Until the slut is turned out of my house, I won't be rid of this spirit. I am a learned man, well versed in the Veda. If he is able to pester me, he must be a Brahmin-demon,[4] not an ordinary spirit. I will pray to him directly: Oh, the first husband of my wife! No, she is not my wife. I will punish myself for saying that. Oh, husband of this girl! You are the real husband, I am not. I will not touch her; will not go close to her. I will not even ask her to serve me. Please save me. Don't kill me. You are a spirit now because you sinned in an earlier life. If you kill me, you will acquire another sin of killing a Brahmin. You will never be free from being a spirit. So please, don't bother me. Kill your father-in-law or kill that Ramap-Pantulu or if not . . . (Sounds of someone crying and yelling in the background.) God, the spirit has come again. (The Disciple comes running and embraces Lubdha Avadhanlu tightly. Minakshi tries to hit the Disciple with a broom. The Disciple escapes and the blow falls on Lubdha Avadhanlu.)

MINAKSHI: You slut, give me my gold. And where are my keys? Tell me, you slut.

LUBDHA AVADHANLU: Why did you hit me? (To the Disciple:) Leave me, don't touch me. (To Minakshi:) I will die if her impure body touches me. Take her away.

(Minakshi pulls the Disciple by his hand and pinches his cheek. The Disciple bites her hand and runs away.)

MINAKSHI: A curse on her mother's house. She bit my hand, Father. It's bleeding! I'll kill her.

LUBDHA AVADHANLU: What a horror. Let me see your hand. (He wipes the blood off.) You are asking her for a gold coin. What gold coin?

MINAKSHI: That bastard, her father gave her a gold coin for me. I believed this jackal of a girl and her pretenses and gave her my trunk and other things for safekeeping. I asked her to save the gold coin too. I don't trust her anymore. I ask her for my gold coin, and she says she put it in the suitcase but lost the key. If she doesn't give me the key, I'll smash her head with a pestle.

LUBDHA AVADHANLU: Don't get too rough. You're insane when you're angry. You might kill her. Be careful.

MINAKSHI: If she dies, that'll be the end. I'll throw the corpse out. Dirty slut, see how she bit me! People say there's no cure for a human bite.

LUBDHA AVADHANLU: Put some red powder on it.

MINAKSHI: I'll smash her head and put that paste on my finger.

LUBDHA AVADHANLU: The doubt is cleared. It's true she was married once. Either her first husband will strangle me or she will bite me and kill me. One way or the other, my death is certain. Why did I buy this expensive deadly wife? I'll drive her out of my house.

That's the way to get rid of him, as well. But where shall I send her? I'll put her on a cart and send her to the city. But what if she doesn't find her father there? She'll be back with the devil of her first husband intact. And I have to pay the rent for the cart too. How do I get out of this mess? How? Maybe I should ask Ramap-Pantulu for advice. Yes, good idea! I'll send this slut to Ramap-Pantulu. He can keep this woman too, in addition to that pleasure-woman. If he wants, I'll sweeten the deal with a gift of ten rupees on top.

(Enter Minakshi.)

MINAKSHI: Father, I can't find the girl anywhere.
LUBDHA AVADHANLU: I hope she hasn't jumped into the well.
MINAKSHI: Who knows?
LUBDHA AVADHANLU: Run and call Gavarayya. You didn't beat her to death, did you?
MINAKSHI: I would have, if I had seen her. I didn't even see her.
LUBDHA AVADHANLU: God, why this new calamity?

(Curtain.)

SCENE TWO. A windowless room in Ramap-Pantulu's house.

(Bhukta, Poli-setti, Siddhanti, and Madhura-vani play cards. Priest Gavarayya watches.)

POLI-SETTI: What a rotten set of cards you deal. You always do this.
BHUKTA: Do I see what I deal? Curse your fate, not me!
POLI-SETTI: Hey, Gavarayya. Off with that dirty knee of yours away from me. It's giving me bad luck. For god's sake, get away from me.
GAVARAYYA: I'll go sit near Madhura-vani.
BHUKTA: Check your cards; maybe I missed one.
POLI-SETTI: Hey, Baepan,[5] you do it because you want to deal wrong. I'll make you pay. You'll go bankrupt.
BHUKTA: But you said you didn't get good cards.
POLI-SETTI: Couldn't I get four aces in the second round?
BHUKTA: (Dealing cards to Poli-setti.) Here, I'm giving you four aces; enjoy them.
POLI-SETTI: Your leather hand only deals out junk cards, never good ones.
BHUKTA: May God make your words come true.
POLI-SETTI: No, don't say so. After all, a Baepan's word carries power, though you are a rotten Baepan. (Looking at the cards.) Yuck, ugly cards!
SIDDHANTI: One. Maybe two.

POLI-SETTI: No, you can't do that. Bid one at a time.
SIDDHANTI: Then one.
POLI-SETTI: One.
MADHURA-VANI: One.
BHUKTA: One.

(Siddhanti thinks.)

POLI-SETTI: What are you thinking? Pick up the cards. You are the playing hand.
SIDDHANTI: What do you have to lose? Two.
POLI-SETTI: You dealt me a Yarborough.[6] What's there to pick up? Two.
MADHURA-VANI: Two.

(Siddhanti thinks.)

POLI-SETTI: Why are you thinking? You are the playing hand. Pick up the cards and win the bid if you can.
SIDDHANTI: If you say so.
POLI-SETTI: Put up the cash before you touch the cards. Do you remember the bid from the third round? You want to play on credit and run away when you go bankrupt?
SIDDHANTI: (Putting his cards down.) The Komati[7] talks big.
POLI-SETTI: You want to fight?
SIDDHANTI: Fight to the finish.
POLI-SETTI: You ruined my game, you Baepan.
BHUKTA: You just complained you didn't get good cards, and now you're whining that he ruined your game?
POLI-SETTI: If I don't make you lose this game, don't call me by my name.
SIDDHANTI: Hey, Komati, will you shut up?
POLI-SETTI: The white man's flag is flying;[8] you can't boss me around. What kind of a game is this anyway? You take forever to pick up the card.
SIDDHANTI: If you open your mouth again, I will mix up the cards.

(Poli-setti indicates by gestures: "I will not talk, you play." Siddhanti plays.)

POLI-SETTI: Hey, Baepan, I have three trump cards. *tamāshā dekho, laṅkā-ke rājāh,* "Watch the fun, King of the Island."[9]
SIDDHANTI: I am going to quit.
POLI-SETTI: I am sorry, extremely sorry. I will never open my mouth again. I will punish myself.
PRIEST GAVARAYYA: I will make an extempore verse on Madhura-vani.

The queen of diamonds is not a queen.
The queen of spades is not a queen.
The queens of clubs or hearts?—No way!
Madhura-vani is the only queen—
the queen supreme whom kings obey.

SIDDHANTI: Gavarayya, your poem is priceless. What a lovely poem you made! Let me make a verse about you.

Gavarayyar,
ever higher
who is equal to you?

PRIEST GAVARAYYA:

There's no one here,
even close,
I'm the most superior.

SIDDHANTI: Here's a king.
POLI-SETTI: Here's a *pŏllu.*[10]

(Madhura-vani plays trump queen.)

POLI-SETTI: No, no. This Baepan fellow revealed under the cover of a poem that Madhura-vani had a queen in her hand. Horrors, horrors. If Gavarayya opens his mouth, I won't play.
PRIEST GAVARAYYA: It has been a long time since I made a verse on Poli-setti. (Inhales snuff.)

Setti's face is fake.
It looks like a pound cake,
and sure his nose looks
like a dark snuffbox

POLI-SETTI: Stop, stop. Are you going to kill me with a wrong syllable in the rhyme?[11] Stay quiet, I'll give you a little money if Siddhanti bids and I win.
SIDDHANTI: The hell with your chatter, I am left with a trump card. I lose my bid. (He shows his cards and throws them down.)
POLI-SETTI: This is the third round you lost. All of you remember. I'm the first to play. Deal good cards, Baepan! Come on! Don't shuffle forever. Horrors, horrors.
SIDDHANTI: You think I will give you a win with a loose shuffle?
POLI-SETTI: You and your leather hand! (Chants:)

God, you came as Lion-Man!
Your name is the mantra
that kills our enemies.

Kills our enemies
Kills our,
Kill sour
Kill sour . . .[12]

SIDDHANTI: There's nothing sour here. Pick up the cards.

POLI-SETTI: Gavarayya is jinxing with his evil eye on the cards. (Continues the chant:)

Your name is the mantra
your name . . .

(Picks up the cards and looks.) Yuck, you dealt me rotten cards.

SIDDHANTI: (Completing the deal, looking at his cards.) *mṛttikā came,*[13] eat dirt!

PRIEST GAVARAYYA: If Poli-setti is so upset with me, I'll go home and rest.

(Exit Gavarayya. Madhura-vani sees him off and returns.)

POLI-SETTI: Got rid of the devil. God, all the cards are rotten. One.

MADHURA-VANI: One.

BHUKTA: One.

SIDDHANTI: One.

POLI-SETTI: Two.

MADHURA-VANI: Two.

BHUKTA: Two.

(Siddhanti thinks.)

POLI-SETTI: There's no point in thinking. Listen to me. Don't bid three.

(A knock on the main door.)

MADHURA-VANI: It's Pantulu.

POLI-SETTI: You said he wouldn't come tonight.

MADHURA-VANI: That's what I thought, but he came. What shall we do now?

SIDDHANTI: Wrap up the game. (He drops his cards.)

POLI-SETTI: To escape your losses? No way. Maduroni,[14] play your turn before you open the door.

MADHURA-VANI: (Puts her cards down, gets up, and says in a soft voice:) Jump over the wall and run.

BHUKTA: We'll leave by the back door.

POLI-SETTI: I am too fat to get through. How do I get out of this?

BHUKTA: We'll leave by the back door. You go hide in the attic.

POLI-SETTI: Help me climb up before you go. What if I slip and fall down?

SIDDHANTI: Your son will be lucky.

(He goes to the backyard.)

POLI-SETTI: Horrors, horrors. Keep the cards as they are. Don't mix them up.

(A knock is heard again.)

POLI-SETTI: (Chants:)

Your name is the mantra that
kills our enemies

(Madhura-vani makes an angry gesture to make him quiet.)

(Siddhanti returns.)

SIDDHANTI: There's a padlock on the back door. Pantulu locked it to catch us red-handed.

POLI-SETTI: (Chants:)

Your name is the mantra
that kills our . . .

MADHURA-VANI: (To Poli-setti:) Shut up. (With a soft voice:) Sit quietly in this room. No noise. I'll release you after he goes to sleep.

(Madhura-vani blows out the lamps, goes out of the room, shuts the door, and bolts it. A knock on the front door again.)

MADHURA-VANI: Stupid Gavarayya. Why does he keep knocking? (Goes to the main door.) Who's that?

PERSON ON THE OTHER SIDE OF THE DOOR: What took you so long?

MADHURA-VANI: I'm sleeping.

PERSON ON THE OTHER SIDE OF THE DOOR: Cards, cards. I'll leave you. I know what you are doing.

MADHURA-VANI: You go wherever you like and leave me alone here all night. Aren't I lonely in the jungle of this village? I have invited friends and we're playing cards. What's wrong with that? It's chilly out there. Come in. You play my game. I'll go sleep.

PERSON ON THE OTHER SIDE OF THE DOOR: A pleasure-woman should never be trusted! I brought a gift for you, and now I've lost my taste for it.

MADHURA-VANI: Whatever I do, it's never enough to make you happy. From now on, I will go with you wherever you go.

PERSON FROM THE OTHER SIDE OF THE DOOR: Stick your neck out. (Madhura-vani sticks her neck out, and the person from the other side of the door puts the gold *kaṇṭĕ* around her neck.)

MADHURA-VANI: (Recognizing the Disciple.) What a trickster you are! How did you learn to speak like Pantulu? You fooled me. (Pulls the Disciple by the arm.) Come into the room. (She takes the Disciple into her room.) Which god gave you these killer-eyes? (Kisses him.) Tell me all the tricks you played in their house.

DISCIPLE: I'll tell you if you promise you won't kiss me.

MADHURA-VANI: Why, am I not good enough for you?

DISCIPLE: If you kiss me, your yucky[15] saliva is all over my mouth.

MADHURA-VANI: True. Adults don't have the sense you have. You scared me for no reason. What punishment should I give you? I'll eat your cheeks.

DISCIPLE: Give me some milk and sugar.

MADHURA-VANI: You can pig out later. First I'll dress you up as a wandering singer. You can go to the village and link up with your guru.

(Curtain.)

(Poli-setti, Bhukta, Siddhanti in the dark room.)

DISCIPLE: (Imitating Ramap-Pantulu's voice from behind the curtain:) You're hiding someone in this room.

MADHURA-VANI: Believe me, there's no one.

(Poli-setti climbs the ladder. Bhukta tries to climb up behind him. After a few steps both of them fall down.)

POLI-SETTI: You've killed me, you lousy Brahmin.

BHUKTA: You fell on me and I was struggling to get up from under you, and you say *I* hurt *you*. Get off of me or I'll bite you.

DISCIPLE: (Again with Ramap-Pantulu's voice:) I hear voices from that room, you slut. It sounds like that Komati fellow. I'll lock them up and call in the entire village to witness the scene.

MADHURA-VANI: No need to lock anything. There's no one there. It's ghosts fighting among themselves. This is a haunted house.

(Madhura-vani opens the door and lights a match. The Disciple steps aside.)

MADHURA-VANI: Why is Poli-setti lying on the floor? Should I sing a wake-up song?

BHUKTA: Where's Ramap-Pantulu?

MADHURA-VANI: Ramap-Pantulu, Shmamap-Pantulu. It was the servant. Nothing to fear.

BHUKTA: I heard his voice.

MADHURA-VANI: I imitated his voice. You're real men, real heroes, aren't you?

POLI-SETTI: (Chants:)

> Your name is the mantra
> that kills our enemies . . .

Does everyone have their cards?

(All of them settle back into the game.)

SIDDHANTI: I mixed up the cards.

POLI-SETTI: Horrors, horrors, I had the ace of spades and I would have won the bid. Horrors, horrors. Maduroni confused all of us. God, I broke my back from that fall.

BHUKTA: Why are *you* whining? *You* didn't get hurt. I was the one who was crushed under your weight.

POLI-SETTI: Reshuffle the cards.

SIDDHANTI: I won't shuffle. My turn is over. You shuffle and deal.

POLI-SETTI: Your turn isn't over.

(Ramap-Pantulu knocks on the door.)

RAMAP-PANTULU: Lakshmi, Lakshmi,[16] open the door.

MADHURA-VANI: It's Pantulu this time.

POLI-SETTI: What to do?

MADHURA-VANI: Jump over the wall and run.

POLI-SETTI: I can't jump.

MADHURA-VANI: I'll lock you up in this room.

POLI-SETTI: Don't put out the light. I'm scared of the dark.

SIDDHANTI: I'll get cut by the glass on the wall.[17] It's not easy to jump.

BHUKTA: I have bad knees. I can't jump.

MADHURA-VANI: (Puts out the light.) Stay here then.

POLI-SETTI: (Chants:)

> Your name is the mantra that
> kills our enemies
> kills our . . .

MADHURA-VANI: Shut up.

POLI-SETTI: I'm done for.

MADHURA-VANI: (Closes the door to the room, bolts it from outside, and opens the main door a crack.) Where did you hide that mystery girl?

RAMAP-PANTULU: What mystery girl?

MADHURA-VANI: How innocent! Where did you hide Lubdha Avadhanlu's charming new bride? You eloped with her and I know what you've been doing all night.

RAMAP-PANTULU: I don't understand what you're saying. Who eloped with who? Who hid the girl?

MADHURA-VANI: I don't care if you have hidden her or not. Where is my gold *kaṇṭĕ*?

RAMAP-PANTULU: Oh, your *kaṇṭĕ*. I forgot. I'm sorry.

MADHURA-VANI: How strange! You forgot me, and you forgot that it was my *kaṇṭĕ*, and you gave it to that girl! You eloped with her, you hid her, and now you come home in the middle of the night like a perfect gentleman.

RAMAP-PANTULU: Has the girl disappeared or something?

MADHURA-VANI: What a game you play! You know very well that she didn't disappear. She is right where you put her.

RAMAP-PANTULU: That Minakshi probably drove her out of the house. I am dead if she drove her away with the *kaṇṭĕ*.

MADHURA-VANI: This is good theater. I don't care if you live or die. I won't let you in unless you bring the *kaṇṭĕ*. (She closes the door.)

RAMAP-PANTULU: I ride the horse eight miles, I come home tired, and I am hit by this cloudless lightning. Did I ever believe that Minakshi would let that girl live? Anyway, who cares if the girl ran away? I'll be lucky if the *kaṇṭĕ* isn't lost. If I go to Lubdha Avadhanlu to ask for it, he'll throw me out for getting him into this marriage. What to do?

(Exit.)

SCENE THREE. Lubdha Avadhanlu's front porch.

LUBDHA AVADHANLU: (Pacing.) Where has she gone? Did she jump in the well and kill herself? If that is true, the police will plunder my house. If she didn't jump in the well, where could she be? She must have gone to Ramap-Pantulu's house. I'm sure that's what happened. What a beautiful girl! It's my bad luck. How soon light has turned into darkness! I was so excited that she was going to mature soon. Maybe she was already mature. Otherwise, how could she look so full? Who knows how many men she has married and killed? (Addressing himself:) You idiot, were you blind? How did you marry a woman who had already seen her blood? You are surely going to hell. You are no different from those bastards who marry widows in Rajahmundry. *Ayyo, Ayyo,* there's no atonement for this sin. Even if you wanted to atone for it, the Sankaracarya will ask for a fee. Brahmins will plunder my house. Even the police are better than these Brahmins. I will quietly give twenty-five rupees to the Head Constable and will leave for Kashi[18] tomorrow night. If I bathe in the Ganges, I will be clean of all sins. I will live in Kashi.

God has taught me a lesson. Why should an old bastard like me want to marry? This Ramap-Pantulu totally ruined me.

(Enter Ramap-Pantulu.)

RAMAP-PANTULU: Lubdha, I hear you mentioning my name.
LUBDHA AVADHANLU: Oh, it's nothing.
RAMAP-PANTULU: You're pacing in the middle of the night.
LUBDHA AVADHANLU: I'm not able to sleep.
RAMAP-PANTULU: Lubdha, Madhura-vani is adamant. She wants her *kaṇṭĕ* back right now. Forgive the inconvenience and bring it to me, please.
LUBDHA AVADHANLU: What *kaṇṭĕ*?
RAMAP-PANTULU: The *kaṇṭĕ* you gave your wife.
LUBDHA AVADHANLU: I gave no *kaṇṭĕ* to my wife.
RAMAP-PANTULU: When you asked me to give her a *kaṇṭĕ,* I borrowed it from Madhura-vani, remember?
LUBDHA AVADHANLU: I never asked you to do anything like that.
RAMAP-PANTULU: So you want to steal that *kaṇṭĕ*? Doesn't your wife have that *kaṇṭĕ* around her neck?
LUBDHA AVADHANLU: Where is my wife? She died long ago.
RAMAP-PANTULU: I am talking of the woman you married a few days ago. Is she not your wife?
LUBDHA AVADHANLU: That once-married slut? No, she is not my wife.
RAMAP-PANTULU: Who's once-married?
LUBDHA AVADHANLU: You yourself said she was married before.
RAMAP-PANTULU: I said it in anger because we had an argument. You shouldn't mind that.
LUBDHA AVADHANLU: No, you spoke the truth. All this is a conspiracy you and that Gunturu Sastullu planned. I know the truth. That slut went to your house. You can keep her too, like you have kept Madhura-vani. Leave me alone. I bow to you, please go.
RAMAP-PANTULU: I ask you to return my *kaṇṭĕ* and you talk crazy.
LUBDHA AVADHANLU: Your tricky girl and your *kaṇṭĕ*—I know both are safe in your house. Don't ask me.
RAMAP-PANTULU: Stop playing games; bring my *kaṇṭĕ* back or else.

(Enter Minakshi with a wet Bhāgavatam text, Asiri holding a stick in his hand and a turmeric-smeared clay pot with a burning flame in it on top of his head, and Priest Gavarayya with an empty bottle.)

PRIEST GAVARAYYA: *Hrīm. Hrīm. Hrūm. Omkāra Bhairavi.*

(Ramap-Pantulu appears frightened.)

MINAKSHI: We didn't find her anywhere. She threw this book in the well.

(Lubdha Avadhanlu appears frightened.)

RAMAP-PANTULU: Who are you looking for?

MINAKSHI: My stepmother.[19] Gavarayya went into the well and looked all over. Nothing else was found in the well.

(Lubdha Avadhanlu is less scared now.)

Father, Gavarayya trapped the Brahmin-demon in this bottle.

RAMAP-PANTULU: What Brahmin-demon?

LUBDHA AVADHANLU: A certain Brahmin-demon came and threatened my little girl.

MINAKSHI: It didn't threaten me. It twisted my dad's throat.

RAMAP-PANTULU: Gavarayya, where do you think the girl has run off to?

PRIEST GAVARAYYA: Her husband snatched her and ran away.

MINAKSHI: Where has he gone? You said he is in this bottle.

PRIEST GAVARAYYA: (Thinks a little and smiles.) Yes, she is in this bottle too.

MINAKSHI: How can a human being get into a bottle?

PRIEST GAVARAYYA: You're very innocent. You think she is really a woman? She is a spirit—a particularly sex-hungry spirit. She was scared of me and moved away every time I came to visit you. I used to wonder why.

MINAKSHI: If you put both of them in the same bottle they may give birth to baby-spirits!

PRIEST GAVARAYYA: Pantulu-garu, see for yourself. Tell me if this bottle is as heavy as two people or not.

RAMAP-PANTULU: Nooo, don't bring it to me.

PRIEST GAVARAYYA: Asiri, you hold the bottle.

ASIRI: I'm not afraid. My cool Goddess Paiditalli[20] blesses me. (Holding the bottle.) Wow, how heavy this is!

PRIEST GAVARAYYA: Put the bottle and the eternal flame down near the basil plant.[21]

LUBDHA AVADHANLU: Please, please, don't leave the bottle in my house. Take it to your house.

PRIEST GAVARAYYA: If my children open the cork thinking this is a bottle of honey, both the ghosts will come back to your house.

LUBDHA AVADHANLU: Then bury the bottle deep in the earth.

PRIEST GAVARAYYA: You think burying spirits is a small affair? There is a big ritual that has to be done. I have to chant mantras and make a fire, and Brahmins have to be fed.

LUBDHA AVADHANLU: And my savings have to be wiped out.

PRIEST GAVARAYYA: Well, if you think so, what can I do? I'll open the bottle and go my way.

LUBDHA AVADHANLU: Why do you want to open the bottle? I'll pay you whatever I can afford; leave the bottle there.

PRIEST GAVARAYYA: You're a smart man. You want to bury the bottle after I leave. If you bury the bottle without the appropriate rituals of pacification, I'll go to hell. I'll open the bottle right now.

LUBDHA AVADHANLU: Don't, don't. You may go on with that stupid ritual stuff tomorrow.

PRIEST GAVARAYYA: Then I'll sleep in your backyard with the bottle under my head. You can go and sleep peacefully.

(Exit.)

RAMAP-PANTULU: Lubdha, come here.

(Ramap-Pantulu and Lubdha Avadhanlu go to one side and talk privately.)

RAMAP-PANTULU: What about my *kaṇṭĕ*?

LUBDHA AVADHANLU: It's in your house.

RAMAP-PANTULU: You say your wife went to my house. But she isn't there and she didn't bring the *kaṇṭĕ* either.

LUBDHA AVADHANLU: Then I don't know where she's gone.

RAMAP-PANTULU: Listen. Don't ask for trouble. Give my *kaṇṭĕ* back to me.

LUBDHA AVADHANLU: *Kaṇṭĕ*, shmaṇṭe. I don't know nothing about it.

RAMAP-PANTULU: If you don't know, who does? Gavarayya says your wife has become a spirit. Maybe you and your daughter killed her.

LUBDHA AVADHANLU: You jackass! (Tries to hit him with a stick.)

RAMAP-PANTULU: You stole my *kaṇṭĕ*. You better watch out!

(Exit.)

LUBDHA AVADHANLU: (To himself:) I wonder what happened to the *kaṇṭĕ*. (Openly:) *Ammī!*

MINAKSHI: Yes, Father!

LUBDHA AVADHANLU: What did she do with the *kaṇṭĕ*?

MINAKSHI: (Thinking.) What did she do with it? I don't know. Maybe she saved it in the trunk. She might be wearing it, Father.

LUBDHA AVADHANLU: Wearing it? Why would a spirit want a *kaṇṭĕ*?

MINAKSHI: Why not, when she has got it for free?

LUBDHA AVADHANLU: Are you sure Gavarayya searched deep inside the well?

MINAKSHI: He searched for an hour.

LUBDHA AVADHANLU: You were there, right?

MINAKSHI: Yes, I was there.

LUBDHA AVADHANLU: She probably went to Ramap-Pantulu's house.

MINAKSHI: Gavarayya put her in the bottle. How could she go?

LUBDHA AVADHANLU: I don't know. It's all confusing to me. Let's go to sleep. This is how our karma goes.

(Exit.)

SCENE FOUR. In Rama-chandra-puram.

(A garden behind the village bar. A pavilion in the garden in front of which stands a Kāḷi temple. A big stool right in front of the image of Kāḷi on which are placed three big bottles of liquor and some empty glasses. Garlands of flowers cover the stool. On one side of the pavilion, Bairagi is seated on a tiger skin, resting his arm on a yoga stick. He is meditating. The young woman, Yogini, serves liquor. The Village Head, Sominayudu, smokes ganja from a pipe. Satani Manavallayya, Jangam Viresa, and the liquor-shop owner, Ramam-dasu, sit around.)

VILLAGE HEAD: Did the earth come first or the sky?

MANAVALLAYYA: Hammer or tongs, what came first?

VILLAGE HEAD: The vertical marks of the Vaishnavites or the horizontal marks of the Saivites—which came first? Hey you, with vertical marks on your forehead, what is my question and what is your counter question?[22] Is the earth the foundation for the sky or the sky the cover over the earth? Those who are learned here, answer my question.

MANAVALLAYYA: The texts say the sky is nothing. That means it doesn't exist.

VILLAGE HEAD: It doesn't exist! If you're blind, it doesn't exist. You think the white man is crazy? Why does he keep looking at the sky through a tube[23] in the city?

MANAVALLAYYA: How could these impure *mlecchas*[24] know the secrets of our *śāstras*?!

VILLAGE HEAD: Hey, you with the vertical marks, this is not about chanting *allāṇḍam bĕllāṇḍam*[25] and eating sweet *pŏṅgali.*[26] What do you know about the power of the white man? There's as much difference between you and the white man as there is between the white man's liquor and country liquor.

MANAVALLAYYA: In the Texts of Counting,[27] the sky, *ākāśa,* means *śūnya,* zero, emptiness, nothing.

VIRESA: The Texts say "earth and sky"—if the earth exists, so does the sky.

VILLAGE HEAD: Ireca,[28] your words are precious.

VIRESA: When it rains hard, people say the sky broke open. If there's no sky, how could it break open?

VILLAGE HEAD: Hurray, Ireca. Why doesn't that man with the vertical marks speak up? His mouth is shut.

(Viresa blows the conch.)

HEAD CONSTABLE: (To the Shopkeeper:) Brother, what's this nuisance?

VILLAGE HEAD: Ireca won. Shouldn't he celebrate his victory?

SHOPKEEPER: If the guru is upset, he will curse us all.

BAIRAGI: (Opens his eyes.) *Śiva-brahmam, Śiva-brahmam, Śivo'ham.*

VIRESA: See friends, he said "Śiva is real."

BAIRAGI: *Rāma-brahmam, Rāma-brahmam, Rāmo'ham.*

MANAVALLAYYA: Now he says Rāma is real. The second word cancels the first word. *Rāmānuja! Rāmānuja!*[29]

VIRESA: *Śiva Śiva, Śiva Śiva!*

SHOPKEEPER: Why are you quarreling? Your Śiva is real. He is shining bright in that bottle. Your Rāma is real too. He is shining bright in this bottle. Haven't you heard the word?!

> Just as in the glass bulb shines the light,
> so does knowledge in your body—if you're bright

BAIRAGI: True, true.

SHOPKEEPER: Guruji, you know everything. The body is the light bulb. Inside it is the ultimate soul. The bottle contains the essence of food. Unless the essence of food is put in the body, the ultimate soul is not awakened.

BAIRAGI: How did you learn this supreme secret, son?

SHOPKEEPER: By your blessing, Guru. (Looking at all present, obviously pleased with himself.) Look brothers, that's what I always say. Unless you come to the arena, how can you see ultimate reality?

BAIRAGI: What's the drink of life that the gods call *amṛta*—it's nothing but liquor. It's to gain this that the gods and demons fought to the death.[30]

VIRESA: *Śiva Śiva, Śiva Śiva!*

MANAVALLAYYA: *Rāmānuja! Rāmānuja!*

VILLAGE HEAD: Stop fighting and listen to words of wisdom, you morons.

HEAD CONSTABLE: Guru, you should make a *rasa-liṅga*[31] and present it to me, your disciple.

BAIRAGI: Sure.

MANAVALLAYYA: Guru, you can make gold. Why don't you spend that gold to build the center in Haridvaram?[32] Why do you ask us for donations?

BAIRAGI: If we spend the gold we make, our head explodes.

HEAD CONSTABLE: Such things are high-level secrets. Don't ask, friend. (To Bairagi:) I suppose it's very cold in Haridvaram.

BAIRAGI: To ordinary mortals, it is. To *siddhas* like us, people of spiritual power, there are no such things as heat or cold, pleasure or pain.

HEAD CONSTABLE: Oh, how fortunate the *siddhas* are!

VILLAGE HEAD: Guru, when did you start from Haridvaram?

BAIRAGI: Two days ago. We visited Prayāga the day before yesterday. Yesterday, we visited Puri Jagannātham. We were passing through this area sky-walking when our movement was stopped at the forest of the village goddess here. Amazed, we looked down and saw, with our yogic eye, a great powerful *yantra,* buried six human-lengths deep in the earth, right under the image of the goddess. So we came down to earth and prayed to her. As we were trying to leave unnoticed, this devotee identified us and begged us to stop.

SHOPKEEPER: I can see a *siddha* miles away, brothers.

VILLAGE HEAD: Yes, yes, you can easily spot a man of the bottle. The goddess of our village is the mother of the world, a cool goddess indeed.

BAIRAGI: *Brahmo'ham. Brahmo'ham.*

HEAD CONSTABLE: Look at the power of yoga. Brahmins who bathe and chant don't have these powers, right?[33]

BAIRAGI: Appearances deceive. They don't lead to knowledge. Hasn't my grandfather Vemana said: *atma-śuddhi leni ācāram' adiy'ela?* What's the use of physical cleanliness when the soul is unclean?

HEAD CONSTABLE: Is Vemana[34] your grandfather, Guru?

BAIRAGI: Yes, it's almost six hundred years since he has gone to that supreme place above.

HEAD CONSTABLE: How old are you, Guru?

BAIRAGI: How can I count that which has no beginning, no end? I am as old as ultimate reality.

VILLAGE HEAD: How precious. Every word we are hearing is precious!

(Viresa blows the conch.)

HEAD CONSTABLE: (Takes the conch from him and puts it away.) Don't drink too much, brother!

SHOPKEEPER: It's not too much yet. If you don't drink until you forget yourself, why drink? Hasn't Vemana said:

> If you drink and drink till you fall on the floor
> you'll know your Lord, and drink some more.
> You've a drinking problem if you do not drink.
> Vemana knows the Vedic-lore.[35]

BAIRAGI: In Kashi, during the reign of Alamghir Badsha[36] a certain rich merchant invited us for enlightened company. He took us in his boat to the middle of the Ganges with large bottles of liquor and served us in golden goblets. By the middle of the night, the bottles were empty. Everyone was out. One Nepali Brahmin and me—we were the only persons left awake.

HEAD CONSTABLE: Amazing!

BAIRAGI: The Brahmin wanted more. Where could the merchant get booze in the middle of the river? The Brahmin was ready to put a curse on the merchant if he didn't serve him more. The merchant fell at my feet. I said, "Relax," poured Ganga water in the bottle, and uttered a chant and the water turned into booze. The Brahmin drank a thousand glasses and belched loudly. There are great men among Brahmins too. For one who knows, the water in the Ganges is nothing but booze.

VILLAGE HEAD: Ramam-dasu is good at turning water into brandy. He adds ten drams for one dram.

(Enter Havaldar Acc'anna.)

SHOPKEEPER: Guru, this is Havaldar Acc'anna. He is a man who knows God. He is the Village Head's nephew, you know.

HAVALDAR: *Rām, Rām.*

BAIRAGI: *Rām, Rām.*

HAVALDAR: (To the Yogini:) Young lady, bring the hookah. (To the Head Constable:) Brother, any trace of that Gunturu Sastullu?

HEAD CONSTABLE: Nothing, brother.

SHOPKEEPER: Ramap-Pantulu says the bride is a widow. The fellow sold her, grabbed the money, and . . .

HEAD CONSTABLE: What do we need all that gossip for?

VILLAGE HEAD: If the police don't care and the Brahmins don't care, should everyone watch helplessly while a Brahmin marries a widow?

HEAD CONSTABLE: If the person who paid the money and married the girl doesn't mind, why should we worry about it? Anyway, where can you find good Brahmins nowadays? Wherever you look, you find young girls being sold to older men and widows getting pregnant, right?

HAVALDAR: Well, this is the Age of Death,[37] brother! However rotten they may be, Brahmins are our gods.

HEAD CONSTABLE: Each one is great in his own way. What matters is knowledge and character, not the caste of your birth. What did Vemana say?

VILLAGE HEAD: He said, go to the policeman for morals and to that Satani fellow for knowledge.

HEAD CONSTABLE: Laugh at me if you like, but in all the districts I have served, I have seen hundreds of widow-pregnancies. If you ask me, I say let widows remarry. My superintendent married a woman with children from a previous marriage and he is very happy.[38]

VILLAGE HEAD: What the policeman says is that a cow with a calf is better than a cow by itself. So if the girl the old Brahmin married is a widow, let us advise your friend Ramap-Pantulu to marry the old man's widowed daughter.

HAVALDAR: That's none of our business. The government, the gods, the Brahmins—they have their faults. We shouldn't concern ourselves with them. We should be devoted to them, that's our duty. (To the Head Constable:) Brother, are white and black the same? Jesus showed one path to the white man, Paigambar[39] showed another to the Muslim, and Rāma showed yet another path to the black man. God said to the white man: Marry a widow. But Rāma said to the Telugu man: Don't marry a widow. I have been to many different countries; their cultures and traditions vary, but there is one God and one morality.

VILLAGE HEAD: Did God Rāma ask widows to do immoral things? After all, women in our castes used to remarry when the first husband died, didn't they?[40]

HAVALDAR: Young lady, refill the hookah for me.

VILLAGE HEAD: The fellow with the vertical marks is kissing her in the corner over there.

YOGINI: (Pulling her hand shyly from Manavallayya.) He is giving me private instruction in secret mantras.

VILLAGE HEAD: I wonder what that private mantra is for? To run away with him at the speed of the wind?

SHOPKEEPER: Brother, why do you say bad things about her? Yogini is deeply religious.

VILLAGE HEAD: I am really sorry. I will punish myself. But Yogini, why don't you teach me what you learned from him?

(Yogini puts a glass of liquor in front of Havaldar.)

VILLAGE HEAD: The girl is moonstruck with the instruction the fellow with vertical marks gave her.

BAIRAGI: Havaldar, don't you want a taste of this juice of joy?

HAVALDAR: A sepoy is ruined if he drinks and a soldier is ruined if he doesn't.[41] The leaf of knowledge[42] is for the man of knowledge, and liquor is for the drunkard.

VILLAGE HEAD: You're now retired from the army; do you still want to serve as sepoy, son?

HAVALDAR: We ate the salt of the Company,[43] so we should serve the Company as long as we have breath in this body. If tomorrow there is war with Russia, I am ready with my gun on my shoulder.

VILLAGE HEAD: The Russian boat travels under the water. Who can you hit with your gun?

HAVALDAR: Just the other day, the English kicked the Russians in the butt. The same thing will happen again. May our queen in England live long.[44]

SHOPKEEPER: The white queen is the incarnation of Goddess Kāḷi you know.

HAVALDAR: No Kāḷi, no nothing. She is the incarnation of God Rāma.

SHOPKEEPER: Guru, Havaldar is a superb singer. You should hear his songs of knowledge. (To Yogini:) Mother, bring my tambura[45] and give it to brother Havaldar.

VILLAGE HEAD: This time, Ireca is giving her private instruction.

SHOPKEEPER: Brother, don't make jokes when great people are present.

VILLAGE HEAD: It's not a joke. I say what I see. Why doesn't anyone give private lessons to me? This time the instruction is very intense. He is not going to let go of her.

(Yogini releases Viresa's hold with great effort and brings the tambura to Havaldar.)

SHOPKEEPER: These are the secrets of knowledge. What is ultimate bliss? Booze in your belly, smoke in your nose, and a girl in your bed.

VILLAGE HEAD: Hey you, shut up! Listen to wise words.

HAVALDAR: Ignorance, ignorance. If we hadn't put Rāma's image on Kāḷi's head, the Company sepoys wouldn't have come here.

HEAD CONSTABLE: Brother, give us a song.

(Havaldar sings:)

pinjarmĕ rahkar chup nai rahnā
kyāre bulbul kaho mulki sunā
—kyāre
yĕkkaḍiki vĕḷtāvu emi cĕppavu,
bolo pinjarme[46]

(Manavallayya blows Viresa's conch.)

HAVALDAR: (Stops singing and puts the tambura away.) This isn't fair.

HEAD CONSTABLE: (Pulls the conch away from his hand.) I'll throw this in the fire. (To the shopkeeper:) Why do you let them bring this here, brother?

SHOPKEEPER: I tell him not to bring it, but he doesn't listen.

HEAD CONSTABLE: If he doesn't, don't let him come to your shop. You'll get the blame for this noise.

SHOPKEEPER: I put away ten conches. He brings an eleventh. What can I do? He is a customer, brother.

VILLAGE HEAD: Let him get dead drunk. Ultimate knowledge should go to his head.

SHOPKEEPER: (Picks up the tambura and sings:)

nāga digurā nā tandrī digurā
digu digu nāganna divya sundara nāga

mudamutŏ repallĕ muddula nāga
ūriki uttarāna ūḍala marri kinda
kŏma puttaloni koḍi nāganna[47]

(Ramap-Pantulu enters as the Shopkeeper is singing, stands at a distance, and gestures to Yogini to come. Yogini talks to Ramap-Pantulu and goes to the Head Constable to say something secretly in his ear.)

VILLAGE HEAD: The girl is now enlightening the Head Constable. Nobody enlightens me. Is it because I am old?

(Yogini goes to the Village Head, puts her mouth near his ear, and pinches his ear.)

VILLAGE HEAD: Hey girl, it's been a long time since I had this much enlightenment!

(The Head Constable goes to Ramap-Pantulu and they confer privately.)

HEAD CONSTABLE: There are no strangers here. Bairagi is our friend.

RAMAP-PANTULU: I was not thinking of friends or foes. It's a real calamity. I need your help.

HEAD CONSTABLE: Any chance of a little cash?

RAMAP-PANTULU: Depends on how you handle it.

HEAD CONSTABLE: Tell me what the problem is.

RAMAP-PANTULU: Lubdha Avadhanlu's new bride ran away with Madhura-vani's gold *kaṇṭĕ.*

HEAD CONSTABLE: Why did she have to run away from her own house?

RAMAP-PANTULU: Minakshi beat her up. We couldn't find her. Get your constables and go look for her.

HEAD CONSTABLE: How can we chase her at this time of the night? Do you think a policeman has ten pairs of feet?

RAMAP-PANTULU: She can go to hell; I don't care about finding her. Just get the old man to give my *kaṇṭĕ* back to me.

HEAD CONSTABLE: What are you talking about? You yourself said that the girl ran away with the *kaṇṭĕ*. How can I get the old man to give it back to you?

RAMAP-PANTULU: The old man *says* that she ran away with it. But I believe he has it in his safe and is refusing to return it to me.

HEAD CONSTABLE: So what do you want me to do?

RAMAP-PANTULU: Say you'll charge him with murder and he'll return my *kaṇṭĕ* to me. You can make some money too.

HEAD CONSTABLE: I see. But what if, as you say, the girl ran away with the *kaṇṭĕ*?

RAMAP-PANTULU: Well, in that case, have him pay its market value.

HEAD CONSTABLE: Will he pay?

RAMAP-PANTULU: That's why I am seeking your help.

HEAD CONSTABLE: I don't believe he'll pay. But let me see what I can do for you. We need two or three witnesses to make a case of homicide.

RAMAP-PANTULU: What about the people right here?

HEAD CONSTABLE: Viresam and Manavallayya are in the third heaven. Havaldar will kill you if you ask him to tell a lie. The Head can't walk the distance at this time of the night. We are left with the shopkeeper Ramam-dasu.

RAMAP-PANTULU: Can't that beggar stand as a witness?

HEAD CONSTABLE: Do you think he is an ordinary beggar in ochre clothes? No, he is a great *siddha* of yogic powers. He will not tell a lie even if you give him a heap of gold as tall as he stands.

RAMAP-PANTULU: He doesn't have to say anything. It's enough if he stands there. Bring him along.

(The Head Constable brings the Shopkeeper and Bairagi.)

BAIRAGI: My kind of people are the best witnesses you can find. If I look with my yogic eye, things appear just as they really happened, in all detail. Let's go. If we can get a little money, it will help the center in Haridvaram.

RAMAP-PANTULU: (To Bairagi:) Who cares what really happened? We need a little imagination here or we can't win. Your reverence should support what the Head Constable tells the old man.

BAIRAGI: Crazy! What's truth, and what's untruth? We are *siddhas*. We can make truth into falsehood and falsehood, truth. Actually, the whole world is a huge lie. Let's go.

(Exit.)

SCENE FIVE. Near the temple doorway.

(Head Constable and Ramap-Pantulu talk privately. The Shopkeeper and a constable stand at a distance.)

HEAD CONSTABLE: Brother, do you want me to lose my job?

RAMAP-PANTULU: If you threaten him a little, will you lose your job? Threatening people *is* your job as a policeman, isn't it? Well, what can I say if you want to shirk your duty?

HEAD CONSTABLE: (Throws out bits of paper he was crushing into balls in his hand.) Brother, Lubdha Avadhanlu is neither a child nor an idiot. How can I threaten him with homicide? If I saw any hope of getting something out of this case—I *am* a policeman, after all—wouldn't I swing into action? If I solve a murder case, surely it will reflect well on my competence. Haven't I sent my assistant into the well in this dark night? If I call this a murder, I will be laughed out of court. I am certain the girl has taken shelter in a neighbor's house for fear of Minakshi's rough hand. Maybe she went to your house, as the old man says.

RAMAP-PANTULU: She did not come to my house, I am telling you. You can't take it easy, telling yourself she is in this or that house. I don't understand how you are so sure about that. I asked you to search for her and you did not. What if the people of this house or that house steal my *kaṇṭĕ* while she is sleeping? If I go home without the *kaṇṭĕ,* Madhura-vani will kick me out—well, not exactly kick me out, but she'll cry and she won't let me live in peace.

HEAD CONSTABLE: If that's what you fear, let me give you some advice.

RAMAP-PANTULU: What's that?

HEAD CONSTABLE: Go to Lubdha Avadhanlu's house and sit there until he gives you back your *kaṇṭĕ.*

RAMAP-PANTULU: Great advice. Why should I go to his house? I'll go home and sleep comfortably.

HEAD CONSTABLE: But you said Madhura-vani won't let you live in peace.

RAMAP-PANTULU: As if you care! If he doesn't give my *kaṇṭĕ* back tomorrow, I will file a civil suit against him. He confessed in your presence. I will include you as a witness.

HEAD CONSTABLE: Oh, is that your game? I am a police officer, and I can't keep my job if I spend my time going around the courts on civil suits and such things. Give me a police complaint that Lubdha Avadhanlu stole your *kaṇṭĕ.* I'll book a case against him and show you my flair.

RAMAP-PANTULU: He admitted he took the *kaṇṭĕ* in your presence. Let's see how well you lie in court.

HEAD CONSTABLE: Pantulu, don't be so clever. He said he didn't know anything about the *kaṇṭĕ.* That's what I'll say in court.

RAMAP-PANTULU: Is that your idea of helping me out?

HEAD CONSTABLE: Why worry for nothing? If you don't see your *kaṇṭĕ* in your house by tomorrow, I'll take the blame.

RAMAP-PANTULU: How can I face Madhura-vani now?

HEAD CONSTABLE: That's your problem.

RAMAP-PANTULU: Please let's go to Lubdha Avadhanlu together. If we both pressure him, he will give in.

HEAD CONSTABLE: We're going round in circles. You've ruined my sleep all night for no good reason. I can't go to Lubdha Avadhanlu again. I told you to go there and sit tight. That's the best advice I can give you. That miserly bastard gave a measly twelve rupees for the four of us, and I had to work my life to its last breath to squeeze it out of him. I'll give my share of three rupees to you.

RAMAP-PANTULU: I lost a golden *kaṇṭĕ* and you give me three measly rupees. What good are they to me?

HEAD CONSTABLE: All the better—we will give them to Guruji.

RAMAP-PANTULU: Well, I'm out of small cash. Looks like I can use those rupees. Throw them this way. (He takes three rupees from the Head Constable.)[48]

HEAD CONSTABLE: Guruji, here's a small offering.

BAIRAGI: Little or a lot, whatever I get goes to the Yoga Center.

HEAD CONSTABLE: (To the Shopkeeper and the junior constable:) Here's your three, and here's yours. (Emptying his hands clean.) *Sāf-jhāḍa,* all gone. Thankless work is my only share.

SHOPKEEPER: (Calling Bairagi to the side:) A fresh supply of excellent brandy came from Madras just today. Have a taste of it before you go to Kashi.

HEAD CONSTABLE: Guruji, goodbye. Pantulu, go grab the old man. I should go to the police station. (To the junior constable:) Kamayya, come, let's go.

(Exit the Head Constable and the junior constable to one side and Bairagi and the Shopkeeper to the other side.)

RAMAP-PANTULU: He gives me a measly three rupees for my *kaṇṭĕ.* (Laughs dryly.) I'll show him. (He picks up the balls of paper thrown on the floor by the Head Constable.) I will send anonymous complaints to the inspector and the tahsildar. The bastard may go to see Madhura-vani now. If I go home I'll have to sleep on the porch. That stubborn slut won't open the door. If I go to Lubdha Avadhanlu's house, he'll grab his stick to hit me. Maybe I should sleep in this temple. What if there are snakes around here? *Chi.* I should get rid of this whore of a woman. I wonder what happened to the girl? If by luck she is found in a neighbor's house, the *kaṇṭĕ* should be with her. What if she committed suicide? No, she wouldn't have. Two people, Gavarayya and Kamayya, searched the well. Maybe she was a previously married girl and her father came quietly and whisked her away. If so, the *kaṇṭĕ* is lost. I should go talk to Minakshi. She might give me some clues, but how to get a hold of her? If I knock, the old man himself might wake up.

(He crosses the street and stands in front of Lubdha Avadhanlu's house.)

I'm famished. If I could get hold of Minakshi, she'd give me something to eat. Who could that be standing under the pipal tree, smoking? (Going a few paces toward him.) Asiri, is that you?

ASIRI: Sir. (He throws the cigar away.)[49]

RAMAP-PANTULU: Are you well?

ASIRI: Not as well as I used to be. You have that woman now, and you are not coming to see *this* woman. No one gives me any money, sir.

RAMAP-PANTULU: You should ask. If you don't ask, even your mother won't give you anything.

ASIRI: That pleasure-woman you keep—she is a bad pleasure-woman, sir!

RAMAP-PANTULU: Tell me, tell me about her. It has been a long time since I gave you any money. Here, take this rupee.

ASIRI: A hundred salutes to you, sir.

RAMAP-PANTULU: You were saying something about Madhura-vani.

ASIRI: She really is a bad pleasure-woman, sir.

RAMAP-PANTULU: Who are her regulars? Who? Tell me.

ASIRI: If anyone approaches her, sir, she gives him a whipping.

RAMAP-PANTULU: I thought you said she is bad.

ASIRI: Of course she is. The other day, when the Head Constable went to her, she set her dog on him!

RAMAP-PANTULU: Tell me, was she mad at you any time?

ASIRI: Why would she be mad at people like me? She only cusses at Brahmins when they go to her.

RAMAP-PANTULU: You're an honest man, Asiri. You speak the truth.

ASIRI: God punishes people who lie, sir.

RAMAP-PANTULU: What's your master doing?

ASIRI: He is sleeping, sir.

RAMAP-PANTULU: I'll give you another rupee. Can you call Minakshi into the hallway?
ASIRI: It's impossible, sir. She is sleeping in the same room as her father.[50]
RAMAP-PANTULU: If you snap your fingers, she'll get up. I know you can do it.
ASIRI: Well, give it to me. I'll see what I can do.

(Ramap-Pantulu gives Asiri another rupee. Both of them enter the house.)

(Curtain.)

SCENE SIX. The hallway in Lubdha Avadhanlu's house.

(Minakshi brings an earthen lamp and puts it on the hallway wall. Ramap-Pantulu makes the wick smaller and kisses her.)

MINAKSHI: You must have lost your way.
RAMAP-PANTULU: I have lost my senses all these days.
MINAKSHI: Did Madhura-vani let you go?
RAMAP-PANTULU: Madhura-vani! Shave her head! I'm going to leave her. Do you have anything to eat? I'm starving.
MINAKSHI: What do I have? Would you like some coconut and soaked lentils?
RAMAP-PANTULU: Give me whatever you have.

(Minakshi brings an iron bowl of soaked lentils and pieces of coconut. Ramap-Pantulu begins to eat.)

MINAKSHI: So you want to leave Madhura-vani?
RAMAP-PANTULU: Yes, I am determined to do so.
MINAKSHI: So you knew about the Head Constable.
RAMAP-PANTULU: Yes.
MINAKSHI: Who told you?
RAMAP-PANTULU: Asiri.
MINAKSHI: My servant Asiri?
RAMAP-PANTULU: Yes, your servant Asiri.

(Asiri peeps in from the main door.)

ASIRI: Hey, are you eating the food offered to the spirit?
RAMAP-PANTULU: Really? Is this an offering to the spirit?
MINAKSHI: (To Asiri:) Shut up, you fool.
RAMAP-PANTULU: No fair, giving me food offered to the spirit.

(Ramap-Pantulu throws the food away, goes into the street, unsuccessfully tries to throw up, and returns.)

I couldn't throw up; what should I do?

MINAKSHI: You don't believe me. It's not an offering to the spirit.

RAMAP-PANTULU: But it was dumped in an iron bowl.

MINAKSHI: As if the spirits eat what you offer!

RAMAP-PANTULU: God! Women are horrible!

MINAKSHI: What did Asiri say about Madhura-vani?

ASIRI: (Peeping in again.) Can I take the food you threw out?

RAMAP-PANTULU: Take it.

(Asiri takes the food in the bowl.)

MINAKSHI: He has more courage than you have.

RAMAP-PANTULU: He's an impure, low-caste bastard. He can eat anything. We are pure. We are Brahmins.

MINAKSHI: Especially the two of us!

RAMAP-PANTULU: Why do you say so?

MINAKSHI: I am a whoring widow and you're my illicit lover. You can't find a purer pair than us.

RAMAP-PANTULU: I came tonight to remove that stigma.

MINAKSHI: How will you do that?

RAMAP-PANTULU: If we marry, we won't be impure any more.

MINAKSHI: What an idea!

RAMAP-PANTULU: Let's marry.

MINAKSHI: Truly?

RAMAP-PANTULU: What kind of oath should I take?

MINAKSHI: Blow the light out while you say it.[51]

RAMAP-PANTULU: Let me read these pieces of paper first, then I'll blow out the lamp. (Reads the pieces of paper from his pocket.) Bastard, he took back the IOU he wrote for the money he owed and short-changed me. I'll teach him a lesson.[52]

MINAKSHI: Who is he?

RAMAP-PANTULU: Never mind.

MINAKSHI: What did Asiri say about the Head Constable?

RAMAP-PANTULU: He said that Madhura-vani unleashed her dog on him.

MINAKSHI: Why?

RAMAP-PANTULU: Because he tried to enter when I was not home.

MINAKSHI: How dumb! (Calls Asiri:) Asiri!

(Asiri enters.)

ASIRI: Yes ma'am.

MINAKSHI: You bastard. Speak the truth. Didn't you tell me that the Head Constable sleeps with Madhura-vani whenever Pantulu is not home?

ASIRI: (Scratching his head.) I did.

RAMAP-PANTULU: You liar, you told me that she set her dog on him!

ASIRI: Sir, a servant should learn to keep his mouth shut. If that woman asks me, am I going to tell on you?

MINAKSHI: Tell her. I don't care.

RAMAP-PANTULU: You bastard liar, don't tell anyone about us. I gave you a rupee, remember?

MINAKSHI: Why did you give him a rupee?

ASIRI: I have a wife and kids, that's why. (He goes out.)

RAMAP-PANTULU: That lying slut, she's cheating on me, eh?

MINAKSHI: You said you knew.

RAMAP-PANTULU: Not this much.

MINAKSHI: Once a woman crosses the boundary, there's no limit—you can't say this much or that much. If a woman is bent on it, even an ocean feels only knee deep. You are a fool to expect a whore to be chaste.

RAMAP-PANTULU: Yes, I was a fool, a big fool. I want to smash her skull. I spent a huge amount of money on her.

MINAKSHI: When are you going to get rid of her?

RAMAP-PANTULU: Tomorrow. Not a day later. Dirty slut. What a game she played, pretending to be a chaste woman!

MINAKSHI: So when are we going?

RAMAP-PANTULU: Where?

MINAKSHI: Are you losing your mind? To Rajahmundry.

RAMAP-PANTULU: Yes, yes. Tomorrow I am getting rid of her and we can run away the day after tomorrow. But would you want to bring your jewelry or leave it to the old man?

MINAKSHI: All I have is my jewelry. I can't lose it. But the key for the box is with my father. What shall I do?

RAMAP-PANTULU: You haven't seen what I can do! Look, with this little iron rod on my key-chain, I can open any box you please. Tell me. Do you know where my *kaṇṭĕ* is?

MINAKSHI: You mean the one given to the girl? She used to put it in my trunk overnight.

RAMAP-PANTULU: I beg you. Will you please check your trunk? I will return the *kaṇṭĕ* to Madhura-vani and drive the slut out.

MINAKSHI: The girl lost the key.

RAMAP-PANTULU: I'll open it with this.

MINAKSHI: Could you open my jewelry box too?

RAMAP-PANTULU: Sure.

MINAKSHI: But you didn't take your oath yet—that you will marry me.

RAMAP-PANTULU: If I blow out the lamp, how can I open the box?

MINAKSHI: I have matches.

RAMAP-PANTULU: Well then. Here I promise I will certainly marry you, and saying this, I blow out this lamp.

(Ramap-Pantulu blows the lamp out, embraces Minakshi, and lifts her off the ground.)

I will carry you to Rajahmundry—like this.

(Lubdha Avadhanlu comes out in the dark and hits Ramap-Pantulu with a stick. Minakshi falls down.)

LUBDHA AVADHANLU: You bandit! You jackass!

RAMAP-PANTULU: God, he's killed me. (Goes limping into the street.)

LUBDHA AVADHANLU: Get out, you slut. You get out of my house too. (He pushes Minakshi out into the street and bolts the door from inside.)

RAMAP-PANTULU: Asiri, he killed me. My leg is broken.

ASIRI: (Softly:) Well, you ate the food offered to the spirit. This is what you get for it. (With a normal voice:) Won't the master kick you if you sneak into his house in the middle of the night?

RAMAP-PANTULU: (To Minakshi:) You go back into the house.

MINAKSHI: I won't ever enter that house again. The hell with the jewelry. Now let's go to Rajahmundry.

RAMAP-PANTULU: Right now?

MINAKSHI: You can marry me whenever you want to. You brought me out of my house. I'll have to live with you. Let's go.

RAMAP-PANTULU: You're like the crazy person who says, "I'm cured. Bring the pestle so I can wrap it around my head." I beg you, please go home.

MINAKSHI: Not as long as there's life in this body. I am never going to go into that house again.

RAMAP-PANTULU: (To Asiri:) Asiri, stay with Minakshi and help her into her house as soon as your master opens the door.

(Ramap-Pantulu runs off. Minakshi runs after him.)

(In front of Ramap-Pantulu's house.)

RAMAP-PANTULU: Open up, open the door quick.

MADHURA-VANI: (From inside:) Why are you banging on the door?

RAMAP-PANTULU: A cheetah is chasing me. Open the door, quick.

MADHURA-VANI: I'll only open it if I see the cheetah.

RAMAP-PANTULU: How can you see it from behind a closed door? It will eat me up before you open the door.

MADHURA-VANI: Did you bring my *kaṇṭĕ*?

RAMAP-PANTULU: Still worried about your stupid *kaṇṭĕ*? I'll give you a ton of *kaṇṭĕ*s.

MADHURA-VANI: Keep all of them yourself. Just give my one *kaṇṭĕ* back to me. Only then will I let you in.

RAMAP-PANTULU: Lubdha Avadhanlu is sleeping. I'll get it from him tomorrow.

MADHURA-VANI: Then you can come into the house tomorrow. What's the rush?

RAMAP-PANTULU: What if the cheetah gets me meanwhile?

MADHURA-VANI: Is she with or without hair?[53]

RAMAP-PANTULU: What's a game for the cat is death for the mouse.

(Minakshi enters and grabs Ramap-Pantulu's arm.)

MINAKSHI: You took an oath by blowing out the lamp. If you don't keep your word, your head will explode.

RAMAP-PANTULU: Get away, you slut.

MINAKSHI: I am your wife-to-be. Where can I go?

MADHURA-VANI: What's that you say? Wife-to-be?

MINAKSHI: He said he would get rid of you and elope with me to Rajahmundry. He took an oath, blowing out the lamp. How can he get out of it now?

MADHURA-VANI: Is she the cheetah you are talking about?

RAMAP-PANTULU: You slut, let go of my arm. Did I ever say I'll marry you? You must be dreaming. (He shakes his arm free from Minakshi's grip and she falls down.)

MADHURA-VANI: Using force against a woman? What a big man you are! Stop lying and keep your word. What does she lack, caste or beauty? You ruined her reputation anyway. Marry her and make amends. I'll open the door, but only after you marry her.

MINAKSHI: When Pantulu embraced me and lifted me off the ground, my father saw it and beat him and threw us out of the house. Pantulu promised me that he would leave you because you are sleeping with the Head Constable; he took a vow. He brought me out of my house; he can't escape marrying me now.

MADHURA-VANI: Of course he can't escape. You won't let go. If he doesn't keep his word, you will take him to court. Pantulu-garu loves courts.

RAMAP-PANTULU: Madhura-vani, you're out of your mind. You're not the master of my house. Open the door.

MADHURA-VANI: Wait, I will bring a welcoming flame[54] to auspiciously invite the new couple into the house. (She goes into the interior of the house from the main door.)

RAMAP-PANTULU: (Peeps through the crack in the door and kisses Minakshi.) See what you did. You told her our secret. Our plan was to run away quietly and marry; we shouldn't make a big fuss about it.

MINAKSHI: Some day or other people will know anyway.

RAMAP-PANTULU: Listen to me and go home.

MINAKSHI: No. I will never go to that house again. This is my home. Madhura-vani will open the door and we'll go in.

RAMAP-PANTULU: Well, wait here for a minute. I'll be right back. (Goes a few paces on the street and stands there thinking.) Stubborn slut. She may really get the welcome flame. Madhura-vani won't open the door and Minakshi won't leave me alone. It's almost morning. I'll go to the pond, brush my teeth and wash, and then think of what to do next. If I leave town for a couple of days, things will settle down. She didn't seem to have opened the door. Whose house does she think this is, and who is she anyway to stop me from entering my own house?

(Enter the Disciple at a distance dressed as a religious mendicant boy, singing and playing on a sitar.)[55]

You crave for a house.
Call it your home.
Where's your home
Little Bird?

RAMAP-PANTULU: Isn't this my house?

DISCIPLE:

North of the town,
in the land of the dead,
there is a house of firewood.
Little Bird!

RAMAP-PANTULU: In the cremation ground?

DISCIPLE:

You may live long years,
but what's truly yours?
You can't take it with you,
Little Bird!

Your life of vanity
is lost in reality

Think of the future,
Little Bird!

RAMAP-PANTULU: It really bodes evil, this song.

DISCIPLE:

Fire's your relative
Wood is your kin.
Who's your mother,
Little Bird?

RAMAP-PANTULU: Relatives? I really have none. I have a sister; she never comes to visit me. And who is the master of the house anyway? A whore inside and a widow outside—together they drove me out of my own home.

DISCIPLE:

Four people carry you.
A few people follow you.

RAMAP-PANTULU: Stupid song; let's go. (He walks quickly for a while.) I hear the song even louder. Maybe he is coming this way.

DISCIPLE:

They wait till you're burned
And turn back home.
No one comes along,
Little Bird.

RAMAP-PANTULU: Crazy song.

DISCIPLE: Pantulu-garu, where are you?

RAMAP-PANTULU: I'd better run or she will catch me. (Runs off.)[56]

(Curtain.)

Act Six

SCENE ONE. In the Brahmin village Rama-chandra-puram.

(The wedding party arrives in the garden on the edge of the village pond. Agni-hotra Avadhanlu stands at one end of the pond and Ramap-Pantulu, brushing his teeth, enters from the other end.)

AGNI-HOTRA AVADHANLU: Get off the carts. Sayibu, there's enough fodder for the elephant.[1] The pond is quite suitable for bathing. Hey, there, who is that on the edge of the pond?

RAMAP-PANTULU: (To himself:) Oh, I forgot all about it. Today is the day when the wedding party arrives. (Loudly:) People call me Ramap-Pantulu, sir.

AGNI-HOTRA AVADHANLU: Has Lubdha Avadhanlu sent you?

RAMAP-PANTULU: What for?

AGNI-HOTRA AVADHANLU: Hasn't he sent anybody to receive us? People call me Agni-hotra Avadhanlu.

RAMAP-PANTULU: Oh, you are Agni-hotra Avadhanlu. What brings you here, sir?

AGNI-HOTRA AVADHANLU: Don't you know about the wedding?

RAMAP-PANTULU: Whose wedding?

AGNI-HOTRA AVADHANLU: Apparently you're not from around here. I am marrying my daughter off to Lubdha Avadhanlu.

RAMAP-PANTULU: Lubdha Avadhanlu is already married.

AGNI-HOTRA AVADHANLU: You are joking. Seriously, how are the arrangements for the wedding going?

RAMAP-PANTULU: No, I am not joking. *You* are joking. Lubdha Avadhanlu's wedding was ten days ago. The word was that you cancelled the match, and he married the daughter of a certain Sastullu from Gunturu instead. He paid twelve hundred for that girl.

AGNI-HOTRA AVADHANLU: Brother, you've got to be joking. Did you want to relate to me as a brother-in-law?[2]

RAMAP-PANTULU: What are you saying? I never lie. This is true, trust me.

AGNI-HOTRA AVADHANLU: Really? With God as your witness?

RAMAP-PANTULU: God as my witness.

AGNI-HOTRA AVADHANLU: *Ayyo, Ayyo.* What treachery. Come with me, I want to break his bones.

RAMAP-PANTULU: No, I can't go to his house. He doesn't talk to me ever since I told him not to marry that Gunturu girl. You go, and I'll wait here for you.

AGNI-HOTRA AVADHANLU: I don't know the way to the bastard's house.

DISCIPLE: (Sings as he comes to the edge of the pond:)

> Who are you,
> and who are your people?
> Illusion binds
> body and soul.

(Ramap-Pantulu looks alarmed.)

AGNI-HOTRA AVADHANLU: What's wrong? You look frightened.

RAMAP-PANTULU: It's a funeral song!

DISCIPLE: (Continuing to sing:)

> Know that you die
> every day!
> Death lies in wait
> every minute!

RAMAP-PANTULU: (To the Disciple:) Quiet! (To Agni-hotra Avadhanlu:) Brother, do you have a copper?

DISCIPLE: She said to come get you.[3]

RAMAP-PANTULU: God, is she coming here?

DISCIPLE: She said, "Never mind the *kaṇṭĕ*. Come home."

RAMAP-PANTULU: What a relief!

AGNI-HOTRA AVADHANLU: Why are you so relieved? What was troubling you?

RAMAP-PANTULU: That's a long story.

DISCIPLE: The cheetah-cub has gone with her father.

AGNI-HOTRA AVADHANLU: Do cheetahs attack this village?

RAMAP-PANTULU: I'm rid of the evil. Here, take this rupee.

DISCIPLE: (Takes the rupee and thanks him.) I am your servant, sir. (Continues to sing:)

> It rains and rains
> at the same time
> it shines.

AGNI-HOTRA AVADHANLU: What's that senseless song? Will you stop it or not? Isn't one rupee enough, you little bastard?

DISCIPLE: Won't you give some too, sir?

AGNI-HOTRA AVADHANLU: I won't. (To Ramap-Pantulu:) Brother, who will show me the way to Lubdha Avadhanlu's house?

RAMAP-PANTULU: (To the Disciple:) Do you know Lubdha Avadhanlu's house?

DISCIPLE: Yes, father.

RAMAP-PANTULU: Avadhanlu-garu will give you something. Show him the way.

DISCIPLE: Let him pay me first.

AGNI-HOTRA AVADHANLU: Take this, you brat.

(The Disciple leads the way, and Agni-hotra Avadhanlu follows. The Disciple starts singing after walking a few paces.)

Hey, pretty girl, what makes you sad?
Hey, pretty girl, what makes you sad?

AGNI-HOTRA AVADHANLU: Who is sad, you brat?

DISCIPLE: No, it's not brat, it's a rat. (Sings again.)

The rats plow the field.
The cats dance along.

AGNI-HOTRA AVADHANLU: What?

DISCIPLE:

A pair of goats
team up as drummers
and go to the festival of fire.

AGNI-HOTRA AVADHANLU: What's this nonsense song?

DISCIPLE:

Their buddy the lizard
picks the flowers
from the jasmine bushes
in the yard.

AGNI-HOTRA AVADHANLU: If you sing any more, I'll kill you.

DISCIPLE: Then I won't show the house to you.

(Agni-hotra Avadhanlu tries to hit him. The Disciple ducks.)

DISCIPLE:

Their buddy the pig
lives under the tank.
Another jump!
Another jump!

(He exits.)

AGNI-HOTRA AVADHANLU: Drop dead, you bastard! Now which way do I go? This way or that?

(Curtain.)

SCENE TWO. Garden on the edge of the pond.

(Agni-hotra Avadhanlu, Ramap-Pantulu, Venk'amma, and others.)

AGNI-HOTRA AVADHANLU: I beat him bad, that son of a bitch. I brought horses and elephants. May the bastard's funeral take place soon. He refused to pay even the travel expenses.

VENK'AMMA: That was our luck. Our fortune was bad, so how can things be different? I told you not to make this match. I had fears right from the beginning. A cat came toward us when we started.[4]

AGNI-HOTRA AVADHANLU: Shut up, you slut. What do women know? Brother, can we make a criminal case out of this? I have an English teacher who is an expert in court matters. We can take his advice too.

RAMAP-PANTULU: You are an old hand at court matters. You don't need anybody's advice. Because I am a local here, I might be able to help you in getting proper evidence, but you don't need any English teachers to advise you. These greenhorns who know a little English may be good for a mechanical word-to-word translation. But in matters of legal strategy, it's veterans like you who should come up with a plan of action and a competent Niyogi like me who should execute it. You don't even need to ask if there's room for a criminal case. You know better than me that we can also sue for three or four thousand rupees of civil damages.

AGNI-HOTRA AVADHANLU: That's what I think too.

RAMAP-PANTULU: It's a done deal. There is nothing to consult about. Let's go right away and hit him with a lawsuit. Bring some cash for expenses.

AGNI-HOTRA AVADHANLU: I don't have a penny on me. I was expecting this ass to pay. I didn't bring any money.

RAMAP-PANTULU: It will be too late by the time you go home and get money. As the saying goes: *śubhasya śīghram*, good things should not be delayed. What do you say?

AGNI-HOTRA AVADHANLU: I am not going to go home until we see the end of this. We'll pawn a piece of my daughter's gold and get some cash.

RAMAP-PANTULU: Then bring it. We'll go to Poli-setti, who will give us some money on it. We have to make friends with him too. Poli-setti was present when you beat up Lubdha Avadhanlu, so he will call Poli-setti as a witness for sure. We have to lure him to our side. What do you say?

AGNI-HOTRA AVADHANLU: Excellent advice. That was my idea too.

RAMAP-PANTULU: See, not everybody can give the right advice. Also, if you ask these English-educated teachers for advice, they advise you against court cases and against false evidence. What do they lose? How can we win cases without any dirty deals?

AGNI-HOTRA AVADHANLU: But our teacher is a decent man and quite smart too. There's nothing he doesn't know in matters of law. I haven't seen a better-behaved person. When you see him, you'll say the same thing.

RAMAP-PANTULU: That may very well be. But you really don't need advice. (Secretly in his ear:) The teacher you talk about is Girisam, right? He is Lubdha Avadhanlu's cousin. Why would he advise you against the interests of his cousin?

AGNI-HOTRA AVADHANLU: That's very true. I didn't think of that.

RAMAP-PANTULU: I am a Niyogi by birth. Diplomacy is my middle name. Pay a little attention to what I say. Send the family back; Girisam can take them home. We should rush to the lawyer and start the suit before Lubdha Avadhanlu does so. Bring something or other to pawn, fast.

AGNI-HOTRA AVADHANLU: (To Venk'amma:) Hey, ask Bucc'amma to come here.

VENK'AMMA: Where is Bucc'amma? Come to think of it, she is probably still sleeping in the cart. (To a person from the wedding party:) Call her, please.

AGNI-HOTRA AVADHANLU: (To Ramap-Pantulu:) We'll get substantial damages, right?

RAMAP-PANTULU: Very substantial. We'll get a lot of money.

A PERSON FROM THE WEDDING PARTY: Her cart is nowhere to be seen. Probably it lagged behind.

VENK'AMMA: But Venkatesam is here. How come he's here? Hey, didn't you ride in Sister's cart?

VENKATESAM: No, I rode the elephant.

AGNI-HOTRA AVADHANLU: You idiot, where is the teacher?

VENKATESAM: I don't know. I didn't see him.

AGNI-HOTRA AVADHANLU: Is the horse here? Where's the horseman?

VENKATESAM: The horseman told me that . . .

AGNI-HOTRA AVADHANLU: Told you what, Idiot?

VENKATESAM: My master . . . last night . . .

AGNI-HOTRA AVADHANLU: Speak up. Last night, what happened last night?

VENKATESAM: . . . got off the horse, and boarded the cart. That's what the horseman said.

VENK'AMMA: Ayyo! I hope they didn't elope.

PEOPLE NEARBY: Really!

VENK'AMMA: That must be what happened, what else? (She slumps to the ground.)

AGNI-HOTRA AVADHANLU: (Trembling with anger.) The teacher has eloped with that beggar of a slut. The jewelry box and my court papers—they are gone too?

VENKATESAM: I put my schoolbooks in Sister's suitcase too.

AGNI-HOTRA AVADHANLU: Dirty son of a bitch. You are at the root of all this. If I'd had a hint of it, I would have killed that crook. I would have buried the bastard six feet deep.

RAMAP-PANTULU: You said the teacher was a good man. What did he make off with?

AGNI-HOTRA AVADHANLU: What did he make off with? Your funeral, that's what he made off with. He eloped with that whore, my daughter. The English schooling of this son of a bitch—that's what has ruined my life.

(He goes to hit Venkatesam, holding him by his hair.)

(Curtain.)

SCENE SIX.[5] Visakhapatnam.

(In a house where Madhura-vani is temporarily staying.[6] Madhura-vani sits on a chair. Enter Karataka-sastri and the Disciple. Madhura-vani stands up to receive them.)

MADHURA-VANI: A thousand bows to my guru. A little kiss to the Disciple. (She kisses the Disciple.)

KARATAKA-SASTRI: Don't spoil my son-in-law, please.

MADHURA-VANI: What son-in-law?

KARATAKA-SASTRI: I am going to marry my daughter to him.

MADHURA-VANI: Will you have the wedding after prison, or have the wedding first and then enter the "holy place"?

DISCIPLE: Sir, what's this, she's talking of jail?

KARATAKA-SASTRI: Nothing. She is just joking.

MADHURA-VANI: Tell him the truth. He will at least have a chance to see his parents.

DISCIPLE: Am I in trouble?

MADHURA-VANI: Big time.

KARATAKA-SASTRI: Please stop joking, or the boy will never trust us adults.

DISCIPLE: What did I do? I did what the guru told me to do. He should take the credit and the blame for it.

MADHURA-VANI: I don't know who did what. But I do know the Head Constable is looking for both of you. He is waiting to shut you up in the "holy place" as soon as he finds you.

DISCIPLE: Is this the "marriage" you promised me?

KARATAKA-SASTRI: If there's any trouble, I will put myself in harm's way to protect you. Don't be afraid.

MADHURA-VANI: Trouble comes to both the guru and the disciple at the same time, so there's no chance of one protecting the other. Perhaps I should save both of you out of kindness. I don't think anyone else can help.

DISCIPLE: You don't need to worry about my guru. He is a grown-up man. He can take care of himself. I'm just a kid, totally innocent. Protect me; your name will be remembered with thanks.

MADHURA-VANI: Will you leave your guru and become my disciple instead?

DISCIPLE: Right this minute. (He puffs his cheeks and hits them both a couple of times with his closed fists to make sounds.)[7] Our friendship ends today. I am not going to play women's roles any more.

MADHURA-VANI: Not even in a play?

DISCIPLE: Not even in a play.

MADHURA-VANI: Do you know what you have to do to be my disciple?

DISCIPLE: I will draw water. I'll cook. I'll wash clothes. I am a Brahmin, so I hope you won't ask me to massage your feet.

MADHURA-VANI: (Laughing uncontrollably.) Is this what you do as a disciple for your guru?

DISCIPLE: There's something more. I will also rub your back.

MADHURA-VANI: You rascal.

DISCIPLE: I'll do whatever you ask me to do.

MADHURA-VANI: You have to kiss me every time I ask you to.

DISCIPLE: I'll kiss you.

KARATAKA-SASTRI: He is a young boy. Why corrupt him? Whatever you want from a disciple, I will do it both on his behalf and mine. If you can, save us, please.

MADHURA-VANI: (Sings:)

> The teacher has become the student
> the student is now the teacher.
> La la la.

If you want to be the student you have to pay the fee.

KARATAKA-SASTRI: What's a game for the cat is death for the mouse.

MADHURA-VANI: You think you're the mouse?

KARATAKA-SASTRI: (Indicating "yes":) Aha.

MADHURA-VANI: You're no mouse. You are a bandicoot. Your disciple is the mouse.

KARATAKA-SASTRI: Well, save him then.

MADHURA-VANI: That's what I am thinking of.

KARATAKA-SASTRI: Two minds are better than one. Tell me what you are thinking, I'll tell you what I am thinking, and we'll make a good plan together.

MADHURA-VANI: Tell me your plan first.

KARATAKA-SASTRI: It's nothing complicated. I will send the twelve hundred rupees in cash and that *kaṇṭĕ* to Lubdha Avadhanlu by insured post, as if it is from Gunturu Sastullu. That will convince Saujanya Rao Pantulu-garu[8] that the murder case is false. What happens next depends on my luck.

MADHURA-VANI: How can you get the *kaṇṭĕ*?

KARATAKA-SASTRI: Only if you are kind enough to give it.

MADHURA-VANI: (Putting her index finger straight on her nose.) Strange, indeed. Brahmins are capable of asking for anything.

KARATAKA-SASTRI: Why do you say that?

MADHURA-VANI: Will I ever see it again?

KARATAKA-SASTRI: Saujanya Rao Pantulu-garu will get your *kaṇṭĕ* back to you. He is an honest man.

MADHURA-VANI: Is he that good?

KARATAKA-SASTRI: Absolutely.

MADHURA-VANI: How good is he?

KARATAKA-SASTRI: There's no one like him in the world.

MADHURA-VANI: I want to see him. Can you take me to him?

KARATAKA-SASTRI: No way. He doesn't allow pleasure-women to see him.

MADHURA-VANI: He is *anti-nautch,* I suppose?

KARATAKA-SASTRI: This is a new disease with English-educated people. There are, of course, different shades among them.

MADHURA-VANI: What shade is Saujanya Rao, and what shade is Girisam?

KARATAKA-SASTRI: There's no comparison. One is a dog and the other is a sacred cow. Saujanya Rao Pantulu-garu is *anti-nautch* in thought, word, and deed. If you, even inadvertently, so much as mention *nautch-girls,* he will say, "I don't want to hear about it." Such clean people are rare. All the others are *anti-nautch* depending on convenience. The entire crowd are heroes only in words. Girisam is the leader among them. Some of them are *anti-nautch* during the day and *pro-nautch* at night. Others are *anti-nautch* in their hometown and *pro-nautch* if they are in a new place. Yet others are *pro-nautch* as long as they have strength and *anti-nautch* when they get too old for pleasure. There are some who are *pro-nautch* as long as they are alive and *anti-nautch* only after their death. But then there are some lucky people who are *pro-nautch* even after their death—they perform Vedic sacrifices to buy entrance to the pleasures of heaven. Weak-minded people like me—we are *anti-nautch* only when no girl is available.

MADHURA-VANI: I know about your morals. But what I hear from the Head Constable is that Saujanya Rao is moving heaven and earth to save Lubdha Avadhanlu. What could be the reason?

KARATAKA-SASTRI: The same reason why fish swim and birds fly.

MADHURA-VANI: You mean helping people is in his nature?

KARATAKA-SASTRI: Absolutely.

MADHURA-VANI: Then why can't you learn a little of that swimming and flying yourself?

KARATAKA-SASTRI: I don't understand.

MADHURA-VANI: Why can't you tell Saujanya Rao the truth of this case and help out?

KARATAKA-SASTRI: Nice advice! The wise say: Swim to the shore yourself first, you can help others cross later.[9] You know what Saujanya Rao will say if I tell him the truth? "Dear Sastri-garu, you committed a crime. There is not much I can do to help you. I am very sad for you." With a lot of pity for me he will send me to jail. He might help my family by sending a little money every month until I am released. I have to save myself from such risk, and that's why I came up with this plan.

MADHURA-VANI: All right, Saujanya Rao is a good man, and if he gets the *kaṇṭĕ*, he will have it returned to me. But what if Lubdha Avadhanlu should take the money and the *kaṇṭĕ* and not say a word about it?

KARATAKA-SASTRI: I will pay you the cost of the *kaṇṭĕ*.

MADHURA-VANI: But if, meanwhile, you should enter the "sacred place," who is going to give me the cost of the *kaṇṭĕ*? Therefore, leave your disciple with me as collateral until you get that *kaṇṭĕ* back to me.

KARATAKA-SASTRI: That's fine.

DISCIPLE: But what about my wedding?

KARATAKA-SASTRI: Didn't I give my word? What do you think I have in my mouth, a tongue or a piece of wood?

DISCIPLE: But what if you should end up in jail?

MADHURA-VANI: That's the right kind of student for the guru.

KARATAKA-SASTRI: In case of such a calamity, I will tell my wife and arrange for your wedding before I go.

DISCIPLE: Just remember you are under a terrible vow to give your daughter to me.

KARATAKA-SASTRI: Madhura-vani, won't you please take the trouble of bringing that *kaṇṭĕ* to me?

MADHURA-VANI: Why; what's the rush?

KARATAKA-SASTRI: If the Head Constable or Ramap-Pantulu should show up, everything will be spoiled.

MADHURA-VANI: I'll fix it if it is spoiled.

KARATAKA-SASTRI: I know you are capable of that.

(Madhura-vani goes in.)

KARATAKA-SASTRI: (To the Disciple:) You don't have to follow every whim of hers. Keep an eye on things and whisper in my ear if anything interesting happens.

DISCIPLE: My style is to follow the commands of my keepers. I wonder what you were thinking of my future when you made me take that female role.

KARATAKA-SASTRI: Even great men make mistakes. Everyone slips some time or other.

(Madhura-vani enters with the kaṇṭĕ.)

MADHURA-VANI: What if the collateral should run away? It's not a dog to be tied up.

KARATAKA-SASTRI: You think any fish can escape once it's caught in your net?

MADHURA-VANI: It's great if my net catches pearls, not rocks and shells.

KARATAKA-SASTRI: Always money. Do you ever think of love and friendship?

MADHURA-VANI: Friendship with people like you, yes. That's why I am trusting you with my hard-earned *kaṇṭĕ*. If my mother knew about this, I wouldn't hear the end of it. Love? Love is lovely only if you have a life. If the owner of a sweets shop has a sweet tooth, that's the end of his business. A courtesan has to suppress her longing for love in her heart. People of my caste, who have to make a living on their short-lived youth—we love only one thing.

KARATAKA-SASTRI: What's that?

MADHURA-VANI: Gold. Once the charm of youth fades, only gold can give me back my luster. I am giving gold to you. You can see how much I care for your friendship.

KARATAKA-SASTRI: Your friendship is beyond reproach. About your youth and charm—believe me, you stay forever young and beautiful like the gods' women.

MADHURA-VANI: Thanks to my mother, who poured her wisdom into my ears, or I would have fallen for the flattery of scholars like you and would have ruined my life like the other pleasure-women of the town.

KARATAKA-SASTRI: Your mother, what a wise woman she is! It's her training that gave you the skill to nourish both your beauty and your learning.

MADHURA-VANI: God knows I would have preferred to be born in a farming family, have a husband, work in his farm taking care of his vegetable garden and plants. That would have given me someone who loved me and looked after me for life.

KARATAKA-SASTRI: What a disappointing thought! If the princess of pleasure-women called Madhura-vani didn't exist in this country, what a loss it would be to God's creation!

MADHURA-VANI: I don't know about the loss to creation, but you would have felt a little lack of help in your present troubles.

KARATAKA-SASTRI: You didn't tell me what your plan was to save us.

MADHURA-VANI: But you were not willing to take me to Saujanya Rao!

KARATAKA-SASTRI: He would throw both you and me out of his house.

MADHURA-VANI: Is he short-tempered?

KARATAKA-SASTRI: No, he is very gentle and soft-spoken.

MADHURA-VANI: Then why do you fear him?

KARATAKA-SASTRI: It's easier to take a beating from a bad person than a mild reproach from a good man.

MADHURA-VANI: I learned something new today. Madhura-vani, the princess of pleasure-women, the crown jewel of creation, is only fit for the company of dogs like Girisam and doesn't deserve to see good men like Saujanya Rao. Because Girisam visited her house, he automatically lost his status and was considered unfit to step into your sister's house. Great scholars like you may of course make a huge effort to locate her in this town, even fall at her feet when they need her. So is the deputy collector a dog too?

KARATAKA-SASTRI: He does not take bribes, but he is a womanizer. He holds high office, so let's call him an English dog. Why, did you catch him in your net?

MADHURA-VANI: What if I did?

KARATAKA-SASTRI: Then we are saved. If he is on our side, the entire case melts like the morning mist. So was this the strategy you were talking about? What a great strategy!

MADHURA-VANI: He is sending messages.

KARATAKA-SASTRI: Go, go, go. Don't lose this opportunity. If you get him, your luck and my luck will have no limits.

MADHURA-VANI: No, I don't want to go.

KARATAKA-SASTRI: You just stabbed me. He is the only one that can save us.

MADHURA-VANI: From now on, I want to keep all dogs at a distance, street dogs as well as English dogs.

KARATAKA-SASTRI: I was just joking when I said he was an English dog. He really is a connoisseur. He gives easily too. In any case, isn't he better than the Head Constable?

MADHURA-VANI: Apparently I lost status in your view when I left the city and went to the village. I kept the Head Constable as a servant, but no more than that. Those few days, he served me instead of the government. Without his help, you wouldn't have been able to get past the boundary of the village. Neither could this young mendicant. Now I know how self-centered people can be.

KARATAKA-SASTRI: Forgive me, please. I offended you. When you refused to see the collector, my heart sank. But let me tell you, I saw with my own eyes how you ruled over the whole village like a queen.

MADHURA-VANI: Why did your heart sink when I said I wouldn't see the collector? Your ways are strange. I suppose Saujanya Rao will be pleased to know this.

KARATAKA-SASTRI: No, no. He will chop my head off.

MADHURA-VANI: Then we will watch him do that.

KARATAKA-SASTRI: You want to acquire the sin of killing a Brahmin?

MADHURA-VANI: You, a Brahmin? Well, as Poli-setti says, Brahmins are Brahmins, no matter how rotten. Take this. (Gives the *kaṇṭĕ* to him.) Will I see it again?[10]

KARATAKA-SASTRI: Don't say that. It will come back to you packed in flowers. I shouldn't embarrass you, but there's no other person like you in the whole world. Except that you are a little nutty.

MADHURA-VANI: It's that nuttiness that helps you now.

KARATAKA-SASTRI: Not quite. Why don't you see that deputy collector and save this poor Brahmin?

MADHURA-VANI: Enough is enough. (She gestures with her hand, telling him to leave. As Karataka-sastri and the Disciple are leaving, she calls:) Sastri-garu!

(Reenter Karataka-sastri.)

Are you going to give your daughter to Mahesam?[11]

KARATAKA-SASTRI: Yes.

MADHURA-VANI: Then make me a promise.

KARATAKA-SASTRI: What's that?

MADHURA-VANI: Promise me that you will not corrupt the boy by making him act in plays and taking him to whorehouses.

KARATAKA-SASTRI: No, I won't anymore. I also want him to be a good boy. (Inhaling a pinch of snuff.) You are my guru, Madhura-vani.

MADHURA-VANI: Brahmins are good at preaching and poor at practice. Your promise is real, right?

KARATAKA-SASTRI: Right.

MADHURA-VANI: Just because you are Brahmins, you can't pull wool over God's eyes, right?

KARATAKA-SASTRI: Now you are scolding me.

MADHURA-VANI: You can't bribe the god of death. I don't think you can send Madhura-vani to him and get him to wipe out all your sins.

KARATAKA-SASTRI: Madhura-vani, I have to go. There is an important errand I have to run. I'll see you later.

MADHURA-VANI: (Collapsing into a chair overtaken by laughter and then composing herself.) Wait one minute. Hey Disciple, remember the song you sang in the village while Ramap-Pantulu stood outside his house, with me inside and Minakshi outside in the quiet of the early morning—that little bird song? Sing that again and teach your guru a lesson. He is trying to save his skin, while because of him, an old Brahmin is about to be sent to the gallows.

DISCIPLE: (Sings mischievously:)

> She has a lovely red nose
> that parrot, my dear. Its . . .

MADHURA-VANI: (Pretending to hit him with a cane:)

> A jail cell is ready,
> if you don't behave . . .

DISCIPLE: (Sings in the right tone:)

> You may live long years,
> but what's truly yours?
> You can't take it with you,
> Little Bird!

KARATAKA-SASTRI: I've got to go, Madhura-vani. I'll see you again. (Leaving the house.) She taught me a good lesson. My hair is turning gray. I should turn my thoughts away from these pleasures.

(Exit.)[12]

Act Seven

SCENE ONE. A street in Visakhapatnam.

(Enter Bairagi followed by several low-caste men.)

RAMANNA: Where's your holiness coming from, Guruji?

BAIRAGI: From Kashi.

RAMANNA: When did you leave, Guruji?

BAIRAGI: We started early in the morning after taking our holy bath in the Ganges.

RAMANNA: How did you get here so soon?

BAIRAGI: We controlled our breathing and came at the speed of wind.

BUCC'ANNA: Hey, you ignoramus, don't you know that yogis have powers? This is the same person who appeared on Śiva's night in two different towns—Uppaka and Simhacalam—at one and the same time.

X LAKSHMANNA: Hasn't the white man set up the wire-post?[1] A letter goes to faraway lands in a minute. Just like that.

BAIRAGI: Ignorance, ignorance.

RAMANNA: What do you know, you stupid bastard? Shut up.

BAIRAGI: There is a bronze temple of Śiva, consecrated by the great Dharma-raja two miles into the ocean from the shore of the holy rocks. I will pray to that god and leave for Ramesvaram tomorrow. Where do I find yogic hospitality here?

RAMANNA: Guruji, there is no yoga center here. But we are all here; what do you lack? Tell us what's new at Kashi.

BAIRAGI: Four days ago, a golden plate fell from the sky into the Vi'sve'svara temple. The Brahmins could not read the inscription written on the plate. We took a look at it. Written on the plate in the secret language of the *siddhas* are two formulas: one for making gold and another for living forever.

RAMANNA: Amazing! Guruji, what do you eat for dinner?

BAIRAGI: Milk, sugar, and bananas. We eat for a fortnight and then live on air for the next fortnight.

RAMANNA: We'll get your dinner ready in a snap. You must come to our Rāma temple, Guruji.

BAIRAGI: Sure. What's new in this town?

LAKSHMANNA: Nothing much. In the Brahmin village Rama-chandrapuram, an old Brahmin killed his wife. He is going to be sentenced, plus the people that gave false witness and the tahsildar too.

BAIRAGI: This town seems to be full of sinful people. We don't want to stay in this town.

RAMANNA: This Lakshmanna is a fool. Don't take him seriously. Guruji, if you leave, how can people like us cross over? And those people don't even belong to this town.

BUCC'ANNA: Here comes the Shopkeeper from that village.

BAIRAGI: Looks like there are a lot of drunks in this town. We don't talk to drunks. Let's turn in to this lane before the Shopkeeper sees us.

(The Shopkeeper runs after them fast and stops Bairagi by the knot of his loincloth.)

SHOPKEEPER: Pay up before you leave.

BAIRAGI: Who is this fellow? He looks drunk. I told you already that this town is full of sinners. Didn't Vemana say: "Don't ever talk to a drunkard?"

RAMANNA: (To the Shopkeeper:) Brother, are you out of your mind? Bow to the guru and beg his forgiveness.

SHOPKEEPER: He is no guru. He drank up all the liquor in my shop and ran away without paying.

RAMANNA: You're nuts. Him, drinking in your shop! How is it possible? He just came from Kashi.

SHOPKEEPER: You might as well say he fell from a hole in the sky. (To Bairagi:) Cough up the cash you owe me.

BAIRAGI: Young man, why do you want to argue with gentle sadhus like us? You must have mistaken me for someone else. A certain mendicant who looks like us has been going around this country. Last time when we found him, we warned him. If you are so keen on money, get an ounce of copper and we'll change it into gold and give it to you. Give half of it to charity and enjoy the other half or else your head will explode.

RAMANNA: What a foolish thing you did, Brother. Do the siddhas who make gold care for money? Fall at his feet and ask for his kindness.

SHOPKEEPER: You can say anything; what do you lose?

(Enter the Head Constable.)

HEAD CONSTABLE: Guruji, how lucky I am to find you. It's like finding God himself. Now I feel safe. There are some urgent matters I need to talk to you about.

BAIRAGI: (Signaling people to let him speak privately to the Head Constable.) Brothers, please.

(Everybody except the Shopkeeper moves aside.)

BAIRAGI: (To the Shopkeeper:) Is it fair to humiliate me in front of the public? You shouldn't reveal secrets of yoga to ignorant people.

SHOPKEEPER: I know your yoga of running away without paying bills. What's secret about your drinking? Everyone is a guru when it comes to that.

BAIRAGI: You ignorant mortal. We *siddhas* don't care for money, we don't pay attention to what we give or what we get.

HEAD CONSTABLE: Brother, I will pay your bill. Don't say foolish things. If the guru sets his angry eye on us, we'll be burned to ashes. Just give us some privacy. (To Bairagi:) Guruji, there is a murder case around my neck. You know, we went that night to threaten that old man to make a little cash. We knew he'd committed no crime, nothing. Then the tahsildar went too. He threatened the old man and squeezed a few more rupees out of him. Ramap-Pantulu, upset that he didn't get his *kaṇṭĕ* back, sent anonymous petitions to the inspector and the police superintendent. Now they're harassing me and the tahsildar, pressing charges that a murder was committed and that I covered it up.

BAIRAGI: Don't you fear, we'll protect you.

HEAD CONSTABLE: That's why I said finding you is like finding God.

BAIRAGI: I'll make your enemies tongue-tied. Write down their names and give them to me. But you used to say the inspector was your friend.

HEAD CONSTABLE: What's friendship for people in high office? However much you bribe them, they don't hesitate to chop your head off quietly when they see a profit in it. My inspector wants to become a superintendent. He hates the tahsildar. Their fight is doing me in.

BAIRAGI: Just watch. By tomorrow the wind will turn in your favor.

HEAD CONSTABLE: It's all in your hands, Guruji. There is a great lawyer called Saujanya Rao. He is helping me a lot. He suggested a way of clearing this case, but it doesn't seem to be that easy.

BAIRAGI: What did he suggest?

HEAD CONSTABLE: If we can find the father of the bride that ran away—a certain Gunturu Sastullu—the case is resolved. But we can't find him anywhere.

BAIRAGI: That's nothing. We can find him tonight. I'll show him to you in the black circle, the *añjanam.*[2]

HEAD CONSTABLE: Then I am saved. Can you also find where that boy, I mean that girl, is hiding now?

BAIRAGI: Yes, you can see that as well.

HEAD CONSTABLE: Can you see her, even if she is a boy?

BAIRAGI: What do you mean boy? How can a girl become a boy?

HEAD CONSTABLE: (To himself:) I don't think it's safe to tell him. (To Bairagi:) I am losing my mind from all these problems. Let's go, we'll go to our house.

BAIRAGI: You go ahead; I'll catch up with you after enlightening these disciples.

HEAD CONSTABLE: I'll cling to your feet until this matter is cleared. If I am out of trouble, I'll give one hundred sixteen rupees for the sacred center you are building in Haridvaram.[3]

(Exeunt omni.)

SCENE SIX.[4] Saujanya Rao's house.

(Saujanya Rao's bedroom on the second floor. A small kerosene lamp on the table. Across from the door to the stairway leading down, a bed with a mosquito curtain in the middle of the room. Saujanya Rao lies on the bed. A bound gilt-edged Bhagavad-gīta *is on the nightstand next to the bed. Girisam sits on a chair nearby.)*

GIRISAM: My mind is in a big *dilemma.* I'm eager to see my cousin out of danger, but I'm troubled by the idea of achieving the goal by the route of untruth. I tried to tell the Head Constable: no false evidence, go get true evidence. But he was furious at my words. Can we not find witnesses who speak the truth, if we tried, sir?

SAUJANYA RAO: Witnesses who speak the truth! What an innocent man you are! Those who speak the truth never enter the court to give evidence, and those who give evidence don't speak the truth.

GIRISAM: Why not?

SAUJANYA RAO: The counsel for the plaintiff is not interested in truth that hurts the plaintiff, and the defense counsel is not interested in any truth that hurts the defense. By the time you begin to cross-examine, witnesses resort to poetry. That's why decent people are afraid to take the witness stand.

GIRISAM: If the advocates themselves make their witnesses tell lies, what can the judge do?

SAUJANYA RAO: He takes notes, until his hand aches, of all the lies the advocates make the witnesses tell.

GIRISAM: Then what's the use of these courts, sir?

SAUJANYA RAO: That's what I have been thinking for a long time. Even senior advocates shamelessly coach their witnesses to tell lies.

Some people gently suggest beginning the argument with a blatant lie. A few old-fashioned people like me are not yet ready for such things but look the other way when our clients tell lies. I'm so discouraged by these compromises that I have cut down on my practice considerably. I intend gradually to give up this profession.

GIRISAM: If every lawyer were like you, there would be no room for falsehood. But sir, I never knew that there was so much corruption in this profession. I can bear anything but untruth, sir.

SAUJANYA RAO: Telling lies is not the only thing. There are many more corrupt practices. There is a need, I believe, for an anti-lawyer movement in this country, like the *anti-nautch* movement we have now. The fault does not lie with the Head Constable. The problem is that no case can be won without some false evidence. You are a young man trained in an honest path, and so the way courts function naturally disgusts you.

GIRISAM: Now then, what will be the fate of my cousin, sir?

SAUJANYA RAO: There is only one way. If we can find that Gunturu Sastullu and get hold of him, we won't need any other evidence.

GIRISAM: If you can suggest a way to catch him, I will catch him even if I have to search all three realms of the universe, sir.

SAUJANYA RAO: I am really delighted at your energy. If there were more young men like you, our country would really improve. I will provide all the support you need to succeed in this search. Since you are free from your own personal problems, you may start right away. However, I am sad that you will have to *postpone* your wedding because of this.

GIRISAM: No need to worry on that account, sir. My mentor has always said: *duty* first, then *pleasure.* Moreover, sir, I have been trained from my youth to control my senses and keep myself busy in some activity or another. I have therefore developed a certain disinterest in pleasures from women. My friends call me the *Napoleon of Anti-Nautch.* I decided to dedicate the rest of my life to *social reform,* so I rejected marriage and joined my guru's movement as his *lieutenant.* But now I have agreed to marry Bucc'amma because her heart is pure and because she is in a pitiable condition, not for sensual pleasures. I love my student Venkatesam, and so I developed a love for her too. She also loves me and has agreed to marry me because she is convinced that it is not bad for a widow to marry. This is a marriage of *true love,* sir, not a run-of-the-mill *widow-marriage.*

SAUJANYA RAO: That's what your guru wrote too. But your cousin might not want to adopt you if you marry a widow.

GIRISAM: I don't think he would reject your advice, sir. But if he does, I am prepared to lose his adoption, but I won't give up Bucc'amma, whom I love more than my life.

SAUJANYA RAO: She is lucky.

GIRISAM: I consider myself lucky—

(A stranger quietly comes up the staircase and stands at the entrance to the room. Girisam looks amazed, stops talking, and drops his lower jaw. Seeing this, Saujanya Rao asks:)

SAUJANYA RAO: What are you looking at? (He turns his face in the direction Girisam is looking and sees the stranger.)

GIRISAM: I consider myself lucky to have gained the love of such a gem of a woman. But still, as the saying goes, *parôpakārah puṇyāya, pāpāya para-pīḍanam:* Helping others takes us to heaven and harming a person leads us to hell. It is utterly sinful to harm a person who quietly lives his life. So I am willing to do anything to help my cousin.

SAUJANYA RAO: (To the stranger:) Who are you, sir?

THE STRANGER: I came on important business, sir. Forgive me, sir, for not informing you ahead of time. I did not see any servants downstairs.

SAUJANYA RAO: Please sit down.

GIRISAM: (Goes and gets a chair and puts it next to his.) Please sit.

STRANGER: No, I'll stand, sir.

SAUJANYA RAO: Please make yourself comfortable. (The stranger sits.) Who are you, sir?

STRANGER: Sir, do I have to tell you who I am?

SAUJANYA RAO: If for some reason you do not want to give your name, you don't have to.

STRANGER: The job I came for does not require that my name be known to you, sir. For some unavoidable reasons, I cannot reveal my name to you. I ask your forgiveness, sir.

GIRISAM: Shakespeare said: *What's in a name?*[5] I translated his line into a line of Telugu verse: *perulonan'emi pĕnnidhiy unnadi.* And as you know, sir, even our texts say that uttering one's own name loudly is improper.[6]

STRANGER: I would have lied about my name if I was dealing with others. I can't tell a lie to you, sir.

GIRISAM: It is said, King Bhoja's presence made even the illiterate speak poetry. Your presence makes anyone speak the truth, sir.

STRANGER: Excepting a rare individual.

GIRISAM: *Such a person should be pitied.* We should be compassionate toward that person.

SAUJANYA RAO: You shouldn't lie to anybody, no matter what.

STRANGER: My mother taught me to be good to good people and bad to bad people. I didn't want to lie to you, sir.

SAUJANYA RAO: Your mother has to be respected. I suggest you follow the first half of her teaching and try to change the second half. Be good to bad people too. Then the world created by the all-merciful God will appear infinitely more beautiful to you. You will be happy and make people who come to know you happy as well. Also, who knows who is good and who is bad? There is always some good in bad things and some bad in good things.

GIRISAM: What a precious message. Suppose there is a bad person—or why take someone else, think of me as that bad person. Being kind to such a bad person is true kindness. Everyone is good to good people like you. Doing good to the person who has not been good to you is the greatest good deed of all—as this perfect gem of a poem from the poet who wrote *Sumati Śatakamu* says:[7]

> Help him who harmed you,
> without saying a word.
> That's the best thing to do
> for your success too.

SAUJANYA RAO: You articulated my thoughts very eloquently.

STRANGER: (To Saujanya Rao:) I will take your advice and will try to be good to bad people too. It is my great good fortune to have you as my mentor. A visit to a good person gives instant results. You said that there is some bad even in good. But I hear that there is nothing bad in the total goodness you are.

SAUJANYA RAO: Only God is totally good. What do people know of my bad qualities?

GIRISAM: Sir, the missionary calls it *original sin.* Our texts call it karma. But this hell of a karma—pardon my language—or *original sin,* pulls a person, no matter how good and however disciplined, to the wrong path. You know it all, sir, I don't have to say this to you.

SAUJANYA RAO: The *Bhagavad-gīta* says: *balavān indriya-grāmo vidvāmsam api karshati.*[8] Senses are powerful and pull toward evil even the most learned of men. Everyone hides his bad side and shows only the good side.

STRANGER: Certain people present good qualities that they do not really possess and create an illusion of goodness about themselves to the world.

SAUJANYA RAO: True. That's why I said only *you* know what is good and bad about yourself, not the outside world.

STRANGER: You can deceive the world with your pretenses only for a short time, sir, but in the long run society will separate the gold from dross. (To Girisam:) What do you say?

GIRISAM: It's getting late—it's past Saujanya Rao's bedtime. If you could say what you came for . . .

STRANGER: (To Saujanya Rao:) The world by nature is uninterested in good. But its eyes are wide open to evil. If people, over time, decide that a certain person is a good man, you can bet that person is truly good. A person like you is rare, sir, even if you cast your net far and wide. Today is the best day of my life because I was able to see you.

GIRISAM: Absolutely.

SAUJANYA RAO: I try to be good. That's the only good quality I have. You didn't tell me what you came for.

GIRISAM: Do you want me to find out and report to you first thing in the morning, sir?

SAUJANYA RAO: I don't think he will tell *you* what his business is. He was reluctant even to say his name.

GIRISAM: Just trying to help, because it's past your bedtime, sir.

STRANGER: Girisam-garu wants to help everybody.

SAUJANYA RAO: Do you know him?

STRANGER: Who doesn't know him, sir?

GIRISAM: It's very kind of him to say that. But really I am a nobody. I frequently give *lectures* and it is possible good people like him have seen me and have developed respect for me. I might have seen this person too. He looks familiar, and I have been racking my brain to remember who he is. But I would like to respect his desire to remain unknown and therefore I will not try too hard to remember. I'll go to bed. You two can talk.

SAUJANYA RAO: So good-night.

GIRISAM: Good-night. (To the stranger:) Are you a Brahmin?

STRANGER: No. I am not.

GIRISAM: (To the stranger:) If so, my salutations *to the unknown.* (As he leaves, he stops at the doorway, looks back toward the stranger and makes a gesture like he is begging for help.)

SAUJANYA RAO: Girisam is a poet, a very fine young man.

STRANGER: To marry a widow and to be *anti-nautch*—are these two things necessary for a person to be a good man, sir?

SAUJANYA RAO: Marrying a widow depends on a man's likes and dislikes, but a man who has connections with a *nautch-girl* can never be called a good man.

STRANGER: Is that all, sir, or are there other requirements—like never seeing a *nautch-girl,* never talking to her, never attending a *nautch* dance, and so on?

SAUJANYA RAO: It is that much better if a person has such principles.

STRANGER: I suppose you are *anti-nautch;* right, sir?

SAUJANYA RAO: Yes.

STRANGER: (Smiling.) Girisam is *anti-nautch* too. Isn't he, sir?

SAUJANYA RAO: Don't you know? He is the guru of *anti-nautch.*

STRANGER: He is my guru too, sir.

SAUJANYA RAO: Is that so? I am glad to hear that.

STRANGER: I have had a question about this for a long time, sir. If you allow me, I'll ask.

SAUJANYA RAO: Ask. What's wrong in asking?

STRANGER: If you don't call the *nautch-girls* to dance, how do they make a living?

SAUJANYA RAO: They can marry and that takes care of it.

STRANGER: You mean marry people like Girisam?

SAUJANYA RAO: No, no way. He is about to marry a chaste widow in a few days. Why would he marry a *nautch-girl*?

STRANGER: I heard that in Japan there are *nautch-girls* called geishas and that men of high rank in society marry them. Come to think of it, I heard this from Girisam. Do you call Japan a civilized country, sir?

SAUJANYA RAO: Yes, it is a civilized country. But should we adopt a bad practice of a great country? I don't think Girisam would ever do such an immoral thing.

STRANGER: Then how do *nautch-girls* who want to marry find desirable men, sir? Or do you think they should marry any man?

SAUJANYA RAO: I don't know. I haven't thought this through. But why can't *nautch-girls* get a good education, live by other professions, and lead a moral life?

STRANGER: If they did, would people like you marry them, sir?

SAUJANYA RAO: What kind of a question is that! I will never marry a *nautch-girl.* I won't even touch one—not even if a pile of gold as high as I stand is offered to me.

STRANGER: What if you should touch her by accident?

SAUJANYA RAO: (Laughing.) I will chop off that part of my body. You are asking strange questions.

STRANGER: Pleasure-women may be bad as a caste. But, sir, as you yourself have said, isn't there some good in everything bad? And isn't good acceptable, wherever it is found?

SAUJANYA RAO: Yes, good should be acceptable wherever it is found. But you didn't tell me what you came here for.

STRANGER: I just came to see you, sir.

SAUJANYA RAO: Do you have to come so late in the night to see me?

STRANGER: I didn't want to take time away from your more important work, sir.

SAUJANYA RAO: I am not doing anything that important.

STRANGER: People say you consider it your calling to help anyone in trouble. Well, sir, I know a person who can be of great help in Avadhanlu's case.

SAUJANYA RAO: If that's so, we'll think of you as a godsend.

STRANGER: But I don't know sir, if I can take that credit.

SAUJANYA RAO: Why, why do you say so?

STRANGER: It's because the job is in the hands of a *nautch-girl.* That's the trouble, sir.

SAUJANYA RAO: We'll give her money.

STRANGER: She is not amenable to money, sir.

SAUJANYA RAO: Then what does she want?

STRANGER: I am afraid what she wants is impossible to get, sir.

SAUJANYA RAO: Tell me anyway.

STRANGER: I doubt if there would be any use telling you, sir. It might just make you mad.

SAUJANYA RAO: I hope she doesn't want me to keep her. That will never happen.

STRANGER: Then I suppose the old Brahmin is unlucky. There is not much we can do to help him, sir.

SAUJANYA RAO: She must be out of her mind. How could she demand such a thing, and how could you carry such an atrocious message to me?

STRANGER: When we talk business, sir, it is necessary that we put everything on the table—good, bad, or otherwise—right, sir? This woman has a crazy desire in her head, totally beyond her station in life. Anyone who is human can see that, sir.

SAUJANYA RAO: Why does she desire me? I am not the most handsome man in the world.

STRANGER: Maybe she likes you for your good qualities, sir.

SAUJANYA RAO: A whore doesn't care for qualities. There must be a catch.

STRANGER: She might have read the *Mricchakaṭika,*[9] sir.

SAUJANYA RAO: A character like Vasantasena exists only in the imagination of a crazy poet. You don't find such people in real life. This is surely a trap. I have no doubt about that. Is there no other way to get her to cooperate?

STRANGER: You ask questions and get angry when I answer. What do you want me to do, sir?

SAUJANYA RAO: Trusting in God, I am trying to kill my anger. You showed a lapse on my part and I thank you for it. Say what you have to say.

STRANGER: If you do not wish to keep her as your pleasure-woman, she is willing to entertain your wish to marry her, sir.

SAUJANYA RAO: I suppose your mother has taught you to mock good people too.

STRANGER: I swear on your God Krishna, I have an innocent reverence for you, sir. I will never, ever slight you in my heart, believe me, sir. It is not fair to blame the messenger for the message. I know these things are not possible. But I had to tell them to you anyway, sir. You are a lawyer, and I thought you might find a way to resolve the knotty problem this *nautch-girl* has posed.

SAUJANYA RAO: Because lawyers are similar to *nautch-girls*? (Laughing.) I concede my defeat. Don't make fun of me. She is a whore and wouldn't refuse money. Tell her to ask for money. Either he will pay it or I will.

STRANGER: If it was a matter of money, I would pay it myself to save the Brahmin, sir. But I told you the woman is not amenable to money. Believe me, sir.

SAUJANYA RAO: But tell me, you said you are a disciple of Girisam. Aren't you *anti-nautch* yourself? If so, how were you able to get all this information from that *nautch-girl*? Or is this a joke to make fun of me or is it a big setup?

STRANGER: I can't say much if you don't believe me, sir. This is no setup, nor does anyone want to make a fool of you. I am really *anti-nautch*. Who in their right mind wouldn't be? But it is my fate to be locked into an association with *nautch-girls*.

SAUJANYA RAO: What fate could that be?

STRANGER: It is this. (The stranger removes the turban and lets down her long hair, turns back, takes off the jacket, puts a shawl across one shoulder, and turns around to Saujanya Rao.) You asked me for my name and place. My name is Madhura-vani. I come from Vizianagaram.

SAUJANYA RAO: (Surprised at first, and then furious with anger, stands up, controlling himself.) What treachery!

MADHURA-VANI: A teacher should not forget his own teaching, sir. There could be something good in what is bad. Moreover, who can determine what is good and what is bad?

SAUJANYA RAO: How treacherous!

MADHURA-VANI: God knows I came here with a pure heart. To you it looks like treachery. There's nothing I can do now. I shall leave.

SAUJANYA RAO: You can leave right away.

(Madhura-vani walks up to the door, leaving behind her turban and coat.)

SAUJANYA RAO: Stop. (Madhura-vani turns around, walks toward Saujanya Rao, and stands at a little distance.)

SAUJANYA RAO: Don't forget your coat and turban.

MADHURA-VANI: That's nothing. I lost my heart here. (She goes a few paces toward the door.)

SAUJANYA RAO: Wait.

MADHURA-VANI: What did I forget this time, sir?

SAUJANYA RAO: You didn't. I did. What about Lubdha Avadhanlu?

MADHURA-VANI: You are famous for your kindness, sir. But God did not create enough compassion for him in your heart.

SAUJANYA RAO: I will do anything reasonable to save him. A *nautch-girl* had never entered my house until today. I have never talked to a *nautch-girl* before. Today, I failed in my vow, and I am very sad.

MADHURA-VANI: You are a wise man. You didn't do anything wrong, sir.

SAUJANYA RAO: I am talking to a *nautch-girl* in the middle of the night in my bedroom. What else is needed?

MADHURA-VANI: You didn't ask me to come here, sir. If *nautch-girls* are your clients, don't you accept their cases?

SAUJANYA RAO: I may or may not. But you are not even my client.

MADHURA-VANI: But I am one who can save your client's life. Whoever I might be, why can't you see me? Apart from that, we dancing girls can go into the temple to see God. Why can't we see worthy people like you, sir?

SAUJANYA RAO: I am ashamed to be called worthy. Don't say that word. *Nautch-girls* might come to see me. But in my bedroom at night?

MADHURA-VANI: If I had told you I was a *nautch-girl,* would you have seen me during daytime, sir?

SAUJANYA RAO: My enemies must have done this. (Gazing at her from head to foot.) Some people are capable of anything.

MADHURA-VANI: If that is so, your own goodness is your enemy, sir. If I help the Brahmin and take no money in return, would you believe, sir, that there is no plot or perfidy in it?

SAUJANYA RAO: If you are so kind a person, why couldn't you help the Brahmin yourself? Why put me in this tight spot?

MADHURA-VANI: Would you then believe that I am a good woman?

SAUJANYA RAO: Yes, if you save that Brahmin.

MADHURA-VANI: May I suggest a compromise?

SAUJANYA RAO: If you stand here long enough before me, I am afraid I will accept any compromise you suggest.

MADHURA-VANI: (Turning her face to one side.) How about a little kiss?

SAUJANYA RAO: Will you agree to do the job with that?

MADHURA-VANI: What else can I do?

SAUJANYA RAO: So all you want is to ruin my vow!

MADHURA-VANI: You don't seem to appreciate that I hit rock bottom in this bargain. Why should I force you to do things you don't like to do? Good-bye. (Starts to leave and goes two paces.)

SAUJANYA RAO: Stop. (Sits on the bed, covering himself with a blanket.) Sit down.

MADHURA-VANI: No, I won't.

SAUJANYA RAO: I will give you a thousand rupees. Take the money and save the Brahmin.

(Madhura-vani starts to leave.)

SAUJANYA RAO: Don't go. You only want a kiss? What a crazy woman you are. What do you gain out of that?

MADHURA-VANI: I don't know.

SAUJANYA RAO: So there is no choice.

MADHURA-VANI: I'm afraid not.

SAUJANYA RAO: Well, I accept, because I have no choice. Strange. One kiss is more valuable to you than a thousand rupees! Well, tell me what help you can render in Lubdha Avadhanlu's case.

MADHURA-VANI: Very simple: The "bride" Lubdha Avadhanlu married is not a girl.

SAUJANYA RAO: (Surprised.) What?!

MADHURA-VANI: But before I go on, I want you to promise me that you will protect all persons involved in this matter.

SAUJANYA RAO: Or else you won't tell me?

MADHURA-VANI: I won't.

SAUJANYA RAO: I will protect them from Lubdha Avadhanlu. But if they have caused harm to anyone else, I can't help there.

MADHURA-VANI: That's enough for me. Now I will tell you. Karataka-sastri dressed his boy disciple as a girl and married him to Lubdha Avadhanlu.

SAUJANYA RAO: So, Gunturu Sastullu is Karataka-sastri?

MADHURA-VANI: Yes, except for a little false beard.

SAUJANYA RAO: What a gutsy thing to do.

MADHURA-VANI: Sir, don't blame him. Agni-hotra Avadhanlu's daughter is his niece. Originally it was arranged that she would be married to Lubdha Avadhanlu. You know that, right? Karataka-sastri planned this strategy to foil that wedding and save his niece. Please see to it that he is not harmed.

SAUJANYA RAO: How strange! Can this be true? Am I sleeping or awake?

MADHURA-VANI: Pay my fee before you fall asleep.

SAUJANYA RAO: I am too poor to pay you.

MADHURA-VANI: That's all the wealth I have. I can't lose it.

SAUJANYA RAO: You are beautiful. I would love to kiss you. My only regret is that it ruins my vow.

(He moves to kiss her.)

MADHURA-VANI: Stop!

SAUJANYA RAO: Why?

MADHURA-VANI: I just remembered I have a vow of my own too.

SAUJANYA RAO: What's that?

MADHURA-VANI: My mother made me vow not to corrupt people who were not already corrupted.

SAUJANYA RAO: So?

MADHURA-VANI: So I shouldn't allow you to kiss me.

SAUJANYA RAO: I am grateful to you.

MADHURA-VANI: May I see that book, sir?

SAUJANYA RAO: Please.

(Madhura-vani opens the book and reads.)

MADHURA-VANI: *The Bhagavad-gīta.* Sir, is this the kind of book good people read?

SAUJANYA RAO: This is a book that converts bad people into good people.

MADHURA-VANI: What does it say, sir?

SAUJANYA RAO: Those who read it find an invaluable friend.

MADHURA-VANI: Who is that friend, sir?

SAUJANYA RAO: God Krishna.

MADHURA-VANI: Will Krishna make friends with a *nautch-girl,* sir?

SAUJANYA RAO: Krishna will make friends with anyone who believes in him. God does not discriminate against anyone.

MADHURA-VANI: So, Krishna is not *anti-nautch*?

SAUJANYA RAO: You are being naughty.

MADHURA-VANI: I'll read this book. I'll turn into a good person by reading this.

SAUJANYA RAO: You may borrow the book if you want.

MADHURA-VANI: Thank you. (Pressing the book to her breast.) I'll take leave of you, sir.

SAUJANYA RAO: (Looking at the ceiling and thinking.) You are a good woman. You are probably the daughter of a good man who took a wrong turn. Can't you give up your profession? Do you need the money?

MADHURA-VANI: Thanks to God, I have enough money. I also know how low my profession is. Why would I continue in a bad life once good people are kind to me?

SAUJANYA RAO: (Pointing to the picture of Krishna on the cover of the book.) I have introduced you to someone who is known to be the greatest of all good people. The closer your friendship with him grows, the less you will think of people like us.

MADHURA-VANI: May I come to see you once in a while, sir?

SAUJANYA RAO: (Hesitates to answer.)

MADHURA-VANI: When I give up my profession?

SAUJANYA RAO: Then you may come.

MADHURA-VANI: (Pressing the book to her chest and folding her hands.) I am grateful to you. Good-bye!

SAUJANYA RAO: Just a word! (Madhura-vani raises her eyebrows as if asking "What?") How do you know Girisam?

MADHURA-VANI: You must forgive me.

SAUJANYA RAO: Tell me, I want to know.

MADHURA-VANI: If you command me to tell you, I cannot disobey. But let him live, poor man.

SAUJANYA RAO: You are only thinking of his life. What about that Bucc'amma? If he is not a good man, her life is ruined.

MADHURA-VANI: (Thinking for a minute.) Yes, that's true. He taught me English for some time. For some time he kept me as his woman as well.

SAUJANYA RAO: How long ago was that?

MADHURA-VANI: Until fairly recently.

SAUJANYA RAO: How strange! Wait a minute. (He goes out of the room and comes back, bringing Girisam with him.) You, Napoleon of *anti-nautch,* do you know this woman?

GIRISAM: Some time ago, there was a foolish young man called Girisam. There was also a beautiful *nautch-devil* called Madhura-vani. Due to his misfortune, he was trapped in her snare, lost his senses, and lived in total darkness. That was then. He remembered the teaching of his guru and came out of that darkness. He reached his guru's feet and came to the right path. That Girisam is this Girisam. That Madhura-vani is this Madhura-vani. She appeared again here, as my misfortune would have it, to drag me down to hell from where I am now, just one step below heaven. Now I have altogether turned a new leaf. I fell into the pit of sin and repented, and I am now reformed. Your nobility lies in helping a repentant sinner like me become a good person. It is not fair to ruin my life. I crave your mercy.

SAUJANYA RAO: How long ago did you leave darkness and enter the light?

GIRISAM: (Remains silent.)

SAUJANYA RAO: (To Madhura-vani:) *You* can tell me.

GIRISAM: What does it matter, sir? Isn't twenty-four hours long enough for true repentance?

SAUJANYA RAO: Amazing! How easily your guru was deceived by your fraud! You were able to deceive me too. I will send a telegram to your guru and tell him to keep you at a distance and to send Bucc'amma to the widows' home in Poona. She will get educated and will marry whomever she likes. Or she will remain single. You tell me you are reformed. If this is true, behave well, go to school, and complete your degree. I will help you with money as long as you are good. Live a decent life. You called Madhura-vani a devil. *You* are the real devil. She did not say a word against you until I insisted. She saved an innocent old-fashioned Brahmin and also saved Bucc'amma from you. She even helped me too. To express my gratitude to her, I want to shake hands with her. (He shakes hands with Madhura-vani.) Napoleon, get out of my house.

(Girisam goes out through the doorway.)

GIRISAM: *Damn it,* the story has taken a wrong turn.

(Curtain.)

The Play in Context: A Second Look at Apparao's Kanyasulkam

Two things that cannot be avoided when writing about Apparao are colonialism and modernity. I will address these issues in this afterword and move on to a critical reading of the play in the context of the social and political conditions of South India in the late nineteenth and early twentieth centuries. I hope to provide a new interpretation of the play in the process.

If one looks at most general accounts of the Indian past, one finds a broad and persisting consensus that India became "modern" only because of its conquest by the British in the later eighteenth and early nineteenth centuries. Historians of the colonial period, including Indian nationalists, are still quite content to divide Indian history into three periods—classical, medieval, and modern—with a subtext for the labels that read Hindu, Muslim, and British. For most Hindu nationalists, India had a great ancient past with dazzling poets, philosophers, and thinkers which was ruined by the invasion of the Muslims. In this view, things began to deteriorate badly in the medieval (especially the late medieval) period. Modernists and modernizers did not dispute this position, and many of them even believed that the arrival of the British gave rise to nothing less than a "renaissance" of Indian culture.

According to this view, whatever the economic or political disadvantages of colonial rule might have been, it was under colonialism that Indian literature began a genuinely new era of openness and creativity. For the great Indian literary leaders of the nineteenth and early twentieth centuries, the literature of the seventeenth and eighteenth centuries was stultified under the weight of literary conventions, making it dull and uninteresting. To top it off, it was also considered decadent and immoral. These writers and thinkers had no lack of admiration for great poets such as Kalidasa, but they firmly believed that the creativity of Indian civilization was in a state of decay and that their own present was deplorably depraved and lost in the maze of an unimaginative adherence to *śastras*—prescriptive ancient codes. Poets had lost their originality, creativity, and ability to reflect and represent the dynamism of life. A truly new era in society and literature began, according to this view, in the twentieth century.

In contrast to this view, one of my collaborators, the historian Sanjay Subrahmanyam, has in the last fifteen years proposed and strongly defended the introduction and use of the idea of the early modern in the context of Indian history. Presenting evidence of historical changes during the period from 1600 on, Subrahmanyam argues in his book *Penumbral Visions* (2001) that the longer period from the fifteenth to the eighteenth centuries was a time of unprecedented historical change both in South Asia and in the regions with which South Asia was in close contact. It was a period of extensive travel, not just between Europe and Asia but also between the Middle East, Central Asia, South Asia, and Southeast Asia. It was also a period of violent conflict between agricultural societies and pastoralists. Finally, while it was a period when the volume and range of long-distance trade increased significantly, it was also a great epoch of empire-building that preceded the rise of the British Empire in India.[1]

Subrahmanyam, David Shulman, and I have questioned in our recent work entitled *Textures of Time* the easy assumption that there was no real history written in India before the colonial encounter. We suggest that by using more nuanced and appropriate techniques of reading that are sensitive to the texture of the text, which is often lost in translation, we are able to identify historical narratives among texts that are either overlooked as bad literature or misread as fiction. We also argue that from the sixteenth century on, a distinct group of literati, whom we call *karaṇams,* emerged who were multilingual and secular and who helped create a new historical awareness. If history is an indicator of modernity, then such modernity emerged for South India well before the British presence, which has been credited with that achievement.[2]

Shulman and I have also discussed in several of our publications elements of modernity in various fifteenth- and sixteenth-century Telugu literary texts.[3] We have demonstrated that modernity in literature was already flourishing during the period from the late fifteenth to the eighteenth centuries. The colonial modernity that had its beginning with the British rule in India is certainly a different kind of modernity, but it is not the only modernity known to Indian literature.

Colonial modernity is perhaps more easily defined by what it is not: It is not "traditional." It rejects the immediate past and presents itself as distinctly different from it. In Telugu, the modern poets of the twentieth century present themselves as singers of wake-up songs at dawn, *vaitāḷikulu,* implying that they signify the end of a dark night. *Navya* and *ādhunika* are two of the most prominent words that poets of the early part of the twentieth century loved to adopt as labels for their poetry. Their mode is to reject the establishment of pundits, prescriptive grammars, and puranic themes. In contrast, precolonial modernity does not define itself as a radical break with the past nor does it deny the significance of the past. It continues the tradition but marks a shift in sensibilities and the way literature is received by readers.

Such a shift occurred during the late fifteenth and early sixteenth centuries in Telugu literature. This was an epoch that also witnessed wide-ranging changes in terms of the structure of social relations. A new elite, mobile in character and no longer quite so rooted in older ascriptive systems, had now come to exercise power; the existence of liquid resources and a far more monetized economy than that of the medieval period provided a propitious context for them.[4] Many of them came from groups such as the Velamas and Balijas, who had creatively diversified their portfolios from a primary investment in land to a growing interest in commerce, but we should also point to the involvement of migrant actors from central and northern India, as far as the Khyber Pass. Many of these actors tried to found small kingdoms within the complex political culture inherited from the fragmented Vijayanagara empire, and its rivals in the Sultanates of Bijāpūr and Golkonda. Tirupati, an already cash-oriented and prosperous temple of South India, grew even richer in terms of resources in cash and kind.[5] Left-handed castes, that is to say castes whose primary orientation was toward trade, rose to political power. This meant in effect that Vaisyas became Kshatriyas. The well-known Brahminic social hierarchy of the four *varṇas,* with its Brahmanas, Kshatriays, Vaisyas, and Śudras all operating in their distinct spheres, began to fall apart. In its place grew a new elite that was more individualistic than previous generations, with a new understanding of status and gender relations. This elite, now the patrons of literature, along with their courtesans (women who exchange sexual pleasure for money), played a prominent role in poetry. The literature of this period began to reflect a new subjectivity that might be called a "modern self."[6] As we shall see below, Apparao's play is a continuation of the literary traditions deriving from this precolonial modernity.

The dominant modes of colonial modernity in the early nineteenth century eclipsed these developments. A cultural amnesia overtook the new middle class, which forgot its immediate past in favor of colonial modernity, which led it to devalue tradition. The new middle class accepted the representation of Indian society as stagnant and decadent and of Indians as a group of people steeped in superstition and immorality, insensitive to human values and incapable of changing.

It is in this context that we come across the characters in Apparao's play. These characters are dynamic, enterprising, creative, funny, intriguing, tough, and they seem to be having a good time besides. Apparao is not presenting a society that is deteriorating, nor is it in any moral crisis. And if there is an occasional violation of the moral order, the play strongly suggests that this society itself is capable of setting it right with a strong sense of purpose and determination. Clearly this is not a society in need of social reform. Apparao also suggests, equally strongly, that the impact of colonialism is debilitating even for a confident society such as this one and that the society's upper castes are losing their fundamental character under the corrupting influence of colonial administration. In this, Apparao is an extraordinarily original writer with an understanding of social reality, very different from many writers of his time, including the more celebrated Bankim and Tagore.

The Colonial Backdrop

By the end of the nineteenth century, most Western-educated and self-described "modern" members of the Indian elite agreed that Indian society was in urgent need of moral reform. Raja Rammohun Roy's famous movement against widow-burning in Bengal had generated a wave of concern among the religious and moral reformers in the West against this inhuman Indian practice. Orientalist studies of India's exotic religious practices and decadent lifestyles—read from works like the *Kāmasūtra*—were making the rounds of English upper-class society. Western missionaries and liberal intellectuals were genuinely worried that the British government in India was not taking a more active role in civilizing its subjects in the colony. However, burned by the bad experience of the Mutiny of 1857, when Indian soldiers and the heads of many princely states had rebelled against the British, primarily (as the British perceived it) for religious reasons, colonial rulers were reluctant to meddle directly with the religious beliefs of their subjects. Since most of the social practices of Indians appeared to be sanctioned by one religious belief or the other, this meant a more or less total withdrawal of the government from any kind of social legislation. However, the British government felt no such reluctance about educating and civilizing Indians by introducing suitable English literary texts into the curricula of schools and colleges so they could see the depraved nature of their own literature and lifestyles by comparison. Thus, by the early decades of the twentieth century, a class of English-educated Indians were in place who were in many respects similar to what Macaulay had hoped for some seventy years before: "a class of persons Indian in blood and color, but English in taste, in opinions, in morals and intellect."[7]

Bengal, the eastern province of British India, had been the center of such activities for a long period before 1900. It was the seat of the British government and the residence of the British governor-general (later the viceroy). The celebrated College of Fort William was seen as the seat of the high intellectual elite. The Asiatic Society of Bengal, founded in the late eighteenth century by the heroic figure Sir William Jones, operated from there. This was where Jones had discovered the significance of Sanskrit, leading to a new discipline of comparative linguistics, the emergence of the Indo-Aryan family of languages, and a new kinship between Indian and Western languages, which also implied a kinship of sorts between the Indian elite (read: Brahmins) and their Western (especially British) counterparts.

It was largely in Bengal (and to a more limited extent in Benares) that the first seeds of the colonial agenda of social reform were sown. Raja Rammohun Roy was among those who led the charge in this first call for a rebellion against a moribund tradition. Despite his own extensive education in Sanskrit, he wrote to the governor-general to ask that the practice of teaching Sanskrit in schools be stopped in favor of the introduction of English instead, English being perceived as the opening to a new world and a ticket to freedom from superstition, misery, and ignorance. The great scholars of Sanskrit in the traditional *pāṭhaśālās* were marginalized, and a new English-educated elite saw itself as creating the beginnings of a "renaissance" in Bengal. For his part, Bankim celebrated a glorious ancient Indian civilization which had been ruined by an alien Islamic invasion and celebrated the greatness of English learning while quietly deploring the lack of freedom of Indians. In his view, India could be revitalized only by a rejection of the hateful imposition of an alien culture imposed by Muslims and by going back instead to the roots of an ancient and profound Hindu tradition.

Later on, Rabindranath Tagore, the Nobel Prize–winning Bengali poet, sang of a national awakening at the end of a dark and troubled night. His poem praised a "Master of the People" (*jana-gaṇa-mana-adhināyaka*), one who would bring India good fortune in the future (*bhārata-bhāgya-vidhāta*). Tagore, who came from a family that was greatly influenced by the reformist Brahmo Samaj, was perceived by many to be the epitome of Indian literary modernity. His grandfather, Dwarakanath Tagore, was a friend of Raja Rammohun Roy, and his father, Debendranath Tagore, had led the Brahmo Samaj following Raja Rammohun Roy's death in 1833. Tagore sang of love, a love that was not polluted by sexuality, and yearned for a spiritual oneness with a nameless god. His *Gitanjali,* or *Offering of Songs,* was a new lyric in Bengali that created a world of new sensibilities.

Under the influence of such Tagorian sensibilities, much of the earlier Bengali poetry was seen as decadent, tastelessly erotic, and immoral. Tagore's plays presented a world free from ignorant superstitions, restrictive traditions, and cruel rituals of animal sacrifice. It rejected a closed and soulless world and heralded a new and a bright beginning. A caste-ridden, superstitious, ignorant, insensitive, and unimaginative past gives way to a new freedom and awakening in Tagore's plays, poetry, short stories, and novels. Tagore was lyrical, romantic, mystical, and idealistic. Together with Bankim and other intellectuals and social reformers, he helped make Bengal the center of avant-garde Indian colonial modernity. Writers in the other languages of late-nineteenth- and early-twentieth-century India looked to Bengal as their role model.

By the late nineteenth century, similar social and literary movements were under way in the south, in the Madras presidency, out of which present-day Andhra Pradesh is carved. Here too, English education was sought after by most upper castes, particularly by Brahmin families, who were attracted to the political power such education gave them and coveted the economic benefits that accrued from it. Many of these groups were already used to serving as administrative assistants to the Nizams of Hyderabad and other Muslim rulers of South India, and they—like Raja Rammohun Roy—were learned in Persian, the language of power during the period of Muslim rule. They were quite comfortable with the idea of shifting their allegiance to the British and to English, the new language of power. It can be argued that they got more than they bargained for. In addition to political power, social prestige, and money, they received access to a whole new worldview through their embrace of English.

Although in past decades Brahmins had opted for administrative jobs under the Nizam, learned Persian and Urdu, and adopted a Persianized style of life, they had kept themselves firmly rooted in their family traditions. Interaction with Arab and Persian cultures had—if anything—strengthened and energized Sanskrit and Telugu and encouraged a healthy multilingual and pluricultural social order. Contrary to the depiction of modern-day Hindu nationalists, Islam did not seek to destroy Hinduism. On the contrary, the presence of Islam opened up a new space in which people of different beliefs, religions, and languages could interact. Poetry, music, arts, philosophy, and the sciences developed in this space—a truly "secular" space, even if it did not carry this name. The new culture generated by the impact of English education was different. It created a wedge between the learning of the past and new forms. Students who went to modern English-language schools studied Western subjects in English, and everything traditional and conventional was marginalized in their minds. The political power of English neatly translated into Western cultural superiority, which was represented simply as modernity. Tradition was devalued as stagnant and backward-looking, dead and decaying. Modernity was seen as a source of vigor and vitality; it was the beginning of a new dawn. Social and moral reform was the order of the day that would wake up a slumbering civilization.

If the British government was reluctant to get directly embroiled in the social and religious practices of its subjects, it was very comfortable with the idea of supporting such social leaders among the natives who were convinced that Hindu society was depraved and that it should morally reform itself. In the case of Bengal, there was a slew of reformers, cultural leaders, writers, and poets who willingly took on this role. In the southern region of Andhra, this role was played in very large measure by Kandukuri Viresalingam (1848–1919). Born in the Godavari delta town of Rajahmundry to a modest Saiva Brahmin family, educated in English and traditional Telugu literature, he took an active lead in advocating moral reform among the Brahmin community of Andhra. He strove to improve the status of Brahmin women by arranging the marriages of young widows whose husbands had died before their marriage was consummated. He also led a movement against a caste called *veśyas* (courtesans, or "dancing girls") or *bogam-vāḷḷu* (pleasure-women), arguing that they lived a sinful life by selling sexual pleasure to men.[8] Popularly known as the widow remarriage and anti-nautch movements (from the word *nāc,* meaning dance), these two forms of social activism were particularly favored by a section of English-educated people who were brought up on the new Christian morals and Victorian values imparted by English education. Sex and sexuality were now associated with sin as never before in either ancient or medieval India.

Viresalingam was especially active in his hometown of Rajahmundry, a town some seventy-five miles away from the *zamindari* town of Vizianagaram in northeastern Andhra. However, the atmosphere in

Rajahmundry was very different from that in Vizianagaram. Unlike the latter, the former was directly ruled by a British collector and boasted a government college with an Englishman as principal. As a result, the cultural scene was much less supportive of conventional scholarship and more accepting of English-style education and its cultural aftereffects. A recent dam built on the Godavari by an enterprising British engineer from Oxfordshire, Sir Arthur Cotton (1803–1899), had made the entire area around the river very fertile. Upper-caste families who owned land enjoyed new wealth and along with it new opportunities for an English education in the newly established schools. The first college graduates of Andhra came from this area. This was fertile ground for Viresalingam. His message of social reform and the need to uplift Hindu society from the moral morass in which it was steeped found a sympathetic following in the Government Arts College at Rajahmundry where he taught. He acquired a position of influence in the colonial administration and popularity among the emerging English-educated middle class but faced severe opposition from orthodox Brahmins. They stood vehemently against any idea of reform, and they even believed that it was sinful for them to deviate from the path prescribed in the normative texts and traditions that regulated social behavior. Upper-caste Hindu society in Andhra was now in turmoil. Heated debates centered on the acceptability of reform and the infallibility of traditional texts which support tradition.

The society in which these debates were conducted included only the small upper-caste layer of Brahmins and an even smaller number of people from Brahminized castes such as Reddis and Kapus. The vast majority of the lower castes did not count in these discussions. In fact, most of these other groups did not really need the social reform agenda that Viresalingam was advocating, as most of their women freely married again if a husband died. However, for this emerging new upper class, the lower castes did not exist. Convinced that that their own caste was all that mattered in society, the leaders of the widow remarriage and anti-nautch movements gave their activities the high-sounding name of social reform, while actually it was only a small-scale caste reform.

The colonial government, which keenly watched every development in public opinion and leadership formation among its subjects, was not opposed to the ideas of social reform and quietly supported it, even as it strictly discouraged any ideas that smacked of politics. Open opposition to the king ruling from England was sedition severely punishable by law, but the arena of social reform was open to all. This policy was in conformity with the ideology of the raj; it implied that the natives themselves accepted the notion that India was morally and socially decadent. This is the social and political context in which Viresalingam worked. He was a dynamic leader, a courageous activist, and a prolific writer. He made a name for himself among the Telugu educated elite. His books sold well, and he commanded an unparalleled influence in the field of Telugu literature and culture. The king-emperor in England awarded him the title of Rao Bahadur, a title similar to "Right Honourable."

Conditions in Vizianagaram, where the author of the *Kanyasulkam*, Gurajada Apparao, grew up, were different. The town was part of a demilitarized princely state, or *zamindari*, whose ruler still held the trappings of kingship, though with no real royal powers. Such *zamindars* knew that they owed their continued existence to the colonial power, and they fully understood the risks of meddling directly in politics. They quickly found that it was far more beneficial to their image to work in the vast arena of culture by patronizing poetry and music. While each of the *zamindars* and *zamindarinis* (there were a few women among this group), competed with the others to demonstrate his or her loyalty to the Queen-Empress, Edward VII, or George V, they also vied with each other to support traditional scholars and poets. Such scholars and poets (who often were orthodox Brahmins), revived Sanskrit learning, extolled traditional Dharmasastra texts, and symbolically elevated the *zamindars* to a status of the legendary Kshatriya kings of the past.

It might look like a contradiction, but these same *zamindars* also took a leading role in the area of social reform. One such *zamindar* in Andhra was the Maharaja of Vizianagaram, Ānandagjapati (1850–1897), whose ancestors had once been powerful kings in the region. No longer a king with real powers, he still held the aura of a king in the imagination of the people. The title "maharaja," great king, which the British graciously allowed him to use, indicated his status among his people. Maharaja Ānandagjapati was very much a maharaja in his cultural role. He was a scholar in Sanskrit and Persian and a true connoisseur of poetry and the arts, and he had gathered around him some of the greatest scholars of his time in fields such as *vyākaraṇa, vedānta, mimāmsa,* and music. He supported a Sanskrit college, a music college, and a modern British-style college in Vizianagaram. An atmosphere of interactive cultural creativity that invited new learning from English into the rich mix of Sanskrit, Persian, and Telugu was gradually emerging in this space.

Apparao: A Brief Biographical Note

Born into a Niyogi Brahmin family, Apparao had imbibed all the qualities of a very competent member of that scribal group. This is the caste that supplied the best of the ministers, royal advisers, and village *karaṇams*.[9] As the best of *karaṇams*, Apparao lived the life of an archdiplomat and politician, carefully observing everything and every person, listening to the wishes and feelings of his master and faithfully working with him and for him, and, in the end, quietly manipulating the reins of power. Apparao never openly flaunted his power, and his body language was humble and obliging. In Maharaja Ānandagjapati's own words, Apparao usually had his head bent down (but observed everything from the corner of an eye) and even while standing held one of his shoulders low in a gesture of submission.

Initially Apparao did not want to write in Telugu; rather, he wanted to be a writer in English and even published a few poems in English. One may wonder why Apparao chose to write in Telugu. One possibility is that he initially did so to please the maharaja. As a member of the Legislative Council, Ānandagjapati had sponsored an unofficial bill to ban child marriages. Apparao's play was conceived as a loyal servant's effort to help support his master's cause.

However, the death of Ānandagjapati in 1897 gave new freedom to Apparao. He began to see a creative space opening up for himself where he could speak freely about a world he had understood long before but had not had the will to express in words. After Ānandagjapati's death, he was appointed the private secretary to the maharaja's widowed younger sister, Appala Kondamamba, who had lost her husband (the Baghela Rajput Maharaja of Rewa) shortly after her wedding. Although she was technically Apparao's employer and supervisor, in reality she was utterly dependent on him. The relationship with his new employer gave Apparao a confidence he had never had before. Intriguing but less widely known information suggests that he was intimate with Kondamamba, spending late nights in her company after all the servants were dismissed, drinking wine and eating meat, two activities that were taboo for a Telugu Brahmin in those days.[10] Apparao made it known to his friends that because of his fragile and debilitated health, he would not engage in any sexual activities, for it could nearly kill him. He admitted going to courtesan houses but only to talk to the courtesans in order to know how they acted and what they did.[11] This was at a time when all his enlightened friends were staunchly antinautch and considered any association with pleasure-women sinful.

Even with the power he acquired after the death of the maharaja, Apparao never removed the mask of a humble servant. He moved, in his own words, like a little beetle in the mud (*kummari purugu*) that is totally harmless but makes holes all over. His real personality was deeply buried under layers and layers of appropriate social behavior and etiquette. He never wrote a letter or spoke to a friend or even made an entry in his diary without an awareness of a world watching him. Even in his creative work, the author in him never speaks directly; he speaks through the many layers of his work or through his characters. It is no wonder that he chose to write plays and poems rather than other genres that would have called for a more direct authorial voice such as the novel or the essay.

Kanyasulkam: The First Version

When Apparao wrote the first version of *Kanyasulkam,* he was deeply devoted to the Maharaja Ānandagjapati, as is clear from the letter he wrote dedicating this work to him. It is an interesting play in its own right, written with intriguing scenes and a lot of drama. Published in the same year another famous writer from the neighboring state of Orissa, Fakir Mohan Senapati, began serializing his novel *Chha Mana Atha Guntha* (Six Acres and a Third),[12] this version, at once brilliantly humorous and tragic, shares many similarities with the Oriya novel. However, unlike *Six Acres,* Apparao's play is more directly oriented toward social reform. Critics agree that the first version is not anywhere as interesting as the second. It is forgotten and would have sunk into oblivion if Bandi Gopala Reddy ("Bangorey") had not traced it and published it with copious notes.[13]

The Second Version: The Present Play

The second version (1909) is the text that has become famous. It has received unparalleled attention for the past fifty years and has been uniformly praised for the inimitable charm of its dialogue and for its great characters, such as Madhura-vani and Girisam. I will set aside, for the time being, a half-century of misreadings of the play as a plea for social and moral reform so that I can proceed to read the play afresh, free from the cultural preconceptions and ideological preoccupations that have characterized the reform-oriented interpretation. In order to do so, we must understand that Apparao wrote the first polyphonic text in modern Telugu.

A Polyphonic Text

I am using a Bakhtinian concept here. In a monological work, the author determines the lives of the characters; he or she is the sole creator and makes them work as he or she wants them to. In a dialogical and polyphonic work, the characters are, in Bakhtin's words, "not only objects of authorial discourse but also subjects of their own directly signifying discourse."[14] The readers hear not just what the author makes them say but what the characters speak from their own world, some of which the author himself or herself does not know. This does not mean that the author abandons a coherent point of view or an ideology. Bakhtin has a more complex understanding of truth than what is generally presented as a simple dichotomy between a systematic unitary theory and chaos. Although the author maintains a coherent position, he or she might create characters who are on an equal footing with the authorial voice, and he or she allows them their points of view without taking upon himself or herself the magisterial authority of deciding what is right. In a polyphonic work there is no dominant voice, no unitary message.

Indian readers are not unacquainted with polyphonic works. The epics, the *Mahābhārata* and the *Rāmāyaṇa,* are dialogical and polyphonic. Their polyphony is what allows numerous retellings with points of view that extend, deviate, contest, and contradict the meaning "intended" by the legendary "author" Vyāsa or Vālmīki. Indian literature has hundreds of such retellings in every language, including Sanskrit. But even if the readers had perceived the polyphony in the great epics, they probably would not notice it in Apparao, for they could not imagine that Apparao, a mere mortal, might belong in the same class as the ancient greats. Furthermore, dominant practices of interpretation of the play, which I will explain later, foreclosed all possibilities of the reader seeing polyphony in Apparao's work.

Reading Apparao: An Interpretive Exercise

I will begin a close reading of the text from the last scene as a point of entry to understanding the polyphony in Apparao's play. In this scene, Madhura-vani enters the bedroom of Saujanya Rao, unannounced and in the guise of a man, when Girisam is present there. (Does Madhura-vani know that this is the opportune moment to make her entry?) From the moment she enters, she is in total control of the situation. Madhura-vani skillfully obtains Sujanya Rao's permission to remain incognito and in the initial conversation indicates that she knows Girisam because he is a well-known man. She knows how long to let Girisam stay and when to get rid of him. At the right time, she suggests that she has come on urgent business, leaving Girisam no option other than to leave her and Saujanya Rao alone. Clearly, Girisam has detected that this stranger is Madhura-vani in man's clothes, but he hopes she will not betray him. The gesture he makes to her as he leaves the room is profoundly indicative of his own desperate desire not to be unmasked.

Madhura-vani enters into a conversation with Saujanya Rao about courtesans and confirms that both Sujanya Rao and Girisam are staunch believers in the anti-nautch movement. She cleverly drops a hint that she has been a disciple of Girisam. As the conversation develops, she cunningly asks Saujanya Rao what would happen to courtesans who reformed. How would they make a living? Saujanya Rao sheepishly answers that he hopes that someone might marry them or that they might get a proper education and live a good life in another profession. Madhura-vani asks if young men like Girisam would marry such women. Saujanya Rao vehemently rejects the idea. Madhura-vani then asks plainly: How then will reformed courtesans find decent husbands? Would he himself consider marrying one? Enraged at the suggestion, Saujanya Rao says he would never marry a courtesan. He wouldn't even so much as touch one. And he bravely adds that if he should touch one by accident, he would cut off that part of his body.

Having allowed Saujanya Rao to dig a hole for himself, Madhura-vani tells Saujanya Rao that she knows someone who would be of great help in his client Lubdha Avadhanlu's case. The trouble is that the woman in question happens to be a courtesan. Saujanya Rao suggests that he would pay for the information. Madhura-vani responds that the woman in question is not amenable to money, and her expectations may be impossible to meet. Here Saujanya Rao takes the hint and asks if the courtesan wants him to keep her and emphatically declares that such an arrangement is out of the question. Madhura-vani forces a break in the negotiation and declares that Saujanya Rao's client is an unfortunate man, since he cannot be saved any other way. Saujanya Rao presses on in the negotiation, convinced that a courtesan would always accept money. Saujanya Rao is searching for some way to get the courtesan to cooperate in the court case (or is he already attracted to Madhura-vani even though she is in a man's guise?). Madhura-vani says that if he does not want to keep the courtesan as his pleasure-woman, she would consider marriage. Outraged by this turn in the conversation, Saujanya Rao demands to know from the stranger how it is that he is in contact with a courtesan if he is also a follower of Girisam in his anti-nautch principles? At this point Madhura-vani removes her turban and coat, revealing her true identity. Furious at this audacity, Saujanya Rao asks her to leave, but as she is leaving he calls her back to further explore any possibility of saving his client. Madhura-vani suggests a compromise. Clearly under her spell by now, Saujanya Rao says, "If you stand here long enough before me, I am afraid I will accept any compromise you suggest." Madhura-vani says, in a captivating voice with the right mode of shyness, "How about a kiss?" Saujanya Rao admits that he would not mind kissing a beautiful woman like Madhura-vani, but he agonizes over breaking his vow never to touch a nautch girl. The audience knows by now that he is helplessly caught in her snare. Once she makes the deal, Madhura-vani tells the lawyer that the "bride" Lubdha Avadhanlu has married is not a girl and that Karataka-sastri dressed his boy disciple as a girl and married him to Lubdha Avadhanlu. Therefore, the whole thing was a hoax. There was no murder. Now Saujanya Rao has to pay up. But just as he is about to kiss her, Madhura-vani springs another surprise on him. She has a vow of her own. Her mother made her vow not to corrupt people who were not already corrupted. So she shouldn't allow him to kiss her. While a relieved (or disappointed?) Saujanya Rao is still recovering from this double surprise, Madhura-vani turns her attention to the book Saujanya Rao keeps at his bedside. It is the *Bhagavad-gīta*. Now comes the sermon. Saujanya Rao tells Madhura-vani that the *Bhagavad-gīta* is a book that converts bad people into good people, and that those who read it would find an invaluable friend in god Krishna. Madhura-vani has one more merciless shot: "So Krishna is not anti-nautch?" This mischievously suggests the irony of Saujanya Rao remaining anti-nautch while he confidently recommends that god Krishna can save her. In the end, Madhura-vani, pretending to be reluctant, reveals that she was Girisam's kept woman for some time. In the end she devastates two strong men: Saujanya Rao and Girisam.

This is a very intriguing scene that can be read at many levels, for there are crucial junctures in the scene that leave room for multiple interpretations. Nearly every line of dialogue has many implications and layers of meaning. The best part of the scene lies in Madhura-vani's skillful use of language in manipulating Saujanya Rao. She assiduously addresses Saujanya Rao as "Sir" all the way through, stroking his male ego while cornering him with her arguments. When she takes off her disguise and stands before him in her own self, she is already certain that Saujanya Rao has fallen for her beauty and charm but waits for him to openly admit it. Once she is certain that she wholly controls his erotic feelings, she drops the "Sir" and addresses him with a confident tone of dominance. From this point onward in the scene, her answers to his requests are curt and monosyllabic: "I won't," "I don't," and so on. She is so sure of her power that she knows that once a man has come into her feminine arena, he cannot escape and she can humiliate him to the hilt. Through the rest of the scene, she has a field day, deflating Saujanya Rao's large ego and playing games with him, to the point that she even makes him believe that she really wants to read the *Bhagavad-gīta* with him, when in fact she has almost certainly read it before since she clearly knows Sanskrit well enough to accurately refer to the *Mṛicchakaṭika,* a rather difficult play in that language. One may even suspect that she also knows that Saujanya Rao himself has not read the *Bhagavad-gīta,* because he has been misquoting it.[15]

But why does Madhura-vani betray Girisam? After all, her task is successfully finished and she could as well leave peacefully. Didn't Girisam, who recognized her in spite of her disguise, save her by not immediately revealing her true identity to Saujanya Rao? If he had even hinted at the true identity of Madhura-vani, Saujanya Rao would have driven her out of his house and would not have had the patience to listen to her, even if she had retaliated by telling on Girisam. Or was Girisam deceived by her disguise too? At least one critic, Kodavatiganti Kutumbarao, thought so.[16] But on reading the scene carefully, it is clear that Girisam does recognize her and even begs her as he leaves to be as kind to him as he has been to her. Again, one can only speculate. The polyphonic nature of Apparao's play makes his characters as intriguing as any complex human beings, and not even Apparao might have been able to give a definite answer to this question. One of Madhura-vani's motives could be that she wanted Girisam under her thumb and that she felt jilted when he opted for a young widow instead. She surely shows a lot of respect for his English and perhaps believes in his chances of landing a big job with the Nawab of Golkonda, but then she could be saying all those flattering words about Girisam just to annoy Ramap-Pantulu, whose male ego she enjoys deflating every time she gets a chance.

Madhura-vani's attitude toward the men in her life is extremely complex. She has to make money through them for a living and she resents that she has to favor all kinds of men, many of whom she does not really care for. She has nothing but contempt for them, and she shows it openly and cruelly once she has made sure that the man is caught in her net. The many inventive ways in which she humiliates Ramap-Pantulu at every possible occasion is evidence of this. She pretends to be very much in love with him but mercilessly makes a fool of him, in public and in private. The idiotic Ramap-Pantulu does not even see this, so blind is his infatuation for her. The way she talks about the Head Constable suggests that she has used him, binding him with her charms. One can never be sure of the truth value of any dialogue in this play because every character says what is right for the occasion, but if we are to believe what she says to Karataka-sastri, she has never allowed the Head Constable to even come close to her. She has a lot of respect for Karataka-sastri for his Sanskrit learning and acting talent, but even he does not escape her critical gaze. But she seems to have a somewhat deeper fascination for Girisam and his English learning. After all, he is her only sophisticated lover.

She can play with male sexual egos by pitting one customer against another and have a lot of fun at their expense. Apparently she never really cares for any man. She has to have an existential contempt for men because as a pleasure-woman she has to constantly play for them and can trust them only at her peril, much less love them. That is the tragedy of the life of a pleasure-woman: If she loves a man, it will be the end of her security and comfort, because no man ever loves a pleasure-woman in return. A trusting pleasure-woman who wastes her best years on an unloving man earns nothing but a free pass to an old age of poverty and misery.

It is important to reiterate that the words of the characters in this play are exclusively situational and do not work when they are taken out of context. They don't always indicate the real feelings of the character because they are meant exclusively for the listener in that specific situation. Apparao's admirers fail to understand this and rather naively quote the words of Apparao's character's as if they were the author's words and/or take them as indicators of the character's true mental makeup. But one thing that Madhura-vani says to Karataka-sastri seems to reveal her real feelings. She says in response to a somewhat flattering compliment that Karataka-sastri pays to her: "God knows I would have preferred to be born in a farming family, have a husband, work in his farm taking care of his vegetable garden and plants. That would have given me someone who loved me and looked after me for life." Acutely aware of her condition as a pleasure-woman who is perceived as an evil in society by modern social reformers, she has possibly developed a deep resentment against all men.

In contrast, Madhura-vani appears to have a soft spot for women. She would do anything to save Subbi from a ruinous marriage, and she can be a trusted friend to Minakshi. She knows of Minakshi's affair with her patron Ramap-Pantulu. Not only does she not feel threatened by Minakshi, but she actually pressures Ramap-Pantulu to marry Minakshi. The support she gives to Minakshi goes beyond her immediate impulse to annoy Ramap-Pantulu. When it comes to women, Madhura-vani seems to be their real friend.

Interestingly, the only "man" Madhura-vani seems attracted to is Mahesam,[17] the disciple of Karataka-sastri. She passionately looks into his boyish eyes and asks: "Which god gave you these killer eyes?" She plays thinly veiled erotic games with him and kisses him on the mouth all the time. Clearly she enjoys this relationship where, beyond being in control, she can live outside her role as a pleasure-woman, since Mahesam is not yet a man and does not view her as such. In a sense, she returns to a more innocent aspect of herself, where desire is just that. She does not have to worry about maintaining a certain dynamic, as she always does when she is working. The boy himself, who is still in his preadolescent age of budding sexuality, does not quite like to be kissed on the mouth. But he seems to enjoy her attention all the same and plays along. Let us remember that he is utterly fascinated by her laugh when he first sees her in his disguise as a girl and tells his teacher that he is watching her so he can get a grip on her laugh. Is that the actor in the boy speaking, or is he already attracted to her? Note also that he takes the gold *kaṇṭĕ* back to Madhura-vani on his own initiative without his teacher's instructions, perhaps knowing that his teacher would not approve of this action. He also plays games with her, imitating Ramap-Pantulu's voice. Finally, hear the naughty song he begins to sing for Madhura-vani, at the end of Act Six, Scene Six when she asks him to sing the funeral song he had sung before.

Does Madhura-vani really change her ways at the end of the play? Does she realize the sinfulness of her profession and decide to read the *Bhagavad-gīta* in order to repent and turn a new leaf in her life? Nearly every twentieth-century critic has thought so. But the fact of the matter is that we do not really know. It is perfectly possible that she is just playing an elaborate game to make a fool of Saujanya Rao, the "modern," Westernized professional who assumes the role of a Catholic missionary who hears confessions and absolves the penitent of his or her sins and provides moral guidance by giving a sermon from the Good Book. Or is it possible that she has realized that times have changed, that no respectable man will come to her door anymore, and that rather than work with low-level village men, she has to make her life worthy of the company of "gentlemen" like Saujanya Rao? Even the author, Apparao, apparently did not quite know the answer. The polyphonic nature of Apparao's characters leaves them free to live their lives as they want, for he, as author, does not control them to make them live according to his plan.

In a similar vein, we may ask: Does Girisam fail and get punished for his folly? That is again the general opinion of the vast majority of critics. They all agree that he is an evil character, that he plays his tricks as long as he can but that in the end Saujanya Rao (with Madhura-vani's help) catches him red-handed and throws him out of his house. Bucc'amma, whose life he would have ruined, is sent to a widows' home and his games come to an end. But the last words Girisam pronounces in the play ("Damn it, the story has taken a wrong turn") leave a huge doubt about whether this interpretation works. Who, after all, was defeated, Saujanya Rao or Girisam? Girisam is too complex a character to be interpreted in any easy way. He is wildly intelligent, always in control, and capable of getting out of any tight corner. He is the only one who is always aware that he is playing a game, that he is a perennial actor in the theater of life. He delivers even his soliloquy in Act Three, Scene Three as if he is talking to an audience before him. Would he have allowed himself to be caught in the last trap he finds himself in? Perhaps not.

One factor that is often overlooked is that Girisam is born with no property worth the name in a Vaidiki Brahmin family. He has no way of finding a wife without paying a bride-price. It would have been a different story if he were born in a Niyogi Brahmin family, in which case he would himself have gotten a dowry. He is self-taught and has an irrepressible desire to move up in society. He has high hopes of making it to the top, and he is not foolish enough to lose his happiness pursuing the ideals of an unrealistic social reform. He has no problem living with the widowed Day-Meal-Woman or with Madhura-vani while talking moral reform. But he also knows these relationships do not last. The only game in town is social reform and he knows perfectly well that he has to play it to gain any prominence at all, which may then lead to the success he aims at. He is no fool to repent and reform himself, for he knows he is not doing anything wrong. True, this story has "taken a wrong turn" for him, but he can always play the role of the hero in another story.

With the powerful characters of Girisam and Madhura-vani so fully occupying the play from the beginning to the end, we have traveled too far from the express aims of social reform—widow remarriage and the elimination of nautch girls. Girisam is the most outspoken leader of the first and Madhura-vani is the subject of the second. With these two characters dealing a death blow to each of the cherished goals of the great movement Viresalingam led, one may wonder what kind of support this play really gives to his causes. In fact, the only true advocate of social reform is Saujanya Rao, who turns out to be the only weak and flat character in the entire play. He is confused, weak-minded, incapable of understanding the dynamics of life around him, and content to mouth shallow platitudes. In the end, all he achieves is to prevent a possible marriage between Bucc'amma and Girisam, and he ends up seeing his own simple-minded adherence to anti-nautch ideals humiliatingly shredded to pieces by a nautch girl. He doesn't even see the contradiction of shaking hands with a nautch girl, thus admitting that his anti-nautch philosophy is wrong, and at the same time throwing Girisam out because of his association with a nautch girl. Indeed, of the play's main characters, he is the one about whose life we know nothing. He does not seem to have a family, he sleeps alone in his bed, and perhaps lives alone in his house. He has a good name as an incorruptible man, but is incapable of influencing any event happening around him, and his altruism looks rather pathetic.

The play thus implicitly lampoons the most respected leader of the movement, Viresalingam himself.[18] Clearly, whatever Apparao's motives might have been in writing the first version of the play, the author of *Kanyasulkam* II (as we may term the later and better-known version), has no interest in social reform and he does not think it has any value except as a colonial sham, largely created by a group of people who want the attention of the press and the *dŏra,* the colonial master. From the foregoing, it seems clear that Apparao saw the shallowness in the social reform movement encouraged by the colonial rulers.

Let us take a look at the central event of the play—the wedding of a child to an old man—the supposed social evil that social reformers were making a song and dance about. As soon as such a wedding is announced, a whole village, across all castes, unites to prevent it from happening. From the priest to the policeman, from the servants to the schoolboys, everyone, including the bridegroom's own daughter, joins hands to foil it, and they make a fool of the cunning middleman who has arranged it and the septuagenarian groom who is foolish enough to fall for the idea. This clearly is not a society that normally allows such marriages to take place. They have come to know that the practice is wrong. Why would anyone make a big issue of reforming such a society unless they were rather simple-minded and naive like Saujanya Rao, who somehow believes that society is decadent and that it is his self-appointed task to remedy it?

Or let us look at the representation of the lower castes in the play at the liquor shop, where a group of them gather to talk to Bairagi, who tells them he can make gold. It is very clear in this scene that everyone is there to have a good time: The Shopkeeper sells his liquor, his customers drink, a religiously initiated yogini entertains them, and no one really believes that Bairagi can make gold. This is hardly a credulous and superstitious society that needs reform.

Apparao stands against the sway of moral cleansing in the name of colonial modernity. Rather than avoiding or masking the sexuality he sees in the society around him, Apparao openly depicts a variety of relationships between men and women. For him, sexuality is an expression of life and a celebration of its dynamic presence in the real world. Apparao sees in the society of his time a worthwhile culture different from the sham colonial culture of social reformers and is determined to represent it in his play. He depicts a population from many walks of life negotiating the best outcomes for themselves and living with positive, uninhibited, and robust energy. His characters are not mouthpieces for meaningless ideals or formless ideologies. Men and women embrace and kiss on the stage and plan strategies to escape from trouble. There is no fear of sexuality, no sermons on morals, and certainly no prudery. Nowhere do they look like ignorant and exploited masses, superstitious people in need of being uplifted by social reform, as most literary critics have read them to be. These people are intelligent and thoroughly rational and capable of making their own decisions in life.

Apparao's characters are going through extraordinary changes politically and culturally and are making appropriate adjustments to maintain the quality of their lives. The two most powerful changes that touch their lives are the colonial administrative system and the language in which it is conducted. The two arms of the government that touch nearly everyone in society are the police and the courts. The Head Constable and through him the police inspector have very prominent roles in the play. We hear a lot about the British-style courts, where disputes are settled in an adversarial system of justice. This system, which is so much a part of the lives of Indians today, is still new to the society of Apparao's time. The language in which laws are written is English, which only a very few people know. English education is not easily accessible, it is expensive, and the schools that teach it are located in faraway towns and cities. As we see throughout the play, this language is both eagerly coveted and severely resisted.

The play begins with Venkatesam, the young son of the orthodox Brahmin family of Agni-hotra Avadhanlu, coming home for his vacation. He has failed his exams, but Girisam, his tutor, assures him that he will lie to his parents about his exam scores, coach him during the vacation, and admit him into the higher class after the vacation. The system of teachers teaching for a salary and giving exams and awarding passes or fails is another new system people are just growing accustomed to. We hear Venkatesam's father Agni-hotra Avadhanlu complaining to his wife that she has put the boy in an English-language school against his wishes. If the boy had stayed home, he could have taught him a good segment of the Vedas. That is the traditional education system in which boys of each caste learn the family trade from their fathers. In this case, the family trade is performing Brahminic rituals and teaching Vedic texts to Brahmin students. Agni-hotra Avadhanlu knows his Veda from beginning to end and can recite it in very complex ways. That is the skill for which he is respected in his community and by which he makes his living. But his wife sees the advantages of an English education. She knows it can lead to high-paying jobs in the new administration. She has seen her neighbor's son, who used to play marbles on the street with disheveled hair, now making a lot of money as the town's munsiff. She wants her son to get a good police job and earn enough money to buy up all the village lands rather than make a meager living like his father by spinning Brahmin threads.

The respect Girisam gets when he speaks English shows the inroads the language has been making into society. Young adults aspire to learn English because it is fashionable. Venkatesam's mother wants to hear her son and Girisam, the teacher who came as an uninvited guest, speak English to each other. And they do. Here is how it goes:

Girisam addresses Venkatesam:

> *My dear Venkatesam,*
> *Twinkle, twinkle, little star!*
> *How I wonder what you are!*
>
> VENKATESAM: *There is a white man in the tent.*
>
> GIRISAM: *The boy stood on the burning deck,*
> *Whence all but he had fled.*[19]
>
> VENKATESAM: *Upon the same base and on the same side of it, the sides of a trapezium are equal to one another.*
>
> GIRISAM: *Of man's disobedience and the fruit of that mango tree, sing, Venkatesa, my very good boy.*[20]
>
> VENKATESAM: *Nouns ending in "f" or "fe" change their "f" or "fe" into "ves."*

Agni-hotra Avadhanlu innocently asks, "What's the meaning of what you are saying?" and Girisam answers with a straight face, "We are discussing what we should read during this vacation and all that." The mother doesn't understand a thing they are saying either, but the very sounds are music to her ears and make her proud that her son speaks like a *dŏra*. She is truly fascinated by the language.

Their reaction is entirely different when they test Venkatesam's Telugu learning. His uncle, Karataka-sastri, a good scholar of Telugu and

Sanskrit in his own right, asks the boy to read a Telugu verse. Girisam suggests a respectable verse from the Telugu *Mahābhārata* by the great poet Nannayya. Venkatesam barely manages to read the verse:

> *nala-damayantul'iddaru manah-prabhavānala-dahyamānulai/ salipiri dīrghavāsaraniśal*

Karataka-sastri stops him and asks, "What is the meaning of *manah-prabhavānala*?" Venkatesam looks up toward the ceiling while Girisam intervenes and says: "How can a young boy know the meaning of such difficult poems?" A surprised Agni asks, "Don't they teach the meanings of poems?" Girisam, with his ready wit, promptly answers: "For now they make them chant the verses like the Veda. In the white man's school they don't care much for Telugu poems. All the time they bombard the students with *jāgraphī, gīgraphī, arthameṭik, alligībra, māthamaṭiks,*[21] and all that heavy stuff." Agni asks in innocent amazement "They teach all that?" Girisam solemnly confirms: "Yes sir, all that and more." Girisam's use of the word "Veda" is crucial. He elevates the mindless memorization of the Telugu verses to the level of Vedic recitation, which the father readily appreciates. But he masks the fact that there is a rupture between the old and new learning.

Agni himself has a love-hate relationship with the English language. He indicates that he hates this dirty language when Girisam utters a few English words at mealtime, but he wants Girisam to translate his legal papers on the cheap. He is easily bamboozled when Girisam flatters him for his knowledge of the law. If only Agni knew English, he would be as great a lawyer as Bhashyam Ayyangar, a famous lawyer in the colonial city of Madras. The powerful role English has in society resonates throughout the play. Ramap-Pantulu says regretfully that if he knew the language, Englishwomen would run after him. Girisam fools practically everybody with his "fluent" English, while Ramap-Pantulu, who hates him, dismisses it as butler English, the kind of pidgin language chefs who cook meals for their English masters speak. Madhura-vani is enamored of it as well, so she has it taught to her by Girisam, apparently in return for her sexual services to him. Mahesam, Karataka-sastri's young Sanskrit student and theater apprentice, has no interest in the Sanskrit *kāvya* of Kalidasa. He reads a verse from the great Indian poet describing the Himalayas and dismisses it as untrue. The Himalayas are not like the poet says—*pṛthivyā iva māna-daṇḍah,*[22] a rod that measures the earth. Girisam has shown them to him on a map. He knows that practical knowledge that makes money comes with English. What good is this Sanskrit? He doesn't trust a Sanskrit book enough to take an oath on it. He would rather borrow an English book for that purpose from Girisam.

The courts function according to the new British-made laws written in English. All court papers are in English and clients are totally confused by the names of the codes and the numbers of sections quoted to them by the lawyers and their touts. The courts are not seen as places of justice that create respect for the law but as places where you can freely lie with no fear of God. The common comparison is between the lawyer and the prostitute, both of whom sell their services to whoever pays the best price. The idealist lawyer Saujanya Rao considers leaving the profession because the system is so corrupt that it cannot be improved. Ramap-Pantulu boasts of his skill in forging any document and producing false witnesses to prove anything in court—something he would not dare to do in a system accepted by the community.

Criminal justice is equally corrupt. Lubdha Avadhanlu faces murder charges without a corpse in sight. The top brass of the police, who have internal grudges with the local police, blame the Head Constable and unjustly accuse him of having covered up a murder in the village. Most people are not affected by what happens in the courts, but they face the police day after day. The Head Constable is present everywhere, from the wedding ritual to the courtesan's house to Lubdha Avadhanlu's house and the liquor store. He personifies law and order in the village and is feared by everybody. Even the bullock-cart driver, whom Girisam lectures for two hours about the National Congress, asks if they will transfer the present Head Constable away from the village.

The lawyers, the police, and the English language represent the face of the colonial government in the play. The new elite created by the colonial culture is going through a process of reform in the face of the new standards of conduct. The bedrock of this culture is sexual morality, which they seek to protect by prohibiting courtesans and encouraging Brahmin widows to remarry.

Compared to the world under the direct impact of English, the society that is not touched by it seems to be doing much better. Its members believe in religion and ritual but carry no superstitious adherence to it. When the priest Gavarayya produces an elaborate ritual to exorcise the spirit that Lubdha Avadhanlu believes has afflicted him, no one except the gullible Lubdha Avadhanlu believes it, but everyone is perfectly willing to go along with the drama to teach the miserly old man a lesson. The illiterate Asiri pretends that the empty bottle in which the spirit is supposed to be locked is too heavy to lift. When a terrified Ramap-Pantulu throws away the lentils and coconut given to him by Minakshi because he suspects they were previously offered to the spirit, the servant Asiri gladly picks them up and eats without hesitation. The Head Constable appears to believe in the powers of Bairagi who says he can locate the missing person through a magical ritual. The Head Constable desperately needs to know the whereabouts of the missing boy who pretended to be the bride so he can be free from the allegations of covering up a homicide. Even under that stressful condition, he hesitates to tell Bairagi that the missing bride is in fact a boy. In the end, his rational sense prevails and he does not reveal that crucial piece of information to the spiritual guru.

Why then did the critics misread this play for so long, seeing in it a deep and thoroughgoing critique of a rotten society in need of social and moral reform? Among the many powerful reasons that determined its fate, both its great popularity and its misreading, the chief reasons are four: the context of the production of its first version, the literary and political atmosphere in the south Indian colonial metropolis of Madras, the influence of Tagore on the Telugu literati, and the later cooption of the play by Marxists who wanted to advance their own sociopolitical agenda.

The context in which the first version of the play was created was the maharaja's interest in social reform. The introduction Apparao wrote for the first play indelibly impressed upon the readers that he was vehemently in favor of reforming a decadent Hindu society with its immoral nautch girls, pitiable child widows, and decrepit old men who wanted to buy child brides. This impression was never erased from the consciousness of the literary community. The author, who subsequently wrote an entirely different play with a diametrically opposite and healthy understanding of society and its people, did nothing to tell his readers how to read the new play. He left only a few hints here and there in his personal letters and diaries. The title remained the same, the preface written for the first edition remained along with a new preface, the characters were almost the same, the theme looked the same, and it still carried the picture of the maharaja to whom the first edition was dedicated. There was no reason to suspect that it was anything but a more interesting elaboration of the first version. One wonders why Apparao, who personally supervised the printing of the play, allowed these symbols to stay. Knowing the complex nature of Apparao, it is difficult to explain. But one cannot rule out the possibility that he intentionally kept the original features of the book. After all, he was still under the patronage of the maharaja's family.

The cultural atmosphere in the modern metropolitan center of Madras was another factor that influenced the reading of this play. There was a strong wave of colonial modernity in that city, where the social reformer Viresalingam was influential. His presence in Telugu literature was powerful. A prolific author, tireless activist, and a prominent public intellectual, Viresalingam ran his own printing press and published a journal to spread his message. A good number of English-educated upper-caste people applauded his social activism, and his literary work received attention among the new literati.

Apparao did not make much of an impact on his contemporaries as a writer. They praised him as a person with worldly wisdom and as a great scholar in the English language, but they failed to see his originality and his greatness. His personal style of lying low and not demanding attention had a lot to do with this. He was more than content representing the maharaja and later his widowed sister in councils and courts and barely asked for the recognition of the literary world. Still, he was very conscious of the greatness of his work and the unique status he had among writers of his time including such great writers as Vedam Venkataraya Sastri.[23]

The third reason for the continued misreading of the play is the influence of Tagore on the Telugu literary sphere. Tagore's fame as a Nobel Prize–winner made him a power to reckon with among a community of Telugu scholars and poets that had been demoted to inferiority under the dominance of English education. English reigned supreme in schools and colleges, and the Telugu pundit was relegated to a secondary status.[24] Into an atmosphere of such internalized inferiority came Rabindranath Tagore with his grand recognition from the West. He was Indian, he spoke of Indian tradition, and he wrote in a language and idiom the West listened to and respected. He spoke the language of internationalism and a universal religion. He was one step above everyone: he was Viśva Kavi, the poet of the world. Telugu poets were totally mesmerized by him. Tagore's influence evolved into a literary movement from which some of the finest new poets emerged. The movement was called the *bhāvakavitvam,* or the poetry of feeling. Since Tagore was quintessentially a product of colonial modernity, there was little space left for a more complex position such as that articulated by Apparao.

Sexuality was the main issue on which colonial modernity in literature established itself. It made a grand statement to the effect that sex was immoral if it was not controlled and limited to a properly wedded man and wife. Despite the subdued public activity of Christian missionaries, Christian morals made a deep impact on Indian intellectuals and poets. This impact was so strong that they began to feel apologetic about the uninhibited erotic expression in literature, art, and sculpture that appeared in all areas and languages of India. All one had to do was look at any temple or palace or even village shrine, read any literary work in any language, or listen to a song or a story in the vast oral traditions of India. Temples displayed sculptures of men and women copulating on their walls, and literary theoretical texts even included the prescription that a description of copulation is one of the eighteen different types of descriptions that makes a poem a *mahākāvya,* a great poem. Descriptions of a goddess always included her high breasts and shapely thighs and buttocks. Past poets presented picturesque details of the body of their heroines from head to toe, including the beauty of their pubic hair. Sexuality permeated the *sṛṅgāra,* erotic poems, the mainstay of all great literature in Indian languages. In religious literature, in the poetry of devotion, Krishna stories described his amorous play with his eight wives, 16,000 cowherd girls, and his special girlfriend Radha. Krishna themes in literature were often explicit to a fault in matters of physical love. Courtesans sang erotic songs for their customers, addressing them as if god Krishna himself was visiting them. Even though there were poems about renunciation, devaluing physical pleasures, and decrying woman as a temptress and as an obstacle to spiritual progress, there was never a strong puritanical streak in Indian literature.

This was the context in which the new Victorianized English-educated middle class learned to be shy of sexuality. Viresalingam led the way by discussing the moral impact of classical authors on their readers. He commented adversely about texts with an excess of erotic descriptions. A few years later, the Cambridge-educated Sir C. R. Reddy declared the bulk of precolonial literature obscene and distasteful. Morality in literature became an issue as never before. Tagore's *Gitanjali* and his other idealistic plays and poems were read in English translation by a large group of this new class. A nameless God and bodyless women parade through his poems while the poet speaks of an ideal love and of a spiritual union with God.[25] If the traditional literati were initially not convinced that Tagore was interesting, they were eventually silenced by his Nobel Prize. It gave him international recognition and a status that was held in awe by modern Telugu poets. English was seen as the doorway to the world, and Tagore had opened it for them.

Under the powerful influence of Tagore, *bhāvakavitvam* poets wrote love poems where love was untainted by sexuality. They called it *amaliana-śṛṅgāra,* unblemished love. Telugu poets, who could not easily dismiss Apparao, had to read him now as another version of Tagore. They even truncated one of Apparao's poems before they included it in their anthology in order to make it work like a *bhāvakavitvam* composition.[26]

The fourth reason that prohibited any possibility of a proper interpretation of Apparao is the co-option of the play by Marxists. Marxist interpretations made eroticism in literature even less desirable than it had been for the Victorians. In their grand agenda for revolution, Marxists assumed that the working class did not enjoy sex. They left untouched the Victorian morality that had taken root in the previous century. Marxist literary critics freely talked of the "feudal" servitude of poets to the decadent pleasures of their royal patrons. They read Apparao's play as a condemnation of the evils of courtesan culture and a call for its reform through the characterization of Madhura-vani.

The high point of Apparao's popularity in the twentieth century began with the attention paid to him by the Progressive Writers' Association, a Marxist-sponsored literary organization that held sway in Andhra during the 1940s and '50s. Critics of this school began calling the twentieth century the Age of Gurajada. The influential Marxist critic K. V. Ramana Reddy, who wrote the only well-researched biography of Apparao, called his book *Mahodayam,* "the Great Dawn," which implied that the period before Apparao was a dark age. Apparao was rapidly transformed into an icon. The famous progressive poet Sri Sri and his nephew Arudra devoted themselves to elaborately praising Apparao. Sri Sri even wrote:

> Follow his footsteps, they are the way to the future.
> Gurajada cures us of stupidity in our nature.

Apparao began to be perceived as one who sought social progress, wrote against religious superstition and sexual decadence, followed simple meters in his poetry, and wrote his play in a spoken language that avoided the artificial literary dialect prescribed for all writing by pundits of his time, thus paving the way for a great cultural and literary revolution. More specifically, his *Kanyasulkam* was read as a testament to the author's commitment to social change, his rejection of a "feudal" society, and his condemnation of the sinful profession of pleasure-women. In general, his voice was perceived as a clarion call to build a new society on a new moral order.

In this reading, Girisam is seen simply as a confidence-man and trickster who is justly punished at the end and Madhura-vani is perceived as a very cultured prostitute who is noble at heart, who saves a young girl from marriage to a decrepit old man and in the end reforms herself to lead a new and morally correct life. Lubdha Avadhanlu, Agni-hotra Avadhanlu, and all the other village Brahmin folk are seen as representatives of a dying age and a decadent Brahmin culture. Ramap-Pantulu is a crook who personifies everything that should be detested in the corrupt and decaying village India. As the Progressive Writers' Association gained ground, Apparao became more and more identified ideologically with Viresalingam, who in turn was connected to Raja Rammohun Roy, Kesabchandra Sen, and other Bengali social reformers. The only thing that distinguishes Apparao from those mentioned above is that none of them is a poet. Viresalingam is a prolific writer, but Marxist writers are content to describe him primarily as a reformer who used his pen as a means to spread his message, whereas they recognize Apparao as a truly great poet. So, in the end, while on the one hand Apparao is celebrated as a great poet and his play is extolled as the greatest work in modern Telugu literature, his work has remained woefully misunderstood.

Partha Chatterjee has convincingly argued that Indian nationalism separated the domain of culture into two spheres, the material and the spiritual. While Indians recognized out of necessity the superiority of the British in the material sphere—that is, in science, technology, economics, and statecraft—they kept the spiritual domain for themselves, unencroached upon by the West, in order to retain their identity. Indian nationalists of the late nineteenth century argued, says Chatterjee, that "not only was it undesirable to imitate the West in anything other than the material domain, it was even unnecessary to do so, because, in the spiritual domain, the East was superior to the West. What was necessary was to cultivate the material techniques of the modern Western civilization while retaining and strengthening the distinctive spiritual essence of the national culture."[27] An exclusive pride in the spiritual superiority of India in the face of the material superiority of the West gave the emerging nation the necessary confidence to fight against the West without giving in to its total domination.

What is problematic in the nationalist strategy as Chatterjee describes it is the assumption that there is such a thing as "India's distinctive spiritual essence" in some pure and untainted state. The nationalists' belief in such a spiritual domain is largely apolitical and ahistorical. They quietly overlook the fact that by the beginning of the twentieth century, this domain had itself been changing over a long period and in the recent past had been fully colonized. This colonization was voluntary and was masked under the cover of cultural revival and regeneration of a forgotten greatness of India. Tagore himself accepted the values of Victorian morality, and his family accepted the Christian concept of a nameless single God when they adopted the ideals of the Brahmo Samaj, which rejected image worship, rituals that included animal sacrifice, and the worship of the multiple gods of Hinduism. The brilliant transformation Tagore was able to bring about in Bengali literary sensibilities was based on a rejection of the sexual and erotic love for God popularized by the poets who preceded him such as Jayadeva, Vidayapati and Candidas. Tagore sang of love, but it was closer to the Christian agape than the erotic love of the Vaishnava poets.

This apolitical and ahistorical celebration of the greatness of an Indian spiritual superiority based on a distant classical and ancient India of the Vedas and the Upanishads, of Kalidasa and Bhavabhuti and other such classical poets, also paved the way for an atmosphere of implied Hindu superiority.[28] That this should have happened despite Tagore's vociferous warnings against the dangers of nationalism and his well-known promotion of an international brotherhood and the religion of man shows the inherent risk of an ahistorical celebration of national spirit.

The theme of a spiritually rich Orient as distinct from the material West is very much a product of the imaginings of the romantics in the West. German romanticism and its related movements clearly influenced this conception, and in turn the aura of a spiritually superior India ensured a red-carpet welcome for the spiritual agendas of Vivekananda and his neo-Vedantic followers. It is not farfetched to suggest that Gandhi's nonviolence, vegetarianism, and sexual abstinence; Radhakrishnan's creation of a Hindu philosophy based on the Upanishads; and Tagore's spiritual poems of the *Gitanjali* found a hospitable climate in the West to no small extent because of the deeply ingrained belief among Western intellectuals of the time in the spiritual virtues of a mystical India.[29]

Apparao does not seem at all invested in this climate. In fact his character Girisam makes fun of it, as when he talks of a new religion. Lecturing to his disciple Venkatesam, he states that he has studied all religions, taken the *essence* of all of them, and created a new religion. He declares, "I am going to spread it in America." The sarcasm is clearly aimed against Vivekananda, who brought a neo-Vedantic refurbished Hinduism to the World Congress of Religions in Chicago in

1895.[30] Later in the same lecture, Girisam ridicules the Upanishads. He says to his disciple:

> See, when I was young, my uncle—who was a firebrand like your father—twisted my earlobes and made me read the Upanishads. In one of those Upanishads—damn it, I forget the name—a student asks questions and a teacher answers them. You are the student and I am the teacher—just like in that Upanishad. If someone records your questions and my answers on a palm leaf, it will be a sacred text—after a couple of hundred years it will be known as *Tobaccopanishad.*

Apparao does not eulogize the greatness of an ancient India, nor does he see a separate spiritual domain from the political. For him, the entire society is a complex but single fabric that needs to be attended to in all its complexity. Neither did Apparao strive to keep his literary work untouched by the influence of the West. Quite on the contrary; he saw that drama—which was considered to be traditional and was actively patronized among the middle class of his time—had been an unimaginative imitation of a theater believed to be practiced in the lost classical past. The playwrights of his time had no idea of what a living theater would look like. They reproduced mythological themes filled with songs and poems and long and unintelligible speeches in a language far removed from living speech. Often even Sanskrit plays of great classical poets such as Kalidasa were adapted to a proscenium stage, which was borrowed from the West, with no idea of how these plays were staged during classical times. He rejected this form of the play and borrowed the structure from Shakespeare and the idea of representing a contemporary social theme from Ibsen. At the same time, he is different from either playwright and stands in his own right as a great writer who showed the world what theater could do in a dynamic society. He saw the need to open himself to the West but kept his feet on his ground. His confidence in his own culture, which gave him the ease to accept influences from the West without the anxieties of material inferiority or pretensions of spiritual superiority, is truly exceptional.

In a long entry in his diary dated August 9, 1901, Apparao writes, paraphrasing a certain Freeman who was speaking about the people of Eastern Europe:

> People of this generation had to live in the midst of two entirely different cultures. One of these cultures has plenty of guidelines, but they have decayed. This culture is emaciated and reduced to its bare bones. It is intrinsically uncompromising, and it is now weak. It is weak because of its

> closed nature. Because the people who represent this culture have closed their minds and because they are socially in low positions—for these two reasons, they are incapable of resisting the defects of Western civilization and foreign beliefs engulfing them like waves of the ocean. About the second culture: This is really energetic in moving forward. It has imbibed the spirit of freedom and rationalism.

Apparently applying the ideas of Freeman to India, Apparao continues:

> Western civilization does help us get rid of some superstitious beliefs, true, but the freedom it teaches is empty of social progress. It is not true freedom. It is only nominal. It doesn't allow others into its fold. Such civilization will lead people into personal weaknesses, instability, and bad habits and leaves them there. It is our primary responsibility to successfully resist these evil influences, defects and bad habits and fight against them.[31]

Apparao is not a revivalist, nor does he want to protect Indian civilization from the influence of Western culture. He sees the weaknesses of Western culture in the form in which it has impacted India. He realizes the strengths of Indian civilization but also sees that it suffers from a lack of self-confidence under colonial rule. A confident culture can both receive what it needs and reject what it does not. It does not need to develop protective barriers. Apparao stands for the rejuvenation of Indian culture so it can stand on its own feet.

In summary, Apparao represents a modernity that is an organic continuation of the past—not the constructed glorious past of ancient times, but the one that had been alive until recently—combined with an intelligent understanding of the opportunities for change that opened up from contact with the English culture. He welcomes change but resists the debilitating colonial discourse of social or moral reform. Perhaps he represents the culture—or at least one of the possible cultures—India might have had, if only the corrupting influence of a colonized mind had not had a full sway in shaping India's destiny in the early and middle decades of the twentieth century.

Note on Names and Castes

Telugu names are usually in two parts, with a third part added if the person has a high-caste status. The first part of the name is the family name, which is used in a formal or a legal context or when the family is referred to. Agni-hotra's family name is Nulaka. The family name is often initialed at the beginning of the name. For example Girisam refers to himself as N. Girisam, and we are not even told what the "N" stands for. The second part of the name is the given name, e.g., Lubdha, Agni-hotra, Ramappa. The third part of the name is a title appropriate to the caste.

Avadhanlu and Sastri are titles of Vaidikis. These were Brahmins who performed rituals, studied sacred texts, and were scholars of Sanskrit. Vaidikis in the play tend to be humble, while Niyogis look down upon them as incapable of handling worldly matters. Based on the family names given, many of the Vaidikis in the play seem to be modeled after a smaller subgroup of Vaidikis called Dravidas, though Apparao does not mention that distinction. For instance, Agni-hotra Avadhanlu, Lubdha Avadhanlu, Karataka-sastri, and Girisam appear to be Dravidas. Girisam does not carry a caste title, perhaps because he is still young and does not have a status in society or perhaps he is modern and does not want to carry a caste title. Dravidas are so called because they migrated from the Dravidian (Tamil) area south of Andhra. This is a famous branch of Brahmins from whom some of the greatest Sanskrit scholars came. A number of Dravida families lived in Vizianagaram in Apparao's days. Dravidas maintained their individual caste identity among themselves, but outsiders generally consider them Vaidikis, as does Apparao.

Pantulu is the title applied to the Niyogis among Brahmins. This is a branch of Brahmins who adopted a secular lifestyle and held political jobs. Niyogis were known to be proud of their status. In the play Ramap-Pantulu insists on an honorific "-gāru" suffixed to his name when people call him.

Setti (derived from Sanskrit *śreṣṭi*) is the title of the merchant caste Vaisyas, locally known as Komatis, as is indicated by the name of Subbi

Setti. Komatis are stereotyped as calculating, reluctant to take social risks, and unwilling to take sides in a quarrel.

Nayudu is the caste title adopted by Kapus in the area of northern Andhra, a group of land-owning, high-caste non-Brahmins who are proud of their martial spirit and leadership status in the society. Somi Nayudu, the hereditary village chief, and the retired army man Havaldar Acc'anna, belong to this caste. Havaldar is a rank in the colonial Indian Army.

Women and low castes have no caste titles; they are known only by their given names. Given names of courtesans often reflect some aspect of feminine beauty, as for instance, Madhura-vani ("One who has an intoxicating voice"). Several women's names may end in an *amma* ("mother"); for example, Bucc'amma (Bucci + amma). Asiri, the servant at Lubdha Avadhanlu's house belongs to a low caste and does not carry a caste title and neither do Manavallayya or Viresa. The latter two persons belong to the non-Brahmin Vaishnava and Saiva castes, called Satani and Jangam, respectively.

The Day-Meal-Woman in the play is never referred to by her given name; her profession has become her name. The practice of calling people by their profession cuts across castes. For instance, the Head Constable, whose caste is not identified but who is clearly of a high caste; the Village Head, a non-Brahmin; and the Siddhanti, a Brahmin are all called by the name of their professions. Some people may have their professional title prefixing their given name, as for instance, Priest Gavarayya.

In three instances Apparao adopts the style of naming his characters by a positive or a negative moral value they represent, a practice much in vogue among writers of moral tales such as *Hitopadeśa* or allegorical novels such as John Bunyan's *Pilgrim's Progress.* Agni-hotra Avadhanlu is so called because *agnihotra* (fire) indicates his short temper. Similarly, Lubdha means miserly and *saujanya* means goodness. Apparao followed this practice when he wrote the first version of the play, which was clearly intended for didactic purposes. He did not change these names when he revised the play.

The birth name of the author, Gurajada Venkata Apparavu, who was a Niyogi Brahmin, is written as G. V. Apparow Pantulu (in English) on the title page of the first edition of *Kanyasulkam.* Modern Telugu critics drop Venkata from his given name and his caste title Pantulu and refer to him variously as Gurajada Apparavu, Apparavu, or Gurajada and spell his name Apparao in English.

On Kinship and Friendship

Telugu people generally consider it improper to call an individual by his or her given name. This practice is fast fading out, but during Apparao's time it was very common. Friendship was not freely recognized as a category of relationship; family was the preferred model for relating to each another. Unless one was outside the social group, people treated each other as if they belonged to one extended family.

In Telugu kinship, relationships are broadly divided into joking and non-joking classes. Joking relationships are those where men and women could potentially flirt with each other. Father-in-law, mother-in-law, son-in-law, brother-in-law, and sister-in-law are joking relationships. Mother, father, brother, and sister are non-joking relationships. Ramap-Pantulu calls Lubdha Avadhanlu "father-in-law" and Girisam chooses to call Bucc'amma "sister-in-law." The choice of these relationships becomes significant when we note that Ramap-Pantulu has an ongoing affair with Lubdha's daughter and Girisam flirts with Bucc'amma. Similarly, a courtesan calls every man that she meets "brother-in-law," signaling that she is potentially available for a sexual relationship with him. Also note that the Day-Meal-Woman gets furious when Girisam calls her "my crazy sister" at Madhura-vani's house in the first act.

People call each other *nestam,* "friend," but only among cohorts in a younger age group such as playmates. Bucc'amma refers to Acc'amma, a woman of her age group, also a child widow, as a friend, but when Girisam claims that the Nabob of Golconda is his friend, we know he is bluffing.

When a kinship term is considered too intimate, the caste title is used to refer to people, with an honorific "-gāru" added to the title.

Performing Kanyasulkam

The first version of *Kanyasulkam* was initially staged in 1892, five years before it was published. The troupe that produced it was Jagannātha Vilāsinī Dramatic Company, which performed Sanskrit plays under the patronage of the Maharajah of Vizianagaram. The decision to perform a Telugu play, written in spoken Telugu, was not easy for the company. Possibly they did this to please the maharaja, and even then they prefaced the play with a prologue written in Sanskrit. The prologue introduces Apparao as an English-language poet, *āṅglabhāshākavi,* who enjoys reading playwrights such as Shakespeare, Molière, and Ben Jonson and who loves to import English style of plays into Telugu. Measured by the reception of the press, especially the English-language press, which gave it rave reviews, the production was a great success.

The second version of the play, which was published in 1909, has not been as easy to perform as the first version. For one thing, it is too long. Apparao did not show much interest in the production of his play. Entries in his diaries show that he was critical of the theater of his time, which produced mythological plays. Deploring the absence of a good theater and and good plays in Telugu, he wrote in his preface to the second version of *Kanyasulkam* (which he wrote in English):

> There is no theater worth the name and no professional actors who practice acting as an art. There are not many good plays either. Modern life with complex social conditions is neglected by play-wrights except for purposes of the broadest farce and poverty of invention is manifested by the constant handling of threadbare romantic topics.

Clearly he had his own ideas of how plays should be written and performed, but it is doubtful if he considered the production aspects of *Kanyasulkam* when he wrote it. The length of the play, the long monologues, and the large number of characters along with incidents nearly impossible to present on stage (as in Act One, Scene Two) indicate that either Apparao did not have any production experience in theater or simply did not care to write a producable play.

For almost a decade after its publication the second version didn't receive attention of the theater groups, while it was popularly read all over Andhra and its main characters Girisam and Madhura-vani became household names. The language of the play and its brilliant dialogues captivated readers, students played parts of it in school theaters, but it did not make it to the professional theater.

The play was staged for the first time in 1924 in Tenali with well-known actors. Great stage and cinema Telugu actors of past decades who played the roles of Girisam, Madhura-vani, and Ramap-Pantalu are still remembered for those roles. Until the 1930s, men played women's roles; Sthanam Narasimha Rao, a male actor, was one of the more memorable Madhura-vanis.

Depite the formidable length of the play, which tests the patience of both the actors and the audience, available information indicates that it was produced in full a few times: at Andhra University in 1939 and in Paralkimidi in the state of Orissa in 1948 and again in 1956. However, the full-length productions have not been very popular.

Famous poet Abburi Ramakrishna Rao abridged it in 1932 and staged it all over Andhra more than 100 times. Ayitam Rajakumari, who is seldom remembered now, was famous for her portrayal of Madhura-vani in those days. A. R. Krishna, a famous artistic director of Hyderbad, continued Ramakrishna Rao's legacy in 1970s. J. V. Somayajulu and J. V. Ramana Murty produced the play with their own innovative changes from 1953 for almost twenty-five years. Countless amateur groups, about which information is not properly available, staged it hundreds of times in various abridgements. In 1976, Sahitya Akademi, India's national academy of letters, published another abridgement of the play by the noted writer Narla Venkateswara Rao. The theme of *Kanyasulkam* became so popular that some writers wrote sequels to it that imagined the afterlife of the main characters.

Kanyasulkam has been staged among the Telugu community in the United States as well. Pemmaraju Venugopala Rao created a new abridgement of the play in 1982 and produced it in Atlanta, Georgia, after which other abridgments of the play were produced in several U.S. cities.

The play was made into a film in 1955 with the changes a popular Telugu feature film requires, the most notable of which is that Bucc'amma and Girisam are married to make a happy ending. Most recently, in 2006, the entire play with no changes, additions, or deletions was broadcast on television over a number of weeks.

Card Game in Act Five, Scene Two

The card game that is played in Act Five, Scene Two is called Bestu-kuḍeḷḷu. During the early decades of twentieth century, it was popular in coastal Andhra Pradesh, including the Visakhapatnam and Vizianagaram areas, but it is almost forgotten now.

Four or more players could play the game. The rules given here assume that four people are playing. Cards 6, 5, 4, 3, and 2 from each suit are removed from the deck; A, K, Q, J, 10, 9, 8, and 7 of each suit are used for playing. Ace is the highest ranked card, followed by king, queen, and so forth. Each game must start with an agreed-upon ante, or initial bet. Each player puts his or her ante at the center of the table.

The thirty-two cards in the deck are shuffled and seven cards, one at a time, are distributed counterclockwise to the four players. The undistributed four cards are left face down at the center.

There are a total of seven tricks to be made. The player to the right of the dealer starts bidding. The bidding starts with one, meaning the player would make one trick with the chosen trump. The next player may continue or pass. The auction continues. The next level of bid is two, and the next is three, and so forth. The highest bidder gets to choose and declare the trump. After declaring the trump, the bidder takes the four cards left face down at the center and removes four cards from his/her hand, which may be same cards just picked up.

Now, the other three players play against the bidder. The object for them is to see that the bidder fails to make the bid tricks. The player to the right of the dealer starts the lead card. The next one should follow with a card of the same suit. In the absence of a card in the suit played, the player can use a card from the declared trump and take the trick. This is called ruffing.

If the bidder makes the tricks he or she contracted for, he or she takes the ante money pooled on the table. If the bidder makes one trick less than the bid, he or she puts additional money equal to the ante of all four players at the center of the table. This is called *bestu.* If he or she is two tricks short, he puts in double the ante money, and so forth. If the bidder fails to make even single trick, he becomes *kudelu.* The amount of money that he or she should place at the center is equal to the number of tricks bid multiplied by the ante. From this game the word *kudelu* acquired the meaning of going bankrupt.

The cards are shuffled again and distributed. The game continues. The player who has bid and lost is usually tempted to bid again to win the pot.

The rules vary slightly from area to area. Auction Euchre may probably come close to this game, if partnerships are removed and the ace is made the highest-ranked card instead of the jack.

(Thanks to Veluri Venkateswara Rao for contributing this explanation.)

Guide to Pronunciation

Long vowels, marked by a macron, are twice the length of short vowels.

The diphthongs e, o, ai, and au are always long. Short ĕ and ŏ are marked.

c is dental fricative, pronounced as ts when followed by a, ā, u, ū, ŏ, and o, and palatal fricative when followed by i, ī, ĕ, and e. In Sanskrit words, c is always a palatal fricative. In Bucc'amma (Bucci + amma) and Acc'anna (Acci + anna) the cc is palatal because it is followed by i before the sandhi. An apostrophe marks the sandhi.

ṭ, ṭh, ḍ, ḍh, and ṇ are retroflex, pronounced by turning the tip of the tongue back to the palate.

ñ is palatal nasal, ṅ is velar nasal.

There are three different sibilants: ś, palatalized; sh or ṣ, retroflex; and s, dental.

A word's final h indicates the visarga of Sanskrit; the vowel preceding it is aspirated.

Proper Names with Diacritics

Characters

Agni-hotra Avadhānlu (Agnihotrāvadhānlu)
Asiri
Bairāgi
Bhukta
Bucc'amma
Bucc'anna
Gavar'ayya (Priest)
Girīśam
Havaldār Acc'anna
Kāmayya
Kām-Bhoṭlu
Karaṭaka-śāstri
Koṇḍi-Bhoṭlu
Lakshm'anna
Lubdha Avadhānlu (Lubdhāvadhānlu)
Maheśam (Disciple)
Madhura-vāṇi
Manavāḷḷayya
Mīnākshi
Poli-sĕṭṭi
Rāmam-dāsu
Rām'anna
Rāmap-Pantulu
Saujanyā Rāv
Siddhānti
Somi Nāyuḍu
Subb'amma
Vĕṅk'amma
Vĕṅkateśam
Vīreśa
Yogini

Places

Krishna-rāya-puram
Rāja-mahendra-varam
Rāma-chandra-puram
Rāma-varam

Notes

Introduction

1. The date of Apparao's birth is reported variously as November 31, 1861, and September 21, 1862. Calculating the date according to the Gregorian calendar from information given in Apparao's horoscope, which records his birth according to the Telugu calendar, is ridden with problems. See Bandi Gopala Reddy (hereafter Bangorey), "Mundu māṭalu," in *Mŏṭṭamŏdaṭi kanyāśulkam* (*kanyāśulkam* First Version), edited by Bangorey (Nellore: Published by Bangorey, 1969), 30–31.

Act One

1. Bonkula dibba (*bŏnku* means "a lie" and *dibba* means "a hill or a mound") is the name of an open public space in front of the fort in Vizianagaram in northern Andhra Pradesh. Local legends derive the name from the story of a French engineer who lied about a scheme for digging for water in the area and fled halfway into the project. Some scholars trace the origin of the name to the Marathi word *bankul*, jail, and say there used to be a jail in the area which fell into ruin. According to another legend, Gurajada Apparao used to spend hours on end in this place chatting away, so his friends called him King of Bunk. K. V. Ramana Reddy (hereafter K. V. R.), *Kanyā-śulkam: Ṭīkā, Ṭippaṇi* (Vizianagaram: Velugu Pracurana, 1991), 10.

2. "Dancing girl" is another term for nautch-girl, a colonial English term (nautch from *nāṭya*, Sanskrit, dance, via Hindi *nāc*) that social reformers of Andhra used for women from a caste called Bogam-vāḷḷu, Sāni-vāḷḷu, or Veśyas. *Bogam* is a Telugu word derived from Sanskrit *bhogam* (pleasure/joy/luxury), and *veśya* is a Sanskrit word assimilated into Telugu. Nautch-girls were courtesans and were kept by upper-caste men as their pleasure-women.

Bogam women were well educated and highly cultured. Some of the greatest singers, dancers, and poets came from women of this caste. Bogam women served as court poets of the Nayaka kings of Tanjore and Madurai. Colonial moralists viewed these women as prostitutes, and the Andhra social leaders of the time adopted the same attitude toward them. A new name was invented to give respectability to them: *devadāsis*, or servants of god, despite the fact that in Andhra, Bogam-vāḷḷu were mostly secular and did not have much to do with temples. In 1956, the government of Andhra Pradesh prohibited dancing by these women and moral activists forced them to reform themselves and live respectable lives.

Among the considerable research that has been done on the *devadāsis* is Frederique Apffel-Marglin, *Wives of the God-King: The Rituals of Devadāsis of Puri* (Delhi: Oxford University Press, 1985); Saskia Kersenboom-Story, *Nityasumaṅgali: Devadāsi Tradition in South India* (Delhi: Motilal Banarasidass, 1987); A. K. Ramanujan, Velcheru Narayana Rao, and David Shulman, *When God Is a Customer: Telugu Courtesan Songs of Kṣetrayya and Others* (Berkeley: University of California Press, 1994); Samanta Banerjee, *Dangerous Outcaste: The Prostitute in Nineteenth Century Bengal* (1998; reprint, Calcutta: Seagull Books, 2000); Leslie Orr, *Devotees and Daughters of God: Temple Women in Medieval Tamilnadu* (New York: Oxford University Press, 2000); Kay K. Jordan, *From Sacred Servant to Profane Prostitute: A History of the Changing Legal Status of Devadasis in India, 1857–1947* (New Delhi: Manohar, 2003); Kalpana Kannabiran and Vasanta Kannabiran, *Muvalur Ramamirthammal's Web of Deceit: Devadasi Reform in Colonial India* (New Delhi: Kali for Women, 2003). However, not much scholarly work has been done on the Bogam women of Andhra. Devesh Soneji is currently engaged pioneering work in this area. See his "Living History, Performing Memory: *Devadāsī* Women in Telugu-speaking South India," *Dance Research Journal* 36, no. 2 (Winter 2004): 30–49. See also Priyadarshini Vijaisri, "Transcending the Devadasi: Reform and Patterns of Sacred Prostitution in Colonial Andhra," in *Space, Sexuality and Postcolonial Cultures*, edited by Manas Ray (Calcutta: Center for Studies in Social Sciences, 2003); Vijaisri, "Contending Identities: Sacred Prostitution and Reform in Colonial India," *South Asia: Journal of South Asian Studies* 28, no. 3 (2005): 387–411; and "The Temple Dancer," in Nancy Paxton, *Writing Under the Raj: Gender, Race, and Rape in the British Colonial Imagination, 1830–1947* (New Brunswick, N.J.: Rutgers University Press, 1999), 83–108.

3. Reference to Benjamin Franklin's *Poor Richard's Almanac.*

4. From John Gay's *Beggar's Opera* (edited by Peter Elfed Lewis [Edinburgh: Oliver & Boyd, 1973]), 60. The opera was first produced in London in 1728.

5. Ibid., 52.

6. Schools run by the colonial government were closed for Christmas, even though Christmas was not a holiday for the vast majority of Indians.

7. Reference to a folktale where a bandit attacks a Brahmin along with a group of other travelers and decides to kill them all. The bandit makes them stand in a row so he can chop off their heads one after the other. As he is about to begin chopping, the Brahmin, who is first in line, asks him to begin from the other end. The bandit agrees, but before he reaches the end of the line, the king's soldiers appear on the scene and the Brahmin is saved.

8. Apparently a term of endearment Girisam uses to refer to his student. It may also refer to a common Telugu usage that describes a person who looks sad as having "Shakespeare's face." Probably derived from the rather sad-looking picture of Shakespeare printed in Indian books.

9. Deccan College at Poona (Pune, Maharastra) was a famous center for both Sanskrit and English education. Its history goes back to 1821, when Lord

Elphinstone instituted Hindoo College, which after some opposition from the Board of Directors of the East India Company, was revived in 1824. In 1864, it was named Deccan College. It was a prestigious center of learning in India during Apparao's time, and it still maintains its high reputation.

10. Girisam quotes a humorous verse in oral circulation about the Lord of Birds (Garuḍa, the eagle), the background of which is the following story:

In Hindu mythology, Garuḍa, the son of Vinata, finds himself and his mother enslaved to his cousins the snakes because his mother lost a wager against his aunt Kadrū about the color of a certain horse standing at the edge of the ocean. Garuḍa, who is enormously mighty, wants to be free and asks his aunt what he needs to do to release himself and his mother from this bondage. She asks for *amṛta,* the elixir of immortality, as the price of freedom. Garuḍa knows that the gods, with the help of the anti-gods, have obtained *amṛta* from churning the ocean of milk. They have tricked the anti-gods out of their share and are carefully guarding it. Garuḍa, who knows where the *amṛta* is being kept, breaks through all the barriers, kills the guards, and carries it off. Indra, the king of gods, chases him with no success and begs him not to give it to anyone. Garuḍa tells him that he is delivering it to Kadrū and her sons to gain freedom from them but that Indra is free to steal it back from them before they have a chance to consume it. Indra does exactly as advised and gets his *amṛta* back.

The joke in the verse quoted here focuses on Garuḍa carrying off the pot of *amṛta.*

11. This is Girisam's invention. No such text exists. Three obscure books with this title are reported in *Bhārati* (January 1952), by Sishtla Ramakrishna Sastri, but they are not what Girisam refers to here. See K. V. R., *Kanyā-śulkam: Ṭīkā, Ṭippaṇi,* 14.

12. A munsiff was a lower-level judicial officer in the British colonial administration; the position was low enough that natives were appointed to it.

13. Most of the books listed by Girisam were actually used in schools during the early decades of the twentieth century. Among them, *Nalacaritra* is perhaps from Nannaya's "Nalopākhyānamu," from his classic *Āndhra Mahābhāratamu* (Hyderabad: Telugu Visvavidyalayam, n.d., photocopy of Ananda Mudranalayamu 1901 edition, 4 volumes), 3.2.2–230. *Rājaśekhara caritra* is, as K. V. R. rightly identifies in *Kanyā-śulkam: Ṭīkā, Ṭippaṇi,* a novel by Kandukuri Viresalingam (1880; 2nd ed., Hyderabad: Visalaandhra Publishing House, 1987). *Venkata Subbarao Made Easy* refers to a kind of Cliff notes written for student use by Rantala Venkata Subbarao (1860–1918), an enterprising educator. Girisam makes up the last title as a joke. See Bangorey, *Mŏṭṭamŏdaṭi kanyāśulkam,* 111–116.

14. Apparently there was a sweets shop set up by a person called Devi, who migrated from North India to Vizianagaram during Gurajada's time. The cakes and other snacks he sold were known as Banaras sweets. K. V. R., *Kanyā-śulkam: Ṭīkā, Ṭippaṇi,* 16.

15. Surendranath Banerjea (1848–1926) was a famous Bengali orator and

one of the leaders of the Indian National Congress. He traveled all over Andhra in support of a national movement against British colonial rule of India.

16. The original song contains English words—*sight, bright, delight, full moon,* and *jasmine*—written in a Telugized spelling.

17. Adult Brahmin men wear a *jandhyam,* a shoulder string that hangs diagonally from the right shoulder across the chest. This indicates their twice-born status. They perform the Gayatri chant during their morning prayers to the sun.

18. Theosophists were members or followers of the Theosophical Society, started by Madame Blavatskey (1831–1891) and Colonel H. S. Alcott (1832–1907) in 1875 in Madras. The theosophical movement attracted a number of English-educated people in Andhra who were taken by its ideas, which provided rational and even scientific explanations for the ancient Hindu practices and rituals. Branches of the Theosophical Society were started in many towns in the area.

19. An English saying that was popular in India during Apparao's time. It means "Take advantage of favorable circumstances; they may not last" (E. D. Hirsh, Jr., Joseph F. Kett, and James Trefil, eds., *The New Dictionary of Cultural Literacy,* 3rd ed. [Boston: Houghton Mifflin Company, 2002]).

20. See "Note on Names and Castes," in this volume.

21. Refers to Girisam's anglicized style and habits picked up from British nationals, who were all Christian.

22. Possibly a nickname of Girisam. The -ḍu ending indicates both familiarity and disrespect.

23. The natives colonial officers employed as butlers and house servants often picked up some English to communicate with their masters. Their broken English is derogatorily called *bŏṭleru inglīshu,* butler English.

24. Like a Tamilian. Hard work that does not pay anything in return is called *arava cākiri,* Tamil labor. An Andhra prejudice against Tamil people holds that they work hard for very little remuneration. Some linguists offer a more generous etymology for this phrase from the Telugu, *aruvu,* credit, hard work done on credit, for a promise to pay later.

25. Menstruating women in Andhra are not allowed to touch others and are secluded from the house.

26. An elaborate bath where the head and body are soaked in oil and washed off with the juice of *kuṅkuḍu-kāya* (*Sapindus emarginatus*).

27. *Firmān* is Persian for "an official order." The Nizam of Hyderabad, whose titles Girisam recites in style, was the last ruler of most of the Andhra region before the British took over.

28. Persian for "courtier," "companion of the Nabob."

29. *Sikka* rupees were legal tender in the Nizam state. Their value was slightly less than the rupees in British-controlled India.

30. Devadatta is the name of the conch Arjuna the great Pandava warrior of the Mahabharata epic blows to announce his presence in battle. Girisam adopts the last line repeated in a series of poems in oral circulation for his mock-aggressive statement. These poems describe Arjuna's determination to destroy

the enemy army, and each poem ends with the statement *"peru kirīṭiye ninada-bhīshaṇa-śankhamu devadattame"* ("[If I do not] my name is not Arjuna and my roaring conch is not Devadatta"). See Veturi Prabhakara Sastri, ed., *Cāṭu-padya-maṇi-mañjari* (Hyderabad: 1913; reprint, Hyderabad: Veturi Prabhakara Sastri Memorial Trust, 1988), 1:292–293.

31. In Telugu marriage ceremonies, the bridegroom ties a pendant-like gold piece strung on a thread, called a *pustĕ, tāḷi,* or *maṅgaḷa-sūtram,* around the bride's neck at the auspicious moment. This constitutes the essential part of the wedding ceremony.

32. Uttering God Rāma's name twice is a way of defending a person as innocent.

33. Sesame seeds are symbolically added to gifts given to Brahmins during death ceremonies. They mark the giving as a ritual act, which brings merit to the giver.

34. "All twelve courts" is a reference to the colonial court system in which one could appeal to successively higher courts, all the way to the Privy Council in London. Twelve is a symbolic number in Ramap-Pantulu's traditional worldview.

Act Two

1. A tax-free village, called an *agrahāram,* gifted by kings to the Veda-chanting Brahmins. This village apparently carries the old name, but perhaps it is not a tax-free Brahmin village anymore. There is a second Brahmin village in the play, Rama-chandra-puram.

2. Christmas.

3. An insulting comment on the way Girisam is dressed. Turaka is a derogatory name for Muslims.

4. Reference to a folktale where someone complains that his pumpkins were stolen. One of the listeners wipes his shoulders self-consciously to check if there is anything on his shoulders that would incriminate him even though he is innocent. The pumpkin referred to here is *būḍida gummaḍi kāya* (*Benincasa cerifera*), a squash with an ashy coating that rubs off when touched.

5. A reference to the Sanskrit theater, which was active at this time under the patronage of the maharaja.

6. The *dammiḍī,* which was in circulation before India went on the decimal system of coins in 1957, is 256th of a rupee.

7. Braided recitation is a complex way of reciting the text of the Veda. The words of the text, for instance abcd, are memorized as abc cba ab bc bcd, and so on. This is to ensure that the text is not altered and no words are lost in the process of oral transmission. Brahmins who accomplished this style of recitation of the Veda were highly regarded.

8. Girisam is being very proper in his approach in order to make an impression on Agni-hotra Avadhanlu. Tradition says that one should never say one's name directly in words such as "My name is . . ." One is required to say

"People call me . . ." For other instances of this usage, see Act Three, Scene Two; Act Six, Scene One; and Act Seven, Scene Six.

9. "Vakil" is Urdu for lawyer, from the Arabic word for spokesperson.

10. "White man" was a term that denoted English people; it both indicated their skin color and recognized them to be of a different race.

11. Lines from the poem "Casabianca" by Felicia Hemans (1793–1835), which tells the heroic story of Casabianca, a young boy of about thirteen years, son of the admiral of the Orient in the battle of the Nile, who stood at his station on his father's orders. The ship had caught fire and all the guns had been abandoned, but the boy refused to leave without his father's permission and perished when the flames reached the powder and the vessel exploded. The tragedy deepens when we learn that the father had died earlier in the same fire and the boy did not know this. This poem was required reading for children in colonial schools. Felicia Hemans, *Selected Poems, Prose, and Letters,* edited by Gary Kelly (Peterborough, Ontario: Broadview Literary Texts, 2002), 300–301. The poem is also in *Poetical Works of Felicia Dorothea Hemans* (London: Oxford University Press, 1914), 396, cited in Bangorey, *Mŏṭṭamŏdaṭi kanyāśulkam,* 119.

12. Lines adapted from Milton's *Paradise Lost,* another required reading in colonial schools.

13. In Andhra, as elsewhere in India, saliva is considered extremely polluting. People do not share food that has been eaten by someone else. *Mānavadharma-śāstra* (5.130) provides a few exemptions to this general rule. A popular verse in oral circulation humorously sanctions a few more exemptions, in a mock-serious *śāstric* tone, from standards of saliva pollution:

pŏgacuṭṭaku satimovikin
agaṇitamugan ūrabavik'
amṛtambunakun
tagan ucchiṣṭhamu led'ani
khaga-vāhanutoḍa kāla-kaṇṭhuḍu palikĕn.

"Women's lips, cigars, ambrosia
and the water from the village well—
they are always pure, people may
share them freely," said Śiva
to the god who rides the eagle.

14. Lines from the eleventh-century poet Nannaya's *Āndhra Mahābhāratamu,* 3.2.24. The verse describes in mellifluous Sanskrit and Telugu words how Nala and Damayanti spent their days longing for each other.

Venkatesam, who was not trained properly, would of course have no idea of the meaning of the words. The story of Nala and Damayanti was prescribed reading in schools. The list of books given by Girisam in Act One, Scene One includes a *Nala-caritra (The Story of Nala).* Girisam seeks to gain some respectability by making Venkatesam recite from a high literary text instead of the mischievous oral verse.

15. Teluguized names of geography, arithmetic, algebra, and mathematics. "*Gīgraphī*" is Girisam's invention to make the subjects sound more impressive.

16. The point she is making is that finding a bride for Venkatesam could be just about as expensive as sending him to school because they have to pay a bride-price. She suggests that even though Agni-hotra Avadhanlu talks of saving money, he still cares enough for his son to pay for these expenses.

17. The bride's party and the groom's party ritually exchange *tāmbūlam*, a small packet of betel leaves and areca nuts, when the match is fixed. Exchange of *tambūlam* symbolizes entering into an agreement—a ritual equivalent of signing a contract.

18. Venk'amma gets the relationship wrong. In the original, Girisam said that Lubdha was his mother's elder sister's son, while Venk'amma thought that Lubdha was Girisam's father's elder sister's son. Both of these relationships translate as cousin. This is a minor error which doesn't make any difference in the story. It only shows that Venk'amma is too agitated to listen to the details of the kinship carefully and that she is more interested in telling Girisam that his lecture will not have any effect on Agni.

19. William Ewart Gladstone (1809–1898), four times prime minister of Britain between 1868 and 1894. He and his opponent Benjamin Disraeli (1804–1881) were popular among the English-educated Indians of the time.

20. Washing one's own feet (and hands) is a requirement before a meal.

21. Rice left over from the night before was soaked in the excess water drained out from boiled rice and allowed to ferment. With spices added, it made a delicious breakfast. Adult Brahmin men, however, considered this food unacceptable for their standards of purity; children and women ate it. Girisam, who is English educated and claims a modern style of life, has no problem eating anything delicious.

22. Brahmin men must pray to the sun at dawn and dusk. Girisam is pretending that he is a proper Brahmin.

23. Ruined-hair: *tala-cĕḍḍadi* is a euphemism for a widow, since widows in this caste were supposed to shave their heads. Even though she hasn't shaved her head, Girisam could have identified Bucc'amma as a widow by other indicators such as the absence of a forehead mark (*boṭṭu*), bangles, and other jewelry that non-widows wore and perhaps also because she wore the plain white sari worn by widows.

24. The disciple is reading Kālidāsa, *Kumāra-sambhava* (New Delhi: Sahitya Akademi, 1962), 3.31.

> *mrgāh priyāludrumamañjarīṇām*
> *rajahkaṇairvighnitadṛsṭipātah*
> *madodhhatāh pratyanilam vicerur*
> *vanasthalir murmurapatramokshah*

> Though blinded by pollen from the *priyālu* vines,
> maddened by passion the deer run

against the wind through the forest, where
falling leaves make rustling sounds.

25. *gītāntareṣu śramavārileśaih*
kiñcitsamuchvāsitapatralekham
puṣpāsavāghūrnitanetraśobhi
priyāmukham kimpurushas cucumba

Between songs the Kimpurusha lover kissed
his girl's face made lovelier with drops of sweat
her makeup smudged a little and her eyes,
drunk on flower-wine, darting wild.

—Ibid., 3.38

26. *varṇaprakarshe sati karṇikāram*
dhunoti nirgandhatayāsma cetah
prāyena sāmagryavidhau guṇanām
parāṅgmukhī viśvasṛjah pravṛttih

It has brilliant color, this *karṇikāra* flower,
but it makes you sad, for it has no smell!
The Creator perhaps doesn't like to shower
all his blessings on a single thing.

—Ibid., 3.28

27. *Bryonia grandis,* a favorite vegetable in Telugu meals.

28. Up north stands Himālaya,
king of mountains, god in his own right,
stretching east and west into the oceans,
straight like a rod that measures the earth.

—Ibid., 1.1

29. The last course in a Telugu meal, which is yogurt with rice.

30. Demosthenes was a famous Greek orator (384–322 BC). Surendranath Banerjea was a famous Bengali orator; see note 15, Act One.

31. Brahmin men say Sanskrit chants at the beginning and the end of a meal, offering water and food to the deities.

32. Obviously, Venkatesam was not at the meal. Children are often given their dinner early in the evening and put to bed, while the adults eat around 9:00. Venkatesam might have slept through the whole scene in the kitchen.

33. *Kanyāśulkam,* money given to the parents of the bride as a price for giving her in marriage.

34. Devotees shave their hair to fulfill their vow to god Vĕṅkaṭeśvara, the chief deity on the hill at Tirupati, the south Indian temple town. The temple maintains a group of barbers, who only shave for ritual purposes. They symbolically shave a part of the devotee's head and leave the person to have a proper shave from a regular barber.

35. See "Note on Names and Castes," in this volume.

36. The *high court vakāltī* was an examination; those who passed were eligible to practice in the courts established by the colonial government.

37. Since girls in Brahmin families are married before puberty, the only single girls suitable for falling in love are widows.

38. The poem imitates the style of "My Mother," by Ann Taylor (1809–1892). See Bangorey, *Mŏṭṭamŏdaṭi-kanyā-śulkam,* 118.

39. Could be a reference to the *Indian Social Reformer,* edited by K. Natarajan, published in Bombay. But this might also be a name made up by Girisam. K. V. R., *Kanyā-śulkam: Ṭīkā, Ṭippaṇi,* 31. Alfred Lord Tennyson (English poet, 1809–1892) was a contemporary of Apparao.

40. The suffix -gāru indicates honor and respect. See "On Kinship and Friendship," in this volume.

41. Actually there was no high court in Jabalpur, a town in Madhya Pradesh State of northern India, but then Agni-hotra Avadhanlu would not have known that. See K. V. R., *Kanyā-śulkam: Ṭīkā, Ṭippaṇi,* 31.

42. Kakinada is an east coast town, now the headquarters of the East Godavari District in Andhra Pradesh. During the early decades of the century, before the railway line connecting Visakhapatnam to Madras was completed in 1893, travel by steamer along the coast was the fastest way to Kakinada, East Godavari District, from the village in Visakhapatnam District, where Agni lives.

43. The original reads *rāmāyaṇamlo piḍakala veṭlāṭa lāga* (like *piḍakala veṭlāṭa* in the middle of the *Rāmāyaṇa*). The meaning of *piḍakla veṭlāṭa,* or its more popular variation, *piḍakala veṭa,* is unknown, but the idiom is used to indicate an unwanted interruption.

Act Three

1. "For two years" is an exaggeration. The marriage agreement is hardly a month old. Agni announces it to the family on the day Girisam comes to their home on the pretext of teaching Venkatesam. Madhura-vani enters Ramap-Pantulu's life at about the same time. Ramakoti Sastry suggests an emendation to two months. See K. V. Ramakoti Sastry, *Maḷḷī Kanyā-śulkam Guriñci* (Hyderabad: Carita Pracurana, 1992), 56.

2. The place of action does not really change from the previous scene. The last scene was Madhura-vani's bedroom. She comes to the front part of the house when Karataka-sastri and his disciple enter.

3. Narada is a popular character in Hindu mythology. He always appears with a vina in his hands and is revered as a great singer.

4. We have to assume that Karataka-sastri does not know that Madhura-vani is now in this village. He has been advised that Ramap-Pantulu is the right person in the village to help him arrange a match for his "daughter" with Lubdha Avadhanlu. He has also gathered that Ramap-Pantulu is easy to influence through his concubine, a new pleasure-woman he has brought from the

city. Being an old hand in dealing with pleasure-women, he thinks he can work on this pleasure-woman and cut a deal with her. He waits for a convenient time to see the pleasure-woman alone and knocks on the door after Ramap-Pantulu has left. He is pleasantly surprised to find his old contact, Madhura-vani, who makes things a lot easier for him than they would otherwise have been. Thanks to J. V. Ramana Murti, who gave this reading; see also Ramakoti Sastry, *Maḷḷī Kanyā-śulkam Guriñci*, 79.

5. A gesture indicating total amazement at something incredible. For a different meaning of this gesture in another context, see note 1, Act Four.

6. Village performers dressed up in various costumes and went from door to door performing for the members of the household.

7. A Sanskrit aphorism attributed to Bhartrihari:

> *eko devah keaśvo va śivo vā*
> *ekam mitram bhūpatir vā yatir vā*
> *eko vāsah paṭṭaṇam vā vanam vā*
> *ekā nārī sundarī vā darī vā*
>
> Serve one God, Śiva, or Vishnu.
> Stick with one friend, rich or poor.
> Live in one place, city or forest.
> Take only one woman, beautiful or ugly.

8. Note that Karataka Sastri adds no honorific -gāru at the end of Pantulu's name. Neither Karataka Sastri nor Madhura-vani have any respect for Pantulu. They feel no compulsion to be polite to him in his absence.

9. Rocks (*raḷḷu*) is a euphemism for money.

10. A variation of Sastri.

11. Remember that Madhura-vani knows that the girl is a boy in disguise. Her jealousy of the new girl is a game to annoy Ramap-Pantulu.

12. Lines from Jayadeva, *Gītagovinda*, 19. For a translation and the original of the song, see Barbara Stoler Miller, *Love Song of the Dark Lord: Jayadeva's Gita Govinda*, hardcover edition (New York: Columbia University Press, 1977), 111–114 and 158–159.

13. Expert lover Karataka-sastri pretends to be an old-fashioned, Veda-chanting, Vaidiki moron who knows his texts but doesn't have a feel for their meaning, thus confirming Ramap-Pantulu's stereotype of Vaidikis.

14. The earlier statement regarding Madhura-vani that Ramap-Pantulu made indicates that she is aggressive in lovemaking. Husbands in traditional families are not supposed to talk about their wives' sexual desire, nor are the wives supposed to have an active interest in sex. This makes it clear that Madhura-vani is not Ramap-Pantulu's wife. Karataka-sastri uses this opportunity to correct his initial "mistaken impression." Obviously he is pretending not to know Madhura-vani from before.

15. Only Niyogis sported mustaches, whereas Vaidikis were not supposed to. The verse is from *Kavi Cauḍappa Śatakamu* (Madras: Vavilla Ramaswamy Sastrulu and Sons, 1973), Verse 18.

16. Minor sons are those who are younger than eighteen years, the legal age of adulthood.

17. According to Hindu law, sons in a joint family have a right to object to the collection of debt incurred by their father when they were minors, provided they can prove that the father behaved irresponsibly and did not care for the interests of the family when he borrowed the money.

18. Zamindar of Urlām is a name for Basavaraju, a famous *zamindar* in Srikakulam District who gave annual gifts of money to Sanskrit scholars according to their academic achievements. Urlām was famous as a center for certification and examination of Sanskrit scholars in different subjects. See Tumati Donappa, *Āndhra Samsthānamulu: Sāhitya Poṣaṇamu* (Waltair: Andhra University Press, 1969), 67–78. Also see Bangorey, *Mŏṭṭamŏdaṭi-kanyā-śulkam*, 151.

19. Scholars in Veda and Śāstra texts wore gold earrings and shawls with gold embroidery.

20. In Indian mythology, Kāma, the god of desire, wields a bow of sugar cane. He hits men and women with arrows of flowers to incite passion. This is a standard trope in all traditional erotic literature. Apparao is perhaps the last writer in Telugu to use this trope.

21. Turakas and Dudekulas are low-caste Muslims. "Turaka" is a word derived from "Turk," and Dudekulas are cotton corders. Both words are used here in a derogatory sense.

22. A Haji Saheb is a Muslim who has completed the pilgrimage to Mecca. The pilgrimage is expensive, and ordinarily only rich and high-class Muslims can afford it. A Haji holds high status among Muslims. This proverb talks about a Haji Saheb who marries into a Turaka family because he has no patience to wait for a suitable woman of his status. (Thanks to Tata Prakasam for helping me with the meaning of this saying.)

23. A verse by Aḍidamu Sūrakavi (ca. 1720–1780). Girisam adapts the verse to his need by leaving out the last line, which names a certain Ponugupāṭi Venkaṭa Mantri, a minister at the Zamindari of Sringavarpukota in Vijayanagram District, about whom the poem was written. See K. V. R., *Kanyā-śulkam: Ṭīkā, Ṭippaṇi* 6; and Adidamu Ramaravu, *Aḍidamu Sūrkavi Jīvitamu* (Madras: Vavilla Ramasvami Sastrulu and Sons, 1955), 19 and 79–80.

24. The English press of the time supported Viresalingam's social reform ideas. Getting one's name in print was a sure way to be noticed by the colonial masters, from which other tangible benefits would follow.

25. *Webster's New Universal Dictionary* (2nd ed.) defines "asses' bridge" as "the fifth proposition of the first book of Euclid, stating that the base angles of an isosceles triangle are equal: so called from the difficulty of learners in grasping it." Girisam uses the word in a literal sense of building a bridge. Also see Bangorey, *Mŏṭṭamŏdaṭi-kanyā-śulkam*, 135.

26. Kashi is the popular name in Telugu of Varanasi or Banares, the holy city on the Ganges. *Kashī majilī kathalu* (Tales from Travel to Kashi), which are modeled after *Canterbury Tales*, were written by Madhira Subbanna Diskhitulu around the turn of the twentieth century and were hugely popular.

27. Rama-varam, an imagined town that reminds us of Raja-mahendra-varam, better known as Rajahmundry, in East Godavari District, from where Kandukuri Viresalingam conducted his reformist activities. See "The Play in Context," in this volume.

28. Sister-in-law is a kinship term Girisam adopts to allow himself room for an erotic undertone in his conversations with her. See "On Kinship and Friendship," in this volume.

29. The entire conversation is an atrocious bluff. "Kapittha" does not mean orange; it means wood apple. Manu's Law Code, the *Mānava-dharma-śāstra,* doesn't say anything even remotely close to what Girisam attributes to it. For a very erudite study of the history of the phrase Girisam uses, see Sistla Srinivas, *Kapitthākārabhūgoḷā* (Visakhapatnam: published by the author, 1999). Amarasimha's text is a dictionary of Sanskrit words and does not include Telugu verses. The verse that Girisam quotes is an erotic verse from oral circulation.

30. See note 15 of Act One. In the list of books mentioned there, we find *Nala-caritra.* Apparently Venaktesam did not read the text and is lying when he says he does not remember it. In fact, there is no such verse in it, either.

31. This is not even a verse. It is an improvisation of Girisam's. The story does include the announcement of a second wedding, but kings do not come running to the wedding, as Girisam claims. In the story, Damayanti falls in love with Nala and marries him, rejecting the hands of the gods who were keen on marrying her. One of the gods, Kali, who was upset at her choice, vows to cause misery in her life. Kali possesses Nala, and under Kali's influence he gambles away his kingdom and abandons Damayanti in the forest. Damayanti, determined to find her husband, reaches her parents' house and sends people to search for him. After ascertaining that Nala is in King Rituparṇa's service in disguise, she asks her parents to announce a second wedding for her on short notice and send the invitation only to King Rituparṇa. She knows that Nala is the only one capable of driving horses fast enough for King Rituparṇa to make it to the wedding on such a short notice. Rituparṇa even wonders, after reaching Damayanti's city, why no one else has shown up. See Nannaya, *Āndhra Mahābhāratamu,* 3.2.2–230. For a translation of the story, see Velcheru Narayana Rao and David Shulman, *Classical Telugu Poetry: An Anthology* (Delhi: Oxford University Press, 2002), 88–113.

32. The Hindu religious authority Śaṅkarācārya never approved of widow marriage. Girisam is bluffing.

33. The term used in the original for this fruit is *jāmi,* a variety of guava. In Telugu, the fruit has erotic connotations. A beautiful young woman is often compared to a just-ripe, succulent *jāmi* fruit.

34. See note 15, Act One.

35. National Congress (The Congress Party), which ruled India for fifty years from 1947, was during the time of the events of this play a small organization of Indians that had been formed to agitate for positions of power in the British administration.

36. This happens to be a quote from *Mānava-dharma-śāstra* (Manu's Law Code), 2–239, though Girisam quotes it from hearsay. He is bluffing about having read all the *śāstras,* which clearly he has not.

37. I left untranslated three pages of the original Telugu text here (Gurajuda Appārao, *Kanyā-Śulkamu: A Telugu Comedy* [Madras: G. Ramasvami Setti, 1909], 63–65).

38. A tahsildar was a revenue officer in the British administration.

39. From *Sumati Śatakamu* (Madras: Vavilla Ramasvami Sastrulu and Sons, 1962), Verse 21.

40. Bangorey traces this poem to Kucimanci Timma-kavi, *Rasika-jana-manobhirāmamu,* an erotic text of the late eighteenth century; see Bangorey, *Mŏṭ-ṭamŏdaṭi-kanyā-śulkam,* 137.

Act Four

1. A gesture a person makes to indicate a taboo.

2. When a woman calls a man by the fictive kinship term brother-in-law, she allows for a potentially erotic relationship with him. See "A Note on Kinship and Friendship," in this volume.

3. Madhura-vani is apparently hinting at the secret sexual relationship between Ramap-Pantulu and Lubdha Avadhanlu's daughter Minakshi.

4. Telugu has two levels of second-person singular, *nuvvu* and *mīru. Nuvvu* is informal, affectionate, or insulting, and *mīru* is formal and respectful (and also plural). Lubdha uses *nuvvu* in this and the next dialogue. Ramap-Pantulu, who insists on getting proper respect, is insulted because he is addressed with an informal "you." Translation fails to carry this nuance.

5. Several exchanges of insults here defy translation. The Telugu insult *vĕdhava,* which Lubdha uses here, literally means a widower or widow. Applied to men, it is a curse, like "bastard" in English. When Ramap-Pantulu wonders aloud who Lubdha is referring to, Madhura-vani takes the word in its literal meaning of "widower/widow" and asks, "Do you want me to be included too?" This implies Ramap-Pantulu's death, since she will not become a *vĕdhava,* widow, unless Ramap-Pantulu dies, which at a deeper level implies that she considers herself his "wife." When Ramap-Pantulu insists that Madhura-vani made him a *vĕdhava,* she repeats the insult with a thin layer of a pun and asks him, "How can you be a *vĕdhava* ['widower'] while I am alive?"

6. Girisam's letter is couched in a high-flown classical literary style called *grāndhika* (book-language). The use of this style for a personal letter is totally ridiculous and adds to the fun. The text of the letter is italicized to separate it from the conversation of the characters. The English words Girisam uses in the letter are in set in Roman typeface.

7. Hindu texts say that Brahmin men who perform their rituals properly go to heaven to enjoy pleasures with gods' courtesans, the most famous of whom is Rambha.

8. Arundhati is the wife of the great sage Vasishta and is considered to be the model of a faithful wife in Hindu mythology.

9. According to Hindu mythology Mārkaṇḍeya, who was destined to die young, embraces Śiva's image in the temple when Yama, the god of death, arrives to take him. Śiva defeats Yama and grants eternal life to Mārkaṇḍeya.

10. See note 7, Act Two.

11. Telugu people use the lunar calendar for counting days of the month for ritual purposes.

12. A *kaṇṭĕ* is a golden rod bent into a circle that women wore around their necks.

13. The elders, *laukyulu,* are Niyogi Brahmins, whose presence at the wedding ensures social approval.

14. Wedding ceremonies lasted five days, except when they were done in a holy place with a famous temple, where the ceremony was concluded in one day.

15. The temple of Kodaṇḍa-rāma-svāmi is a local shrine, not a recognized holy place by any stretch of the imagination. Karataka-sastri invokes a ridiculous local legend about the temple to elevate its standing. His plan, obviously, is to leave town as fast as possible and keep Ramap-Pantulu out of the whole thing. Note also that Ramap-Pantulu has gone to a nearby town to invite the elders to the wedding. Lubdha Avadhanlu falls for the idea because it saves him money.

16. The reader should recall that Minakshi already knows that the bride is not a girl and that she is just playing along. As he has been advised to do by Madhura-vani, Karataka-sastri has bribed her to cooperate in this false wedding. In fact, she has a deeper motivation to stop her father from marrying a young girl in a real wedding.

17. Remember that Siddhanti has also been bribed.

18. A *gaḍiya* is a period of twenty-four minutes. There are seven and a half *gaḍiyas* in a *jāmu,* and eight *jāmus* make a day. This is how time was measured in precolonial Andhra.

19. Siddhanti quotes Sanskrit aphorisms to appear learned.

20. This is a critical moment. If anyone else should take over the responsibility of giving the ritual bath to the bride, the secret will be out. Minakshi skillfully manages the job herself.

21. A verse in oral circulation. The complete verse is:

> *niyyogi leni cāvaḍi*
> *ayyayyo vaṭṭi rota adiy eṭlannan,*
> *vayyāri gubba canṭiki*
> *payyĕda len'aṭlu mantri bhāskara-rāyā.*
>
> An assembly without a Niyogi,
> is utterly vulgar—alas—to compare,
> it's like a woman with lovely breasts,
> who doesn't have a sari to wear.

This verse is given with a modified second line in Veturi Prabhakara Sastri, ed., *Cāṭu-padya-maṇi-mañjari.* See K. V. R., *Kanyā-śulkam: Ṭīkā, Ṭippaṇi,* 42.

22. Ramap-Pantulu wants people to think that Madhura-vani is totally devoted to him, though he himself constantly suspects that she is having an affair with the Head Constable.

23. Apparently, even the thought that his new bride could be a widow is enough to scare him.

24. Brahmins don't eat food cooked by any other caste. The cooks for the wedding feast must also be Brahmins.

25. The chant Girisam refers to is called *Camaka,* which has a long list of things the chanter is asking gods to provide. It is 4.7 of *Taittirīya Samhitā,* which is a part of *Black Yajurveda.*

26. According to Hindu cosmology, the earth is ringed by several concentric oceans—first the salt ocean, then oceans of sugar-cane juice, wine, clarified butter, milk, whey, and fresh water.

27. The Eastern Ghats are a mountain range on the east coast of India.

28. Monkey-sticks is a game called *koti-kommacci,* which children play on the branches of trees.

29. A *pandiri* is a temporary structure erected with bamboo poles and covered with palmyra leaves. Built for weddings, it provides shade for the guests and is also a symbol of a happy occasion in the house.

30. The first lines of a popular hymn *Bhaja govindam,* also called *Mohamudgara,* attributed to Śaṅkarācārya, available in many editions; for instance, *Bhaja govindam athavā mohamudgarah* (Delhi: Parimal Publications, 1998). The hymn is supposed to have been composed by Śaṅkarāchārya when he saw an old scholar memorizing rules of grammar.

31. A prestigious brand name of an expensive soap imported from Britain.

32. Rambha, Menaka, Ūrvaśi, and Tilottama are the names of pleasure-women of gods in Hindu mythology.

33. The giving tree, or *kalpa-vṛksha,* is the tree in heaven that grants all wishes.

34. "Out of the house" is a euphemism for menstruating. Women having their period are considered unclean and are not allowed into the house for the three days of menstruation.

35. The original is *golla-bhāma,* literally a girl from the cowherd caste, a character from the popular Bhāma-kalāpam, a dance drama of the Kūcipūḍi tradition.

Act Five

1. Brahmin Lubdha Avadhanlu will be polluted if the low-caste Asiri enters his bedroom.

2. See note 28, Act Three, and "The Play in Context," in this volume, for more on Rajahmundry.

3. Śāpara chants; apparently chants to ward off spirits.

4. It is believed that Brahmins who do horrible crimes during their lifetime become Brahmin demons, or *brahma-rākṣasi,* after their death.

5. "Baepan," which I adopted from the original "Baepanayya," is a derogatory form of "Brahmin."

6. A Yarborough, called *lāntaru* in Telugu, is a hand containing no cards higher than nine. So called after Charles Anderson Worsley (1809–1987), 2nd Earl of Yarborough, who is said to have bet 1,000 to 1 that such a hand would not occur.

7. Komati is the caste to which Poli-setti belongs. People of this caste, who are merchants, prefer to be called Vai'sayas, a Sanskrit word indicating a high social status, and feel that calling them by their caste name is disrespectful.

8. The Englishmen are ruling.

9. This is Hindi; a catchy phrase used by street performers referring to Rāvaṇa, the ten-headed demon of the Rāmāyaṇa.

10. A *pŏllu* is a waste card. See "Card Game in Act Five, Scene Two," in this volume.

11. It was believed in Andhra that you could die if a poet composed a verse about you with certain syllables in certain places. For instance, the syllable /ta/ in the sixth place in a line kills the person to whom the verse is addressed.

12. The verse is from Seshappa-kavi's *Narasimha-śatakamu,* a text of devotional verses addressed to Nara-simha, the Man-Lion avatar of Vishnu. The text is popular in northern Andhra, perhaps because of the Simhacalam temple, whose deity is Nara-simha. Poli-setti repeatedly chants a single line from this text, pronouncing conjunct consonants inaccurately.

13. *mṛttikā* means soil or dirt. *mṛttikā ca me* is a part of a Sanskrit text often chanted at Brahminic rituals. The text is popularly called *Camaka,* and it consists of long list of things the chanter wants the gods to provide for him. Each item in the list ends with a *ca* ("and") and *me* ("to me"), while at the end comes the finite verb, *kalpatām* ("may [they] be provided"). Also see Scene Five of Act Four, where Girisam talks about this chant.

14. A typical feature of the Telugu dialect of uneducated non-Brahmins is to drop aspirates and the intervocalic /v/. Also, the /a/ after the dropped /v/ is uttered as a closed vowel, closer to /o/. Thus, "Madhura-vani" becomes "Maduroni."

15. The original is *yĕṅgili.* An object touched by another person's saliva is *yĕṅgili.* The object must be washed if it has to be used again, and if it is food it is unusable for others. People go to extreme lengths to avoid *yĕṅgili.* Mixing of saliva is not *yĕṅgili* between a husband and wife and between a mother and her young children. Also see the verse Girisam stops Venkatesam from singing in Act Two, Scene One.

16. "Lakshmi" is apparently Ramap-Pantulu's name for Madhura-vani. It is said that there was a very well-known pleasure-woman called Maha-lakshmi in Vizianagaram during Apparao's time and that she was kept by the Maharaja himself. Legends are told about her willfulness and skill in singing. In the first version of the play, Girisam's pleasure-woman is named Maha-lakshmi.

17. Pieces of broken glass are often stuck to the top of the compound wall to prevent thieves from jumping over it.

18. See note 26, Act Three.

19. Subbi is Minakshi's father's second wife; therefore, technically, she is Minakshi's stepmother. She is a little girl, and Minakshi referring to her as stepmother heightens the fun.

20. A goddess in Vizianagaram.

21. A small fort-like structure is built with mud and bricks around the basil plant (*tulasi*); this is a usual fixture in the backyards of Brahmin houses. The women of the household worship it.

22. The Vaishnavites, the devotees of Vishnu, wear a U-shaped white mark with a vertical line of red ocher in the middle on their foreheads. The Saivites, the devotees of Śiva, wear three white horizontal marks across their forehead. Among the people sitting in the village bar, Manavallayya is a Vaishnavite and Veresa is a Saivite.

23. Telescope.

24. "*Mlecchas*" is a derogatory Sanskrit word for non-Hindus.

25. A ridiculing imitation of the words from the Vaishnava sacred text *Tiruppallāṇḍu* by Priyāḷvār, which begins with "*Pallāṇḍu, pallāṇḍu.*" See *Nityānusandhānamu* (Madras: Vavilla Ramaswami Sastrulu and Sons, 1953), 24.

26. *Pŏṅgali* is a sweet rice pudding offered to Vishnu in the temple and eaten by the devotees as god's gift, *prasādam.*

27. *Gaṇita-śāstra* (mathematics).

28. In the Village Head's non-Brahmin dialect, the word initial /v/ does not exist, and palatal /s/ is replaced by a /c/. Thus "Viresa" becomes "Ireca."

29. Rāmānuja (1037–1137 CE) is the first guru of the Vaishnavas. They utter his name at every occasion as a sign of devotion to him.

30. Gods and anti-gods churned the ocean to obtain the essence of eternal life, *amṛta,* from it. Once they acquired it, they quarreled among themselves for it. See Wendy O'Flaherty, *Hindu Myths: A Sourcebook* (Baltimore: Penguin, 1975), 273–280.

31. Mercury shaped in the form of a liṅga, an image of Śiva. Apparently only *siddhas,* people of religious power, can make mercury, which is not a stable element, stay solid.

32. Refers to Haridvar in the foothills of the Himalayas, a sacred site for Hindus.

33. Non-Brahmin religious gurus practice yoga that is not textual. It is different from the yoga in textual Hinduism and is less well known. The songs Havaldar Acc'anna and the Disciple sing belong to this tradition. Bairagi and the Shopkeeper seem to exploit this tradition to make a living, but no one seems to be overly concerned about their fraud. The Village Head is aware of their pretensions, as may be noted by his sarcastic remarks.

34. Vemana is the name of an eighteenth-century yogi to whom are attributed iconoclastic verses, all of which end with the line *viśvadābhirāma! vinura vema!,* the meaning of which is unclear.

35. A verse made up by the Shopkeeper in the style of Vemana's verses.

36. Apparently Akbar, who ruled 1556–1606.

37. The age named Kali. This is the last in the Hindu cycle of four ages, when all values deteriorate and the number of sinners increases until all creation is finally destroyed.

38. Apparently an Englishman. High-level posts in the colonial administration were mostly reserved for Europeans.

39. The Prophet Mohammed.

40. The Village Head refers to the custom of *māru-manuvu,* which was in practice among lower castes. The upwardly mobile lower castes, to which the Village Head belongs, prohibited remarriages to their women in order to achieve social respectability by emulating the upper castes, whose widows were not allowed to remarry.

41. A sepoy was a native recruit in the colonial army. "Soldier" referred to white recruits.

42. "The leaf of knowledge" refers to marijuana. A man of knowledge is called *jñani,* one who knows the ultimate reality in yoga.

43. The British East India Company, which ruled India during the period 1757–1857.

44. Queen Victoria (1837–1901). The war referred to here is the Crimean War of 1854–1856.

45. A tambura is a stringed instrument.

46. This is a Sufi religious song in Urdu, where the soul is compared to a bird and the body, its cage.

> You live in the cage and say nothing.
> Dear little bird, say something.
> Say something.
> Where do you go, why don't you say,
> Say something—in the golden cage . . .

47. The song is a popular cobra song that appeals to the snake to withdraw the poison from the person he has bitten.

> Come down my cobra, my lovely cobra,
> Gently get off, you're divine, you are handsome.
> Come down in joy, snake of Repallĕ!
> You live there in the anthill, north of the village
> Under the big banyan tree, all male snake!

48. Niyogis are too proud to accept gifts, so Ramap-Pantulu doesn't ask for the rupees with words such as "Please give them to me."

49. People of lower status do not smoke in front of their superiors. Thus, the low-caste servant Asiri does not smoke in front of the Brahmin Ramap-Pantulu.

50. It might sound strange now, but the practice of family members sharing the same bedroom was not unusual in Andhra during this time.

51. One of several practices of taking an oath. If a person who made such an oath went back on his word, God would punish him.

52. The pieces of paper in Ramap-Pantulu's pocket are the ones the Head Constable trashed in the last scene. We can infer that the Head Constable has used Ramap-Pantulu's complaint about the gold *kaṇṭĕ* to threaten Lubdha Avadhanlu with a criminal case and as a result has been able to get him to write off a personal loan. Lubdha has returned the Head Constable's IOU but has not written on it that the debt has been paid in full. The Head Constable has torn up the IOU, thus destroying any evidence that he ever received a loan from Lubdha.

Ramap-Pantulu is talking aloud to himself here as he looks at the discarded pieces of the IOU and realizes that the Head Constable has benefited financially from the situation and won't be pressuring Lubdha to return the *kaṇṭĕ* or its money value, let alone pursuing a murder investigation against him. Thus, Ramap-Pantulu's plan to use the Head Constable to pressure Lubdha to return the *kaṇṭĕ* has been foiled.

53. Reference to the practice of Brahmin widows shaving their heads. But not all widows shaved their heads. For instance, Minakshi, Bucc'amma, and the Day-Meal-Woman did not shave their heads.

54. Traditionally, a flame of burning camphor is brought on a brass plate to the doorway to ritually invite the newlyweds to their home.

55. Apparao collected this song from a mendicant singer named Jangam Mallayya of Draksharamam. See the editorial note in Gurajada Apparao, *Lekhalu, Gurjada Racanalu,* vol. 5 (Vijayawada: Visalaandhra Pracuranalayam, 1958), 10.

56. Refers to Minakshi. Apparently Ramap-Pantulu thinks that Minakshi is chasing after him. This scene and the next create an eerie atmosphere with a funeral song and a confused, sleepless Ramap-Pantulu, who has not eaten all night, in a surreal state of mind during the wee hours of the morning.

Act Six

1. Sayibu is a colloquial variant of Saheb, an Urdu word often used for people in position of power. The colloquial variant is used for Muslim men of low status.

2. See "On Kinship and Friendship," in this volume

3. Refers to Madhura-vani. This and the following words of the Disciple enhance the surreal nature of the scene.

4. The cat is a bad omen in Telugu culture. People believe that if a cat comes toward you as you leave home on any business, that business will fail.

5. Scenes Three, Four, and Five are not translated; they are summarized below. Apparao wrote these short scenes for his first version and used them in the present version almost verbatim. Their usefulness for the narrative is minimal and they are not of the same literary quality as the rest of the play. These scenes are invariably edited out when the play is performed. According to reports from his contemporaries, Apparao was under some pressure to keep the printers busy; he was literally completing the play as it was being typeset. Possibly he

wanted to gain some time to concentrate on his concluding scenes and sent off these scenes unchanged to the press.

Scene Three: Agni finds that he is out of cash to pay for court fees. Ramap-Pantulu advises him to pawn his gold bracelet. When Agni reluctantly pulls the bracelet off his wrist and gives it to Ramap-Pantulu, the latter grabs it to cover his own fees for advising Agni. Meanwhile an advocate named Nayudu enters. Ramap-Pantulu tells him that Agni has given the brief to another advocate, who knows English. Nayudu gets upset and threatens to badmouth Agni to the deputy collector.

Scene Four: In a soliloquy, Lubdha repents his past deeds. He regrets marrying his daughter Minakshi to an old man, thus dooming her to widowhood in the prime of her youth. He regrets his own foolish desire to marry a very young girl in his old age. He trusts and hopes that Saujanya Rao will clear him of the murder charges of which he has been falsely accused. He decides to let his daughter go the widows' home, if she so prefers, and he himself will retire to the sacred city of Banares. Ramap-Pantulu enters to pressure Lubdha for money to bribe the inspector and the deputy collector. Lubdha resists. Saujanya Rao enters and drives Ramap-Pantulu out. Lubdha confesses his sins to Saujanya Rao and offers to surrender all his property to him if Saujanya Rao succeeds in getting him out of his troubles. Saujanya Rao rejects the offer and asks Lubdha to make a donation instead to the Social Reform Association in Rajahmundry.

Scene Five: Karataka-sastri admonishes his Disciple for not returning the gold *kaṇṭĕ* to Lubdha. He says that it was a mistake to take it to Madhura-vani, who didn't acknowledge it and kept insisting that she did not get her ornament back and pressured Ramap-Pantulu to bring it to her. A frustrated Ramap-Pantulu complained to the police and they used the complaint to foist a murder case against Lubdha. Karataka-sastri now wants to go to Madhura-vani to ask her to give the *kaṇṭĕ* to him as a favor so he can mail it to Lubdha along with the bride-money Lubdha has paid. He hopes this will resolve the murder accusation against Lubdha and assures Madhura-vani she will get her *kaṇṭĕ* back in the end. (One wonders how a murder case can be withdrawn by the prosecution if the accused provides evidence that he got his money and gold back. Apparently Karataka-sastri doesn't understand how the British legal system works.)

6. Obviously, Madhura-vani has left Ramap-Pantulu and shifted her residence from his village to Visakhapatnam, the district headquarters and a big city.

7. A children's ritual game of declaring an end to friendship.

8. Saujanya Rao is an idealist advocate. The character will have a major role in the next act.

9. Karataka-sastri quotes the Sanskrit saying *svayam tīrṇah parāms tārayati.*

10. This is the last we hear of the *kaṇṭĕ.* We have to assume that Madhra-vani got her ornament back when the murder case was resolved.

11. The Disciple's name.

12. Scene Seven is not translated. Here is a summary of the scene:

Saujanya Rao tries to convince Agni that selling girls is wrong. He advises Agni to marry his second daughter Subbi to a suitable young man and give Bucc'amma the property that belongs to her and let her live in the widows' home. Agni resents this advice and storms out of the lawyer's office.

Act Seven

1. Telegraph.

2. *Añjanam* is a divination ritual in which collyrium (mascara) and oil are smeared on the palm and a child is asked to say what it sees in this spot. The ritual is used to divine the location of lost properties or people.

3. Haridvar, a holy place in Uttar Pradesh.

4. Scenes Two, Three, Four, and Five are not translated. Here are the summaries:

Scene Two: Agni's case against Girisam for abducting Bucc'amma fails because of the incompetence of his lawyer. The judge finds no valid information regarding the alleged abduction or any reliable evidence that Bucc'amma was a minor. Agni is laughed out of court, while his advocate refuses to represent him unless he is paid more money.

Scene Three: While interviewing Poli-setti regarding his testimony, Saujanya Rao finds out that Poli-setti does not want to testify in court after all. Poli-setti says that he was not even in town on the day the alleged murder occurred. Previously, under pressure from the Head Constable, who was also trying to clear his own name, Poli-setti had agreed to testify that he had seen the bride jump over the wall and run away.

Scene Four: Lawyer Nayudu encounters Agni on the street and advises him to drop the case against Girisam. He presses Agni for his lawyer fees and extracts from him a promise to give a cartload of red peppers as payment. Girisam happens by and pretends to bow to Agni's feet. He grabs Agni's legs and makes him fall down and escapes.

Scene Five: Girisam goes to Lubdha's house pretending to help him with the court case. Girisam asks Lubdha to legally adopt him so that he could look after his affairs. The Head Constable and the Shopkeeper arrive and wonder where Bairagi has gone. The Head Constable still hopes Bairagi will magically locate the missing bride. (The Head Constable knows the bride is a boy, but Bairagi doesn't.) The Head Constable asks the Shopkeeper to testify for him, but the Shopkeeper refuses. Girisam dismisses Bairagi and his magic as superstition. The servant Asiri also wiggles out of giving testimony. He swears he hasn't seen anything regarding the bride running away. Priest Gavarayya declares that Bairagi is sitting outside, invisible to everybody else. When Girisam dismisses the whole thing as a hoax, Priest Gavarayya protests that yogis refuse to stay where "unbelieving Christians" gather. He calls the invisible Bairagi to follow him and leaves. As he leaves, he refuses to stand witness to anything about the bride. Thus, by the end of this scene, Lubdha has lost the support of all possible witnesses. The defense is totally in shreds.

5. Romeo and Juliet, II.2:

What's in a name? That which we call a rose
By another name would smell as sweet.

The line translated by Girisam is in a Telugu meter called *teṭa-giti.*

6. See note 8, Act Two, on telling one's own name. Girisam gives his own interpretation to the convention. He says that saying one's own name loudly is a sin, suggesting that the stranger could say his (her) name in a soft voice.

7. *Sumati Śatakamu* (Madras: Vavilla Ramasvami Sastrulu and Sons, 1962), Verse 16.

8. For all the love Saujanya Rao has for the *Bhagavad-gīta,* he has apparently not read that book carefully. The line he quotes is not from that book. It is popular as an aphorism and is from *Mānava-dharma-śāstra,* Manu's Law Code, 2.215.

mātrā svasrā duhitrā vā na viviktāsano bhavet
balavān indriya-grāmo vidvāmsam api karṣati.

She may be your mother, sister
or your own daughter—
don't sit alone with her.
Senses are powerful and pull toward evil
even the most learned of men.

9. In the *Mṛicchakaṭika,* a play in Sanskrit by Śūdraka, a pleasure-woman, Vasantasena, falls in love with a poor but honest Brahmin and marries him.

The Play in Context

1. Sanjay Subrahmanyam, *Penumbral Visions: Making Polities in Early Modern South India* (Delhi: Oxford University Press, 2001).

2. V. Narayana Rao, David Shulman, and Sanjay Subrahmanyam, *Textures of Time: Writing History in South India 1600–1800* (New Delhi: Permanent Black, 2001).

3. See the afterwords to V. Narayana Rao and David Shulman, *The Sound of the Kiss, Or A Story That Must Never Be Told* (New York: Columbia University Press, 2004); and *The Demon's Daughter: A Love Story from South India* (Albany: State University of New York Press, 2006). Also see D. Shulman, "Who Invented Modernity in South India and Is It Modern?" in *Comparing Modernities: Essays in Homage to Shmuel N. Eisenstadt,* edited by Eliezer Ben-Rafael and Yitzhak Sternberg (Leiden: Brill, 2005), 395–412.

4. See Velcheru Narayana Rao, David Shulman, and Sanjay Subrahmanyam, *Symbols of Substance: Court and State in Nayaka-Period Tamilnadu* (Delhi: Oxford University Press, 1992).

5. See the afterword to V. Narayana Rao and D. Shulman, *God on the Hill: Temple Poems from Tirupati* (New York: Oxford University Press, 2005).

6. See Narayana Rao, Shulman, and Subrahmanyam, *Symbols of Substance,* 57–112; A. K. Ramanujan, Velcheru Narayana Rao, and David Shulman, *When God Is a Customer* (Berkeley: University of California Press, 1994).

7. G. M. Young, ed. *Speeches by Lord Macaulay with His Minute on Indian Education* (London: Oxford University Press, 1935; reprint, New York: AMS Press, 1979), 359.

8. For the etymology of the term "nautch-girl," see note 2 in Act One.

9. For more on *karaṇams,* see Narayana Rao, Shulman, and Subrahmanyam, *Textures of Time,* 93–139.

10. Pusapati Rajakumari Devi's reminiscences of Apparao, reported by Puripanda Appalaswami. Rajakumari Devi is, by an extended relationship, a grand-niece of Maharaja Ānandagajapati. See M. Chalapathi Rau, ed., *Gurajada Commemorative Volume* (New Delhi: South Delhi Andhra Association, 1976), 5. Biographies of Apparao, which tend to be hagiographic, do not mention this or any other incident that could look unflattering to his image. K. V. R., *Mahodayam: jātīya-punarujjīvanamlo Gurajāḍa sthānam* (Hyderabad: Visalaandhra Publishing House, 1969), which is otherwise well researched and responsibly written, is no exception to this.

11. Arudra, "Madhura-vāṇi pātra: Punah-parśīlana," in Bangorey, *Mŏṭṭamŏdaṭi-kanyā-śulkam.* Aruda's essay is reprinted in Modali Nagabhushana Sarma and Etukuri Prasad, *Kanyā-śulkam: Nūreḷḷa samālocanam* (Hyderabad, Visalaandhra Publishing House, 1999), 456–462. According to Arudra, Apparao recorded in his diaries observations of the pleasure-women the Maharaja was associated with. Arudra also reports from a secondary source that Apparao admitted to his friend Gidugu Ramamurty that he visited the houses of pleasure-women himself. Also see K. V. R., *Mahodayam,* 117–118.

12. Translated by Rabi Shankar Mishra, Satya P. Mohanty, Jitindra K. Nayak, and Paul St-Pierre (Berkeley: University of California Press, 2005).

13. Bangorey, *Mŏṭṭamŏdaṭi kanyāśulkam.*

14. As quoted in Gary Saul Morson and Caryl Emerson, *Mikhail Bakhtin: Creation of a Prosaics* (Stanford, Calif.: Stanford University Press, 1990), 231–268. My presentation of Bakhtin's concept of polyphony follows chapter 6 of this book.

15. See note 8, Act Seven.

16. Kodavatiganti Kutumbarao, "Kanyā-śulkam Noṭs," in Sarma and Prasad, *Kanyā-śulkam,* 687–724.

17. Sripada Gopalakrishnamurti notes this in his "Madhura-vāṇi," in Sarma and Prasad, *Kanyā-śulkam,* 463–468.

18. Racamallu Ramachandra Reddy, a perceptive critic of modern Telugu literature, notices that Apparao does not have sympathy for the social reform movement Viresalingam led. However, he concludes that this is due to a streak of extremism (*viparīta-dhoraṇi*) in Apparao's psychology. "Gurajāḍa manastatvamloni viparīta dhoraṇi" (Samvedana, 1969; reprinted in *Gurajada Commemorative Volume,* New Delhi: South Delhi Andhra Association, 1976, 61–67).

19. See note 11, Act Two.

20. See note 12, Act Two.

21. See note 15, Act Two.

22. Kālidāsa, *Kumārasambhava,* 1.1.

23. Apparao makes trenchant critical remarks about Vedam Venkataraya Sastri's work in two of his private letters, written in English, to Vangavolu Munisubrahmanyam, a younger contemporary. Telugu translations of these letters are published in Apparao, *Lekhalu, Gurajāḍa Racanalu,* 5:86–97. They are reproduced in Sarma and Prasad, *Kanyā-śulkam,* 770–774.

24. For more detailed information on the status of the Telugu Pundit, see my "Historical After-Essay," in Velcheru Narayana Rao, *Hibiscus on the Lake: Twentieth Century Telugu Poetry from India* (Madison: University of Wisconsin Press, 2003).

25. For an excellent study of Tagore's ideal of love, see Sudipta Kaviraj, "Tagore and Transformations in the Ideals of Love," in *Love in South Asia: A Cultural History,* edited by Francesca Orsini (Cambridge: Cambridge University Press, 2006), 161–182.

26. See Narayana Rao, "A Historical After-Essay," especially 284–286.

27. Partha Chatterjee, *The Nation and Its Fragments: Colonial and Postcolonial Histories* (Princeton, N.J.: Princeton University Press, 1993), 120.

28. See Rosinka Chaudhuri, "Hemchandra's Bharat Sangeet (1870) and the Politics of Poetry: A Pre-History of Hindu nationalism in Bengal?" *Indian Economic and Social History Review* 42, no. 2 (2005): 213–247.

29. See Richard King, *Orientalism and Religion: Postcolonial Theory, India, and the "Mystic East"* (London: Routledge, 2005), especially 118–142.

30. I am indebted to David Shulman for this observation and its formulation.

31. Apparao originally wrote this in English. I was not able to find his diaries, and the entry here is translated from the Telugu translation of Avasarala Surya Rao, *Mahākavi Ḍairīlu, Gurjāḍa Racanalu 3,* 2nd. ed. (1954; Vijayawada: Visalaandhra Pracuranalayam, 1961), 174–175.

GURAJADA APPARAO (1861 or 1862–1915) is regarded as the father of modern Telugu literature, primarily as a result of the popularity of *Kanyasulkam,* although he also published poetry and short stories and wrote two other plays, left unfinished.

VELCHERU NARAYANA RAO is Krishnadevaraya Professor of Languages and Cultures of Asia at the University of Wisconsin–Madison. Along with co-author David Shulman, he was the 2004 recipient of the A. K. Ramanujan Prize for Translation from the Association for Asian Studies for *Classical Telugu Poetry: An Anthology.*